THREE WEEKS IN
QUEBEC CITY

Also in the
History *of* Canada Series

*Death or Victory: The Battle of Quebec
and the Birth of an Empire,* by Dan Snow

*The Last Act: Pierre Trudeau, the Gang of Eight
and the Fight for Canada,* by Ron Graham

*The Destiny of Canada: Macdonald, Laurier,
and the Election of 1891,* by Christopher Pennington

*Ridgeway: The American Fenian Invasion
and the 1866 Battle That Made Canada,* by Peter Vronsky

*War in the St. Lawrence:
The Forgotten U-Boat Battles on Canada's Shores,* by Roger Sarty

The Best Place to Be: Expo 67 and Its Time,
by John Lownsbrough

*Death on Two Fronts: National Tragedies and the Fate
of Democracy in Newfoundland, 1914–34,* by Sean Cadigan

Ice and Water: Politics, Peoples, and the Arctic Council,
by John English

*Trouble on Main Street: Mackenzie King, Reason, Race,
and the 1907 Vancouver Riots,* by Julie Gilmour

THREE WEEKS IN
QUEBEC CITY

THE MEETING THAT
MADE CANADA

CHRISTOPHER MOORE

General Editors
MARGARET MacMILLAN and ROBERT BOTHWELL

ALLEN
LANE

ALLEN LANE

an imprint of Penguin Canada Books Inc., a Penguin Random House Company

Published by the Penguin Group
Penguin Canada Books Inc.
90 Eglinton Avenue East, Suite 700, Toronto, Ontario, Canada M4P 2Y3

Penguin Group (USA) LLC, 375 Hudson Street, New York, New York 10014, U.S.A.
Penguin Books Ltd, 80 Strand, London WC2R 0RL, England
Penguin Ireland, 25 St Stephen's Green, Dublin 2, Ireland (a division of Penguin Books Ltd)
Penguin Group (Australia), 707 Collins Street, Melbourne, Victoria 3008, Australia
(a division of Pearson Australia Group Pty Ltd)
Penguin Books India Pvt Ltd, 11 Community Centre, Panchsheel Park, New Delhi – 110 017,
India
Penguin Group (NZ), 67 Apollo Drive, Rosedale, Auckland 0632, New Zealand
(a division of Pearson New Zealand Ltd)
Penguin Books (South Africa) (Pty) Ltd, 24 Sturdee Avenue, Rosebank,
Johannesburg 2196, South Africa

Penguin Books Ltd, Registered Offices: 80 Strand, London WC2R 0RL, England

First published 2015

1 2 3 4 5 6 7 8 9 10   (RRD)

Copyright © Christopher Moore Editorial Ltd., 2015

Manufactured in the U.S.A.

LIBRARY AND ARCHIVES CANADA CATALOGUING IN PUBLICATION

Moore, Christopher, 1950-, author
Three Weeks in Quebec City : the meeting that made
Canada / Christopher Moore.

(History of Canada)
Includes bibliographical references and index.

ISBN 978-0-670-06525-7 (bound)

1. Québec Conference (1864).
2. Fathers of Confederation.
3. Canada--History--1841-1867.
I. Title. II. Series: History of
Canada (Toronto, Ont.)

FC476.M66 2015   971.04'9   C2015-900011-4

eBook ISBN 978-0-14-319450-7

Visit the Penguin Canada website at www.penguin.ca

Special and corporate bulk purchase rates available; please see
www.penguin.ca/corporatesales or call 1-800-810-3104.

CONTENTS

INTRODUCTION TO THE HISTORY OF CANADA SERIES

Canada, the world agrees, is a success story. We should never make the mistake, though, of thinking that it was easy or foreordained. At crucial moments during Canada's history, challenges had to be faced and choices made. Certain roads were taken and others were not. Imagine a Canada, indeed imagine a North America, where the French and not the British had won the Battle of the Plains of Abraham. Or imagine a world in which Canadians had decided to throw in their lot with the revolutionaries in the thirteen colonies.

This series looks at the making of Canada as an independent, self-governing nation. It includes works on key stages in the laying of the foundations, as well as on the crucial turning points between 1867 and the present that made the Canada we know today. It is about those defining moments when the course of Canadian history and the nature of Canada itself were oscillating. And it is about the human beings—heroic, flawed, wise, foolish, complex—who had to make decisions without knowing what the consequences might be.

We begin the series with the European presence in the eighteenth century—a presence that continues to shape our society today—and conclude it with an exploration of the strategic importance of the Canadian Arctic. We look at how the mass movements of peoples, whether Loyalists in the eighteenth century or Asians at the start of the twentieth, have profoundly influenced the nature of Canada. We also look at battles and their aftermaths: the Plains of Abraham, the 1866 Fenian raids, the German submarines in the St. Lawrence River during World War II. Political crises—the 1891 election that saw Sir John A. Macdonald battling Wilfrid Laurier; Pierre Trudeau's triumphant patriation of the Canadian Constitution—provide rich moments of storytelling. So, too, do the Expo 67 celebrations, which marked a time of soaring optimism and gave Canadians new confidence in themselves.

We have chosen these critical turning points partly because they are good stories in themselves but also because they show what Canada was like at particularly important junctures in its history. And to tell them we have chosen Canada's best historians. Our authors are great storytellers who shine a spotlight on a different Canada, a Canada of the past, and illustrate links from then to now. We need to remember the roads that were taken—and the ones that were not. Our goal is to help our readers understand how we got from that past to this present.

Margaret MacMillan
Warden at St. Antony's College, Oxford

Robert Bothwell
May Gluskin Chair of Canadian History
University of Toronto

We are a democratic people.
—George Brown, 1864

ONE

October 10, 1864:
La Vieille Capitale

"Since Saturday we have had the world's bleakest weather," lamented the Quebec City correspondent of the Montreal newspaper *La Minerve* on Monday, October 10, 1864. "It is too bad for our visitors. Quebec City is so beautiful when the weather is good." Instead, on Saturday night, "a white shroud of snow covered the ground, and a penetrating frost chilled us hand and foot. On Sunday, we might have been somewhere in Siberia. Today the white shroud has grown dirty, and you cannot put a foot off the sidewalk without plunging into mud." The wooden sidewalks were not much better than the streets. The English writer Anthony Trollope found while visiting that "the boards are rotten, and worn in some places to dirt. The nails have gone, and the broken planks go up and down under the feet, and in the dark they are absolutely dangerous."[1]

The visitors for whom *La Minerve* grieved were the delegates who had arrived for the British North American constitutional conference, beginning that morning at the legislative building. Thirty-three delegates from five provincial legislatures—Newfoundland, Nova Scotia, New Brunswick, Prince Edward Island, and Canada*—had come to Quebec City pursuing the old idea of uniting into a single nation all the provinces of British North America, an idea proposed frequently for fifty years without effect, and now suddenly revived. The threat to British North America from a massively armed and not always friendly United States encouraged the small and barely defended provinces to think of uniting for mutual protection. The rapid expansion of distance-annihilating railroads and steamships spurred visions of a continent-spanning new nation, bound by rail. A political crisis in the Province of Canada—present-day Ontario and Quebec—had stimulated the search for new and larger unions. And there was the sheer ambition of the thing. "Do we wish to live and die in our insignificance?" cried Joseph Howe of Nova Scotia when the idea of union was discussed in Halifax that summer, though he would come to oppose the plan these delegates would craft in Quebec City. His rival, Charles Tupper, foresaw Nova Scotians enjoying "a far higher status" as citizens of a transcontinental nation than as a small Atlantic coast community.[2]

In the Province of Canada, a broad coalition committed to remaking the union took power in June 1864. In September, eight cabinet members from that coalition travelled by steamship to Charlottetown to present their proposals to delegates of the legislatures of the three Maritime provinces. In the brilliant sun of Charlottetown, the Maritimers endorsed "confederation," a federal union of all the British North American provinces. Confederation carried the promise of westward expansion to British Columbia on the Pacific coast, and of rail links between the Maritimes and "the Canadas." During the six days at Charlottetown, this confederation had generated a shared purpose among the usually fractious politicians of British North America. But they had discussed

* In 1864, "Canada" meant the territories of the St. Lawrence–Great Lakes system, roughly today's Quebec and Ontario, then united into a single province of Canada. Citizens of the Atlantic provinces did not then think of themselves as Canadians.

the matter mostly at the level of general principle. The nuts and bolts of a formal union remained to be placed and tightened down. There would be confederation only "if the terms of union could be made satisfactory."[3] A longer meeting, a true constitutional conference, would be needed to discuss and ratify those terms of union, the principles and the practicalities upon which a new nation could be built. Early in October, British North American politicians were on the road again, this time to Quebec City.

In those days, they came usually by train. Quite suddenly, steam trains had become the way one travelled in British North America—but not yet between Atlantic Canada and Quebec City. No rail line yet linked all the provinces of British North America. Fortunately steamships, as new as, almost as fast as, and often more comfortable than steam trains, filled the gap. "The boats are very fine," wrote one traveller on the steamships that plied between Montreal and Quebec City in 1864, noting that they were "three storeys high and like floating hotels," although "they shake very much and the lamps swing with the motion, not agreeable."[4]

For Maritimers travelling to the constitutional conference, a special steamship cruise had been arranged. In the 1850s, the province of Canada had commissioned a private shipping line to outfit three steamships to carry mail and tend the buoys and lighthouses of the Gulf of St. Lawrence. When the company got into financial trouble, the government found itself owning the ships. In August, the "government steamer" *Queen Victoria* had carried the Canadian cabinet from the dock at Quebec to anchorage in Charlottetown harbour in barely sixty hours. In early October, *Queen Victoria* sailed again, this time to bring Maritime delegates to Quebec City.[5]

Queen Victoria's first call was Pictou on the gulf coast of Nova Scotia, where Nova Scotia's delegates had come up from Halifax to meet the steamship. Premier Charles Tupper of Nova Scotia came aboard with three Conservative colleagues and two members of the Reform opposition, along with wives and daughters eager to renew the festivities many of them had enjoyed during the Charlottetown sessions. The next stop was Charlottetown, where *Queen Victoria* picked up Colonel John Gray, the Conservative premier of the island, and members of his cabinet, and also leaders of the Island's Reformers—and more wives and daughters. Then the steamer made the short crossing to Shediac, New Brunswick, to collect another group of government and opposition members from the New Brunswick delegation, and more wives and daughters—again, no sons were included, and the daughters were all single and of marriageable age. Leaving Shediac early Friday morning, October 7, *Queen Victoria* made steam for Quebec City, offering the passengers "every comfort and luxury that could be desired."[6]

The mood was festive. *Queen Victoria*'s deck "was seldom deserted by promenaders during daylight and long after dark," wrote Edward Whelan. Whelan, a member of the Prince Edward Island legislature and a delegate to the conference, was a Charlottetown newspaperman who kept copious notes for his paper, *The Examiner*. As they steamed up the broad St. Lawrence, he reported, the promenaders on deck were driven indoors by gales and snow squalls. The storm slowed the ship's progress, and the travellers reached Quebec City in darkness on Sunday, October 9, too late to share the sight sailors had marvelled at for centuries: the city and its mighty rock rising where the great river narrowed "like an island above the surface of the ocean," as the Quebec navigator Joseph Bouchette once put it.[7]

Not all Maritime politicians heading for Quebec City were aboard *Queen Victoria*. Some had opted for the one railroad then available for travel from the Maritime provinces to Quebec City—the one through the United States. Prince Edward Island's opposition leader and former premier, George Coles, his wife, and his daughter Mercy Anne boarded a steamer in Charlottetown at 3 A.M., and crossed to Shediac, New Brunswick. "I was very ill, it was so rough," Mercy recalled in her diary, but a train waited at Shediac to carry them to Saint John, where they joined George Coles's fellow Reformer, New Brunswick's premier

Leonard Tilley, and other delegates and their families. Tilley was "the only beau of the party," with five single ladies, Mercy Anne reported, and she was flattered by his attentions. Tilley was forty-six to her twenty-six, but he was a widower and, though her language in the diary is guarded, she may have been considering him as a potential suitor. From Saint John, the steamer *New Brunswick* took them down the Bay of Fundy to Portland, Maine, where they boarded the Grand Trunk passenger train north into Canada. They were expected: at the junction for Quebec, a special train requisitioned by the government of Canada waited to carry them along the branch line to Lévis Junction, across the river from Quebec City.[8]

In 1850, not even fifteen years earlier, the British North American provinces boasted barely a hundred kilometres of railroad. Travellers moved at the speed of stagecoaches and sailing ships. In winter, as the Canadian engineer Thomas Keefer wrote bitterly, "far away in the south is heard the daily scream of the steam whistle, but from Canada there is no escape, blockaded and imprisoned by ice."[9] In 1849, the reform-minded Canadian government of Louis-Hippolyte LaFontaine, newly empowered by something called "responsible government," enacted legislation to provide financial underpinning for railroad bond issues. A railroad boom began, and soon the navvies were swinging their hammers. By 1864, the province of Canada alone boasted three thousand kilometres of railroad.

Canada's principal railroad, the Grand Trunk, now ran from Sarnia in the west through Toronto and Montreal. At Montreal, the hub of this network, the mighty Victoria Bridge, an engineering marvel completed in 1860, carried the rail line across the St. Lawrence, and the Grand Trunk continued downriver past Quebec as far as tidewater at Rivière du Loup. From Montreal, another line ran southeast to Portland, Maine. Maritimers still made do with relatively short local lines, but they too were planning new railroad projects everywhere, and they nursed bold aspirations for lines to Quebec City and Montreal and down into the United States.

Not that train travel was luxurious. "One might just as well try to write on horseback," Mercy Coles wrote about diary-keeping on a train. The first Grand Trunk trains took fourteen hours to travel from Toronto to Montreal, and at first they had no dining or sleeping cars. Soon after confederation, a new member of Parliament from southwestern Ontario boarded a train at Strathroy on his way to his first parliamentary session. He had to change trains at London, Hamilton, Toronto, and Prescott, with long waits each time, and he arrived in Ottawa exhausted after twenty-four bumpy hours. Grumpy too: at some point his new umbrella had been stolen from the overhead rack.[10]

Train travel carried risks greater than delays and petty theft. In June 1864, a Grand Trunk passenger train rattling through Beloeil in Quebec's Richelieu Valley crashed through an open drawbridge, and ninety-nine people died in the wreck. "The Grand Trunk is in very bad repair," the politician George Brown grumbled a few months earlier. "Almost every day we hear of accidents."[11] Despite the dangers and discomforts, the railroads enabled resourceful travellers to make journeys in speed and relative comfort, like the one bringing these Maritimers toward Quebec City. The American writer Henry James, who would visit Quebec City a few years later, described his trip north from the United States by train as "a dreary night journey through crude, monotonous woods," until the railroad line emerged onto the south shore of the St. Lawrence. Then suddenly "beyond it, over against you, on its rocky promontory, sits the ancient town, belted with its hoary wall and crowned with its granite citadel."[12]

Mercy Coles and the Maritime politicians taking the train to Quebec travelled in daylight, but they reached Lévis station too late on Saturday afternoon, October 8, to appreciate Henry James's view of the citadel city. It was dark when they took the ferry across the river in heavy rain and rode carriages up to the Upper Town. After some confusion about their destination, they found their way to the Hotel St-Louis inside the city walls on Rue St-Louis, "a very nice hotel and every comfort one can wish for," in Mercy's opinion. Two delegates from Newfoundland had already arrived, but the storm-stayed passengers from *Queen Victoria* would not join them until the following evening. Journalists from as far as London and New York, executives from all the leading railroad companies, and other interested parties who had swarmed to Quebec for the conference had been dispatched to the Russell House some blocks away.

The Hotel St-Louis, Quebec City's leading hotel from the 1850s until the Chateau Frontenac was built just down the street in the 1890s, would be a hive of activity throughout the conference, and not only for the Maritimers. Several of the Canadian delegates, indeed, were also residents of the hotel. Six months earlier, George Brown had been renting "very good quarters—a good sitting room and a closet as bedroom" in Madame Langlois's house on the north side of the upper town, "with a glorious view of the St. Charles" river. But Madame Langlois sold the house in May, and Brown joined other parliamentarians who roomed at the Hotel St-Louis.[13] On Saturday night, Mercy Coles encountered him in the hotel drawing room as soon as she had changed her dress and ventured downstairs. She had met Brown and most of the other Canadian politicians in September, during their mission to Charlottetown; at the time Brown had written to his wife that the Coles daughters were "educated, well informed and as sharp as needles."[14] Brown himself had only returned from Toronto that morning, sped down overnight in a private rail car—being a cabinet minister had perks, he noted appreciatively—and they all reunited like old friends. "Mr. Cartier, John A. Macdonald, and McGee arrived in a minute," Mercy reported, and with instinctive Victorian formality, they arranged themselves to go into the dining room. "Mr. Cartier took Ma to dinner, John A. took Mrs. Pope; we had a splendid dinner." Friendships forged at Charlottetown were renewed, and Macdonald's aide, Hewitt Bernard, promised Mercy they would all have "grand times." There would be an even larger gathering at the hotel the following evening when *Queen Victoria*'s passengers arrived. "What a Babel when they came in!" she told her diary. [15]

As a governor general's wife was soon to say, Quebec City was already "one of the most famous landscapes of the world," and the confederation delegates and their families were eager to explore what Edward Whelan called "the ancient and historic city" and its "mazy, crooked, narrow and bewildering streets."[16] In 1864, Quebec was a city also being transformed by steam and iron. Since Champlain's day, and long before, Quebec had commanded the narrows of the St. Lawrence from its rock above the river, controlling all traffic and trade between the wide Atlantic world and the interior of Canada. The city's guns had long defended the entry to the continent, and its docks and warehouses dominated its trade. Upstream from Quebec City, only local shipping traffic ventured. In the 1850s, however, shipping began to travel past the city. Powerful steamship engines and the dredging of the riverbed allowed ships swift passage upriver, right past the older city to Montreal, the emerging commercial capital and railroad hub. In the new age of steam and iron, Quebec City's businesses were shifting to Montreal, particularly the international commerce that depended on British capital and operated mostly in English.

Montreal, the new point of exchange between the steamships and the American continent, grew rapidly in the 1860s, but Quebec City's population levelled off at about fifty thousand people. That population was about 40 percent English in the 1860s, but would grow steadily more French-speaking. Was Quebec City about to become what Montrealers were already beginning to call it: the *vieille capitale*, a folkloric, historic place that business had passed by? Slower growth would indeed preserve its historic ambiance, its walls and ancient buildings, but in 1864 the city was still the centre of government for the province of Canada and the residence of the governor general of all British North America. Quebec was still the military capital of British

North America, with a garrison of red-coated British soldiers and their officers, and fortifications of stone and earth framing the town. It remained a centre of commerce, law, and culture. Many of the great institutions of French Canada—the Catholic bishop's cathedral and palace, the Séminaire de Québec, Université Laval—were found inside the ancient walls in the Upper Town neighbourhoods atop the cliffs, mingled inextricably with long-established English institutions, such as the Anglican Cathedral, the English-language college, and the homes of leading anglophone business families. The civic government was similarly mixed. Adolphe Tourangeau, a lawyer and businessman, had recently succeeded Thomas Pope as mayor of the city, though his plan to demolish the town's gates and even the walls themselves as part of his modernization campaign had been thwarted. The city remained divided between the stylish Upper Town inside the walls and the working-class Lower Town along the riverfront, but in recent years the Grand Allée had been laid out, leading westward beyond the St. Louis Gate, through new developments and past the Plains of Abraham to Spencer Wood, the elegant park and residence of the governor general.[17]

Quebec City had not yet yielded cultural leadership to Montreal, either in English or French. Since 1824, the Literary and Historical Society of Quebec, mostly but not exclusively English, had been maintaining a library and collecting historical records. And at Octave Crémazie's bookshop, many of French Quebec's leading intellectuals and writers could often be found in the backroom gathering place. Crémazie himself, honoured as "le poète nationale" for his tributes to French Canada's culture, no longer joined them; he had fled to Paris to escape his extravagant debts. His shop remained a gathering place for poets, journalists, antiquarians, and artists such as the painter Théophile Hamel. Quebec was also home to Cornelius Krieghoff, whose paintings of *habitant* life were already popular among English-Canadian collectors. Both of French Canada's leading historians lived in the city. François-Xavier Garneau, ailing and elderly in 1864, had been inspired to write his *Histoire du Canada* by Lord Durham's ill-considered remark that the French Canadians were a people without history, but Garneau was a free thinker and somewhat anti-clerical, so the church hierarchy preferred the more deferential *Cours d'Histoire* of Abbé Ferland, dean of arts at Université Laval. More popular than either, both in French and in English translation, was the nostalgic historical novel *Les Anciens Canadians*, recently published by the elderly lawyer and former seigneur Philippe Aubert de Gaspé.

If trains and steamships were draining trade from Quebec City, they could at least bring visitors. Anthony Trollope visited in 1861, observing, "The best part of the town is built high upon the rock—the rock which forms the celebrated plains of Abram; and the view from thence down to the mountains which shut in the St. Lawrence is magnificent." The homespun American humourist Artemus Ward came in 1865, and wrote home, "The streets don't lead anywheres in particular but everywhere in general. The city is built on a variety of perpendicular hills, each hill bein' a little wuss than t'other one."[18] Ten years earlier, the English world traveller Isabella Bird found Quebec "most picturesque ... all novel and original," and was struck by its military air. "Guards and sentries appear in all directions; nightfall brings with it the challenge '*Who goes there?*' and narrow gateways form inconvenient entrances to streets so steep that I wondered how mortal horses could ever toil up them."[19]

Now came all these politicians from all the provinces of British North America, paying court to the traditional pre-eminence of the city by bringing the crucial constitutional negotiations to be settled there. Journalists and political aides and railroad lobbyists followed them. While the delegates got the newly built Hotel St-Louis, these observers were dispatched to the older Russell House, across town on Côte du Palais. A decade earlier, Isabella Bird had found the guests at the Russell "lively and amusing," although the hotel was "composed of three of the oldest houses in Quebec," had "no end of long passages, dark winding staircases, and queer little rooms," and was "haunted to a fearful extent by rats."[20] Around the constitutional summit would develop a social and commercial festival to brighten a cold, damp autumn. The governor general and his court, the politicians and civil servants, and the civic elite, both French and English, would all be drawn in, inspiring Edward Whelan to tell his Charlottetown readers that the Maritimers were in danger of forgetting their mother tongue and returning home "talking a strange conglomeration of English and excessively bad French."[21] Shopkeepers, hoteliers, and *caleche* drivers would prosper. Whatever those upriver parvenus in Montreal might think, Quebec in these few weeks seemed to recover its place as the key city of British North America. It warmed the hearts of Quebec City to see the steamships arriving crowded with Montrealers whenever one of the great balls of the confederation conference was about to be held.[22]

There had been a long gestation to this constitutional conference. It had emerged from fierce rivalries among the provinces and within their governments, and from equally fierce clashes of both ideology and ambition among the politicians involved. The meeting at Quebec had drawn together several provinces, more than thirty delegates, and many contending interests. At the heart of the project, however, stood three men, all from the province of Canada, all between the ages of forty-five and fifty, all veteran politicians, and all vying for leadership in the conference and in the new nation they would discuss. They were a francophone from Montreal, George-Étienne Cartier; a Scots Canadian from Toronto, George Brown; and a second Scot, John A. Macdonald, from Kingston. Their tactical alliances, their three-cornered rivalry, and their visions for confederation would be central to the whole process.

TWO

Before the Conference 1: John A. Macdonald's Worst Summer

Saturday, August 27, 1864. After a spectacular thunderstorm during the night and steady rain all morning, the cabinet of the Province of Canada assembled about midday in the legislative building on the cliff edge high above Lower Town, within the walls of Quebec City. Confederation planning demanded the parliamentarians' attention, and one minister had yet to arrive: John A. Macdonald, the attorney general for Canada West.

As they waited for Macdonald, eleven other cabinet ministers helped themselves to lunch from a sideboard and took up business that did not require the attorney general's participation. Then it was 1 P.M. Then it was 2 P.M. Finally Alexander Galt, the finance minister, sent a runner to Macdonald's home to remind him his presence was required. He returned with Macdonald's promise to join the ministers immediately. But it was 3 P.M. when Macdonald arrived, and they saw why he had been unavailable.

He was "bearing symptoms of having been on a spree," his fellow minister and longtime rival George Brown wrote.[1] "He was half drunk."

Once arrived, Macdonald availed himself of "potations of ale" from the sideboard, even as the cabinet moved on with the one urgent item on the agenda. The whole cabinet was to board *Queen Victoria* at the city wharf on Monday, bound for Charlottetown. There they would meet representatives of three Maritime provinces and present their confederation project. The confederation opportunity had blossomed so rapidly that there had been no prior consultation with the Maritimers about anything more than the invitation to attend. No one knew how they might respond to the nation-building program on which the Canadians had formed their new government. The Canadians' case for confederation had to be complete, confident, and carefully prepared. Everyone in the delegation needed to understand and support the offer they would make—no doubters, no backsliders, no diversions on untested ideas. The cabinet had been working out details of the constitutional plan all summer. This afternoon, they had to wrap up what Brown called "the important discussions of three days on the constitutional changes."

For the next two and a half hours, Macdonald worked with the rest. Evidently his sobriety, or lack of it, was tacitly ignored. Most of his colleagues had seen him dealing with vital issues in worse condition. Even in his cups, Macdonald could be a formidable participant in anything to which he put his agile mind.

Success! By the end of the afternoon, the ministers had settled "all about our trip to Charlottetown and our course when there." Six weeks of intense work were bearing fruit. The summer had been demanding for everyone in cabinet. In a few dramatic days back in June, these twelve parliamentarians had formed a coalition from the three factions they led. Macdonald's anglophone Conservatives from Canada West and George-Étienne Cartier's mostly francophone Bleus, the conservatives of Canada East, were longtime allies, accustomed to working in harness, though rarely without tensions. Never before, however, had they jammed themselves together with George Brown's rival faction, the impassioned

Reformers from Canada West who had helped keep the other two groups united against them for a decade. Now, after years of rivalry, with the fall of yet another divided Parliament about to provoke another general election that would settle nothing, the three groups had come together on the promise of fundamental constitutional reform: a federal union between Canada East and Canada West, and an approach to the Maritime provinces about joining them in a broad confederation of all the British provinces of North America. Through July and August ("been in council five hours, and the heat is oppressive," Brown wrote to his wife Anne on August 8), the members of the new government struggled with this ambitious plan in closed-door sessions, tantalized by the possibilities of nation-making glory, fearful of bitter failure, and always competing for primacy. Amid the burdens of administering a vast and fractious province, they needed to turn the airy promise of a grand union of all the British North America colonies into a feasible—and politically saleable—set of proposals. They had reason to be edgy: federation was a goal that generations of British North Americans had been hearing about—and failing to bring about. No time remained for further tinkering. At the end of the afternoon, with the preparations finally done, several cabinet members probably needed a drink as badly as Macdonald had earlier.

Then Macdonald struck. They could not adjourn yet, he declared. Cabinet must take up the matter of the Ottawa building contractors. The file on the Ottawa contractors was old business. It hardly seemed to need immediate action, not on the last full day before the ministers sailed for Charlottetown with the fate of confederation in their hands. For fifteen years, the capital of the Province of Canada had moved every few years: Montreal, Kingston, Toronto, and Quebec City had all filled the role in their turn. In 1857, a new, permanent capital had been chosen: Bytown, the lumber town on the Ottawa River that divided Canada East from West. The future capital was renamed Ottawa, and magnificent parliament buildings were already under construction on Barracks Hill, newly reborn as Parliament Hill. The original plan had been to provide a permanent capital for the Province of Canada. Now the city might become the capital of a larger Canada, composed of all the confederated British North American provinces.

Whatever the buildings' destinies, the contractors had begun to bicker with the government as soon as the work began. They demanded more money. The government replied that payment would be made when more work was done. Even the work already paid for was incomplete, according to the public inspectors. This squabble over fees had been an irritant for two years, through every change of government and many construction delays. Now, with steam practically up on the boat to Charlottetown, right at the climax of the vital constitutional planning that was the new government's reason for existing, Macdonald brought up the contractors' demands once more. The builders needed a decision, he said, a quick arbitration and prompt payment. He had with him a list of arbitrators.

George Brown, who had been chairing the constitutional discussion in his new cabinet post as president of the council, was as eager as anyone to see the new parliament buildings finished. Brown had been up the Ottawa River that summer—for the first time in his life—to inspect the construction work in the capital-to-be. He had been hugely impressed. The Victorian Gothic towers rising above the river were "really magnificent," he wrote, a great capital worthy of a great people.[2] But Brown was not sight-seeing. He was a cabinet minister now. After fifteen barren years in opposition complaining about government waste authorized by Macdonald and his friends, Brown was now putting his own signature on expenditures. He was as responsible as Macdonald for the public money being spent, and being cabinet colleagues for ten weeks had not persuaded the two men to trust each other. If there were going to be any arbitration, Brown needed to be sure the government—his government—would select impartial arbitrators. He wanted no panel packed with cronies of John A. The decision about arbitrators would have to wait, Brown declared in response to Macdonald's blunt demand, at least until he could vet the names on Macdonald's list.

John A. blew up. He insisted, "loudly, fiercely," the thing should be settled then and there. He demanded that his friends in cabinet stand with him. Brown had only brought two of his own party into cabinet. The rest of the twelve were Macdonald's and Cartier's men, old allies to each other, old rivals to Brown's Reformers. Brown recognized a test: was this government truly a coalition, or was it John A.'s to command? He laid down his own ultimatum. If the cabinet approved Macdonald's arbitrators, he declared, "then he would not stay in the council one moment more." On the eve of the mission to Charlottetown, the coalition would come apart, and the government must fall. The confederation plan would fall with it. George-Étienne Cartier, the pivot of the triangle that linked Brown and Macdonald, said not a word. The confederation alliance trembled.

Alexander Galt took alarm. An anglophone Quebecker whose loyalties bridged the Conservative–Reform divide, Galt had been promoting federation for years. To safeguard its prospects now, he floated a compromise that was really the postponement Brown demanded: let the choice of arbitrators wait. Cartier, dominant among the Bleus who held the balance, must have given his approval, because Galt's motion for delay got through with only one contrary voice: Macdonald's. John A. then burst out furiously that since his friends were deserting him, he would not hold office another day. But George Brown guessed that the vote had ended the crisis. John A.'s resignation threat was an empty one—"He will not think of it when he gets sober," Brown wrote to Anne Brown that night. The next day, the cabinet postponed the whole matter until the return to Quebec City. The appointment of arbitrators dropped down cabinet's agenda; when it came back six weeks later, it would be dispatched in a moment. The coalition government endured, along with the pursuit of confederation.

For once, John A. Macdonald, the smooth parliamentary operator with unrivalled gifts for reading a room and guiding its deliberations, had failed to wrong-foot George Brown by goading him to some act of furious principle. This time, Brown got what he needed from his threat of resignation, and Macdonald's own threat had been exposed as a bluff. John A.'s own closest allies had measured their reliance on Macdonald against the pettiness of the issue he was raising, and then against the vital place Brown held in the confederation plan. They had drawn back from Macdonald. The attorney general could not provoke Brown into walking out and did not dare walk away himself. He was forced to let the whole cabinet see his demand as bluster, as the drink talking. Cartier's signal of support for Brown's new place at the table had compelled Macdonald into acquiescence. For John A., it was a low moment in a long, low summer, a bitter and discouraging time of too much drink and too few victories, personal or political.

Macdonald had come to politics in the 1840s, a young man with an eye on greatness. Born to a struggling family on the edge of poverty, its genteel status forever slipping away, he had built a thriving legal career very young and was soon a man of business and politics in his hometown of Kingston, the effective head and breadwinner of his family when barely out of his teens. He had an eye for power and a knack for persuasion from the very beginning, and he soon put them to use in politics: elected at twenty-nine, a cabinet minister at thirty-two, and the coming man among Upper Canadian Conservatives by the mid-1840s. He went out of power, still in his thirties, in the great Reform triumph of Baldwin and LaFontaine in 1848, but he bided his time and let the Baldwin–LaFontaine coalition come apart.[3]

When George-Étienne Cartier replaced Louis-Hippolyte LaFontaine as leader of the broad French-Canadian parliamentary bloc, Macdonald watched French Canada lose confidence in its partnership with Baldwin's heirs among the Canada West Reformers, and he deftly put forward his own bloc as the alternative. In 1856, Cartier and Macdonald put together their first government. George Brown was rebuilding the Reform bloc, but now it was Macdonald's Conservatives who had the alliance that was the key to power. For the next several years, Macdonald and Cartier were in and out of power, but mostly in, and as attorney general Macdonald became a master of government business. He drafted new legislation. He dealt with the American republic across the border as it slid into civil war. He corresponded with the separate Maritime colonies of British North America over perpetually vexed tariff and railroad proposals. Above all, he dealt with the fractious, independent-minded legislators and their unstable alliances, learning the parliamentary business of putting together majorities. He became the most gifted politician in the province, the best tactician, the liveliest stump speaker, and the most tireless campaigner and organizer too. Macdonald looked like a brilliant success.

Early in 1864, however, it all seemed sour to him. Not quite fifty now, John A. was a widower, his young son left with his in-laws back in Kingston, his law practice there near collapse for lack of his attention. He and Cartier had lately come back into power after a spell of opposition, but theirs was a government with the barest of majorities, with all the usual factions deadlocked and divided, and with little likelihood they could hold all their supporters together. With Brown's Reformers catching the mood of Canada West, Macdonald's bloc was dwindling. His own seat at the cabinet table depended more than ever on Cartier's support. After twenty years of struggle, he was talking of getting out of the "dreary waste of colonial politics" where there was "nothing worthy of ambition."[4]

That spring, the politicians began to talk of federal union again. To end the constant factional quarrelling within the Province of Canada— French and English, Reformers and Tories, Canada East and Canada West—perhaps they should consider letting its eastern and western parts run their own affairs again. On George Brown's motion, the legislature struck a committee on constitutional options. The idea of a federal union that would divide Canada West from Canada East was in the air.

Macdonald opposed it. Certainly he opposed the committee and the federal project just because it was George Brown's work. Macdonald had tolerated previous federal proposals from governments he was part of, but he had no obligation to Brown and no wish to further Brown's program. His opposition ran much deeper than that, however. His reading of politics—indeed, his whole life experience—persuaded him that strength and success lay in concentrating power, not diffusing it.

Macdonald was a Kingston man, and Kingston had been built on the river trades, an economic satellite of Montreal more than of Toronto. Kingston needed no new barriers placed across the lines of trade that kept it prosperous. John A. was a man of the 1860s, too, and looking south he saw the American federal union torn apart and flung into civil war by regional rivalries and the weakness of central authority. He was also a British Empire man, with Britain both his birthplace and the root of his political faith. In Britain, no one doubted where sovereignty and power resided: it was in Parliament alone, and in the cabinets that parliament empowered. Macdonald was a Scot, but he did not pine for the ancient autonomy of Scotland or Wales or Ireland—or for Canada West either. In his heart, he believed that power had to reside somewhere, and power was always his lodestone. Instinctively, he doubted the viability of any political system that diffused power across several governments.[5]

There was his own situation, too. For all his political successes, Macdonald's access to power had always been frustratingly shared and circumscribed, always depending on his followers' vital role as minority partners to Cartier's Bleus. A federal union would end the value of that link. He would then be a Canada West politician exclusively, and a self-governing Canada West promised to elect Brown's Reformers, cut Macdonald off from his Canada East allies, and relegate him to an eternal minority.

So he opposed the federal initiative both on principle and from political calculation. When Brown proposed that the legislative committee consider the federal idea, Macdonald declared it was not worth discussing—that any British North American union should be a complete union, not a federal one. Look what the Americans' experience of federation had brought them, he declared in March 1864, in the debate on the motion to form the committee. "We should have a legislative union in fact, in principle, and in practice."[6]

This time, the tide was running against John A. He lost that vote, joined the committee to continue his opposition, and was outvoted twelve to three. "A strong feeling was found to exist among the members of the committee in favour of changes in the direction of a federative system," the committee reported on June 14, 1864.[7] Macdonald, in the minority of dissenters, continued to insist that only a strong union, a legislative union—one government, one legislature—could hold together these weak and fractured colonies.

These were surely Macdonald's sincere convictions on display. True, he had given support to federation proposals, such as Galt's plan of 1858, that had been what the opposition called "ministerial myths"—worthy notions likely to come to nothing. All his life, before confederation and after, Macdonald spoke for and acted on the belief that Canada needed a strong central government. Brown's committee's recommended move in "the direction of a federative system" was never a way he preferred going.

The same day that the committee opted for a federal solution to Canada's problems, the shaky Macdonald–Cartier government was defeated on another matter. "We have had great times," George Brown wrote to his wife. "On Tuesday we defeated the government by a majority of two."[8] With the government denied the support of the legislature, another general election loomed, promising only another deadlock. Instead, the fall of the government changed everything. In the span of a day, John A. would reverse his position and plunge into negotiations for precisely what he had inveighed against: federal union.

Having tested the waters in the constitutional committee, George Brown, the pillar of dogged opposition for fifteen years, the one factional leader who could never be enticed into supporting the government, stood in the legislature after defeating the government and hinted that this time he might offer that support. He did not even insist on seats in a reconstituted government. He required only two things: a federal plan that would let Canada West control its own vital affairs and "rep by pop," representation by population. Macdonald and Cartier had maintained their partnership for almost a decade on a firm, determined rejection of both these old demands. They had consistently stood for preserving the union of Canada East and West under a single parliament, and they stood for each section having equal voting power in the legislature, no matter what imbalance of population developed between them. Both rules were understood as safeguards for French Canada, to ensure the francophone population in the Province of Canada could never be outnumbered, outvoted, or eventually assimilated.

Now George-Étienne Cartier was changing his mind. The master politician of French Canada was suddenly willing to reconsider federalism and rep by pop as well, and Brown was responding to his signal. Macdonald's quick strategic mind tallied the consequences. He could stand on principle and continue to oppose federalism and its weaknesses. But if Cartier and Brown, leading the largest blocs in Canada East and West, agreed on a federal partnership, then Macdonald's refusal to go along would only consign him to opposition, to the fringes. Better, he calculated, to be on the inside shaping the terms than outside condemning them. In the next few days, Macdonald, on behalf of the Macdonald–Cartier government, began to negotiate terms for a new alliance. He insisted that Brown come into the government and bring his party with him. They must join a coalition, not just give independent outside support for a federal plan, as Brown had preferred to do. Macdonald bargained hard on the distribution of seats in the new cabinet: Canada East held six of the twelve, all from Cartier's Bleus and their allies, Macdonald insisted on three for his supporters, and Brown settled for just three Reformers in a cabinet of twelve. Macdonald also ensured that the coalition would pursue "confederation"—a union of all of the British North American colonies, not just the "federation" of Canada East and West. This was not just "the glory argument," though uniting all of

British North America was an enticing prospect. There were Conservative governments in the Maritime provinces, and Macdonald could envision potential allies in the event Cartier and Brown lined up against him.

That summer, however, the mass of votes behind the Canadian coalition were still Brown's and Cartier's. The policy was theirs, too: a federal union, the type that Macdonald feared, opposed, and had argued against. No wonder that as the Canadian cabinet spent the summer working out the details of the federal union Canada would propose to the Maritime provinces, Macdonald's frustrations and irritations grew, and were taken out in absenteeism and drinking. Finally, at the climax of the planning, he was goaded into something very much out of character: an inept, drink-fuelled, and embarrassingly unsuccessful attempt to break the coalition apart and remove Brown from the planning, just as the mission to Charlottetown prepared to set sail.

THREE

Before the Conference 2: George Brown's Best Summer

George Brown was on fire in the summer of 1864. He was a big, hard-driving, serious man of forty-five, wealthy, successful, and positive about most things—even his positive hatreds, of which he had more than a few. Back in the 1840s, newly arrived from Scotland, he had founded the Toronto *Globe*. Publisher Brown improved the newspaper's presses, expanded its frequency, and got it distributed all over the province.[1] Editor Brown made it the liveliest paper around, one that reflected and shaped the politics of his prosperous, growing, ambitious readership, in Toronto and across southern Ontario. *The Globe* became Canada West's leading newspaper and the foundation of Brown's fortune and reputation, even as he poured boundless energy into his farm property in Oxford County, his new Toronto home on Wellington Street, and his unrelenting political commitments. In 1862, he had married for the first time at forty-three, and in 1864 he was a proud husband and the doting father of baby Maggie. That summer, Anne Brown, toting Maggie, had sailed to Edinburgh to visit her family. Brown, often an absent spouse, was a faithful correspondent. He worked ferociously long hours, travelled constantly, and generally left his wife and daughter at home in Toronto during parliamentary sittings while he lived in cramped rooms in Quebec City. During this most important summer of his political career, he had sent his family to Scotland, always promising his imminent departure to join them, just as soon as this confederation business was taken care of. Meanwhile he inundated Anne with his letters full of affection and longing, full of requests for photographs of the baby, and full of sometimes indiscreet details about the confederation negotiations.

Politics was the one unrelenting frustration of Brown's life, nagging at him like the back trouble and sciatica for which he kept promising to seek treatment. He had been nearly always in opposition, rocklike in his beliefs yet constantly outmanoeuvred and derided. Frustrated by his inability to get anything done, he talked constantly of the day when Canada West's grievances would be addressed and he could give up political life for his true vocation of journalism.

In June 1864, Brown found his political life transformed. As if he had been pounding his head against a wall and suddenly found it collapsing in front of him, he abruptly became a member of a broadly based government coalition. And not just any member, but one whose own long-derided principles and demands were suddenly government policy. Dazed and joyful, he plunged into the responsibilities of office, and his energy for the task was unlimited.

Early in August, Brown left Toronto, where he had been campaigning, to take part in the cabinet sessions in Quebec City. He had business interests in New York State, so he took the Great Western Railway via Hamilton and Niagara Falls into northern New York. Two days out from home, he wrapped up his American business and took another train north to Ogdensburg, New York. There he crossed the St. Lawrence at midnight in a thunderstorm to await the Grand Trunk passenger train scheduled to come through Prescott, Ontario, at 2:30 A.M. Instead, word came of a train wreck near Kingston: no eastbound service. Brown crossed back to the American side and caught a steamship downriver to Montreal ("a fine run down the rapids"), telegraphing ahead for the Quebec City steamer to await his arrival. He got to Quebec City with time to spare, just four days out from Toronto—a trip that would have been inconceivable just a few years before.[2]

Soon after, Brown made his dash by train and river steamer to Ottawa to inspect the new parliament buildings under construction. In opposition, Brown would have thundered against governmental waste and cronyism in the construction project. As it was, however, the monumental Victorian Gothic buildings rising "on a high promontory, seen all around for a grand distance and amid scenery nowhere surpassed" enchanted him. They were a capital worthy of a great people, he wrote, and the sight inspired in him a vision of the far future. "A hundred years hence the people will fancy the men of their days were giants in imagination."[3]

Six months earlier, in February 1864, after enduring hours of George-Étienne Cartier's "screeching" in the legislature, Brown had said of his political foes, "I would a thousand times rather go out of public life than be at the mercy of such people." Yet by the end of June, he was constantly riding the trains and riverboats back to Quebec City to chair cabinet discussions with these same people—and the discussions were being driven by the principles he had pushed forward for years. Brown liked rolling up his sleeves, bulling his way through the complications, and getting things done. The cabinet sessions of 1864 were the best opportunity he had ever had to apply that zest to governance. "I don't think any of us appreciate the immensity of the work we are engaged in," he wrote. He was not shrinking from it.[4]

What were these principles Brown took such pride in and was finally getting a chance to apply? As a youthful editor, George Brown had lived in a colony and chafed at its subjection. In the mid-1840s, the Province of Canada had an elected assembly, but the governor appointed by the British government truly ruled. The governor chose his own advisors and campaigned hard to get his supporters into the assembly.

He controlled the Crown's funds, no matter how the assembly might want them spent, and for instructions he looked to Britain, not to the colonial legislature. Brown, a traditional British parliamentary democrat, would have none of such arbitrary rule: to be legitimate, he believed, a government must be accountable to a parliament. He and his newspaper were fierce in support of Robert Baldwin, Louis-Hippolyte LaFontaine, and the alliance that united Toronto and Montreal, francophones and anglophones, for the sake of "responsible government"— the campaign to make the governor a ceremonial figurehead who took direction from a cabinet that was accountable (that is, "responsible") on a daily basis to the elected representatives of the people of the Province of Canada. When that campaign triumphed in 1848, Brown exulted in the victory, and in his newspaper's part in it. It was all the sweeter because John A., already his rival, had preferred the influence of having the ear of a powerful governor to the accountability that had triumphed. Macdonald had defended the old regime and gone out of power with it.

By 1851, when Brown first entered Parliament, he was still dedicated to representative democracy, but he had cooled on his party's leaders. Baldwin and LaFontaine intended to make a success of the union forced on the Canadas in 1841. By jamming anglophone Canada West and francophone Canada East together in a single province with a single legislature and government, Britain had intended this union to ensure the assimilation of the troublesome French. Baldwin and LaFontaine had turned the tables. They campaigned for tolerance and cross-cultural partnership in a union based on equality and political alliance, and they built an English–French political alliance that shifted authority from the appointed governor to the elected majority—their elected majority. That French–English alliance remained the two men's fundamental goal, not merely a tactic by which to achieve responsible government. It became a political vocation for Baldwin, who was elected in Rimouski, and LaFontaine, who was elected in York. Baldwin sent his daughter to a

French school in Quebec City. English and French, they urged, could prosper together, and the union could prosper too.[5]

Brown, a passionate supporter of LaFontaine and Baldwin's campaign for colonial self-government, was less moved by their goal of French–English unity. His people were Canada West's people: British to the bone, Protestant to a man, and to Brown's mind, far more go-ahead and less priest-ridden than the people of Canada East. Brown's Scots Presbyterianism had bred into him a horror of "established" state churches. A man should face God directly, he believed, not through priests, bishops, and popes, and no religious hierarchy should meddle in secular matters. Those convictions made Brown a relentless foe of the Roman Catholic Church and its influence over life and politics in Canada. Brown said he opposed only the way that the Catholic hierarchy meddled in politics, but it was a distinction not much appreciated in French Canada, where he was denounced as a bigot and a fanatic, nor among non-French Catholics. Brown complained that the Irish Catholics pouring off the immigrant ships in the 1840s and the 1850s were as ignorant and priest-ridden as the French Canadians.

If anything angered Brown more than the "priestcraft and state-churchism" he saw prevailing in Catholic Canada East, it was the equal voting power that the union of 1841 had given to Canada West and Canada East. This was precisely the kind of cross-cultural compromise Baldwin and LaFontaine accepted and exalted: two equal sections, one French, one English. To Brown, it simply gave Canada East control of the union while larger and wealthier Canada West provided most of the money. His attacks on French-Canadian domination of the union and of Canada West—"French-Canadianism," he came to call it—confirmed his status as the bogeyman of French Canada in the 1850s and into the 1860s. As Brown's Reformers turned against the partnership with French Canada in the mid-1850s, John A. Macdonald, as British and Scottish as Brown (though less rigorously Presbyterian), saw and seized the opportunity. If Brown was going to split the Canada West Reformers from LaFontaine's heirs, Macdonald's Canada West Conservatives would step into their place. They would defend the union of French and English from the seats of power.

Brown wholeheartedly agreed that the self-government Baldwin and LaFontaine's coalition had achieved in 1848 was the bedrock of Canadian public life. But with self-government achieved, were voting rights linked to population size—rep by pop—not an equally vital principle for free peoples? As a journalist, Brown had supported Baldwin in freeing Canada West from the misrule of autocratic British aristocrats and their local flunkies. He rose in active politics on his promise to set it free from the new menace: French Canada's big voting bloc and its control of Canada West's destiny, particularly when abetted by John A.'s Tories. The way to free Canada West, Brown had come to believe, was to remake the union itself, to free Canada West from Canada East and put each political entity in charge of its own affairs. He began groping toward a separation, or rather, a federal union: two strong, autonomous provinces linked by "some joint authority."[6] This was the principle his old enemies had fought against for a decade and more—and now, miraculously, had accepted.

"We have been hard at work with our constitutional discussions for two days and everything goes as well as we could possibly hope for," Brown wrote to Anne Brown during the hot summer of 1864. "I do believe we will succeed. The discussion today lasted from 12 till ¼ to 6 and from first to last it was highly interesting—most deeply interesting."[7]

FOUR

Before the Conference 3: The Veto Power of George-Étienne Cartier

"He has the happy quality of being always thoroughly well pleased with himself," an observer once said of George-Étienne Cartier, and Cartier did seem to be sailing through 1864 with precisely that cheerful certainty.[1] He had turned fifty during the Charlottetown meetings: four months older than Macdonald, four years older than Brown. That summer, while George Brown was lit up with enthusiasm and John A. sulky and hard-drinking, Cartier was outwardly unruffled by the great political change he had set into motion in June. In public, he spoke with calm confidence about his confederation decision—and his authority to make it. Through all the constitutional events that would follow, observers would speak of his good cheer, his attentions to the ladies, and his enthusiasm for singing and playing the piano.

In the working sessions, Cartier spoke less than Brown, the impulsive fountain of ideas, or Macdonald, the skilful manager of discussion. He could afford to be silent, sure as he was that the votes required to make things happen or prevent them from happening were his to direct.

He seems to have been mostly silent in the exchange of resignation threats between Brown and Macdonald over the Ottawa contractors in late August. But his choice was clear; it had been clear all summer. He would not permit the partnership with Brown's Reformers to be broken. Rep by pop and federalism were his policies now. If that was intolerable to Macdonald, it was Macdonald who would have to go.

Until June 1864, George Brown had been a useful foil to George-Étienne Cartier. For many years, Brown's railings against the malevolent influence of Catholic priests and bishops had been a great help to Cartier in rallying French-Canadian voters against the fanatical Protestant foe. Brown's contempt for "French domination" in the union enabled Cartier to position himself all the more firmly as the loyal and dedicated defender of a political system once intended as the doom of French Canada, now turned into its shield and protection. As Brown came to personify Reform thinking in Canada West, Cartier had redefined LaFontaine's francophone Reform bloc into his own, more conservative "Bleu" caucus. Just months before they went into coalition together, Brown had been fuming about "that little wretch" Cartier, and Cartier had been mocking Brown's endless, futile opposition.

Yet Brown and Cartier were not entirely alien. Long before their rivalry began, Cartier's Reform credentials had been stronger than Brown's. Cartier came from an old political family; his grandfather had been elected to the colonial assembly of Lower Canada in 1809. He himself had been engrossed with politics from his law student days in the 1830s, when the movement against autocratic rule was led by Louis-Joseph Papineau and his Patriot Party. Young Cartier became one of his organizers.[2]

When rebellion against the governors and their cliques flared in both colonies in 1837, George Brown was a teenager in Glasgow. John A. joined the loyal militia in Toronto. Cartier, however, went out with the Patriots and then fled for his life as their insurrection collapsed. That taste of armed conflict, when he stood with the farmers of

St-Denis-sur-Richelieu against British troops, convinced Cartier that his future lay in political work, not revolutionary violence. Later he was proud to say he had been a rebel for the sake of his people, but he always insisted he had fought for a good parliamentary motive, opposing not the government itself but only "a minority which desired to dominate the majority."[3] In the responsible government struggle of the 1840s, when Brown the young Toronto journalist swung his newspaper behind Robert Baldwin and Macdonald boasted of his loyalty to the Queen's governor, Cartier the young Montreal lawyer worked for Louis-Hippolyte LaFontaine. He became a propagandist and arm-twister for LaFontaine, though he maintained radical credentials by his marriage into the Fabres, a leading Patriot family. LaFontaine enunciated the high principles of parliamentary democracy and cross-cultural partnership, but it was young campaigners like Cartier who got articles into the newspapers, got out the election crowds, and built up the French-Canadian voting bloc that elected the LaFontaine–Baldwin government in 1848—when Cartier himself was first elected, four years after Macdonald first became the member for Kingston.

LaFontaine retired from politics in 1851, and Cartier gradually made himself dominant among the francophone politicians of Canada East. Responsible government—and Canada East's large cohesive voting bloc—had secured the political power of French Canada. LaFontaine's supporters had achieved most of their goals, and could drift to the innate conservatism that was still strong in French-Canadian society. In a government where once-autocratic governors now did the bidding of the elected members, francophone politicians like Cartier enjoyed access to power positions as never before. They soon entrenched the use of the French language and legal code—"*notre langue, nos institutions, et nos lois,*" as the slogan went. They continued to make reforms—such as the abolition of the seigneurial system of landholding—that they would have fought if imposed by a British governor and his anglophone councillors. Beyond that, they were content to conserve the traditional structures of French and Catholic society. The Reform Party built and led by LaFontaine gradually became Cartier's more conservative Parti Bleu.

Not that Cartier had mutated into some nostalgic reactionary. Though he often represented the farmers of rural Verchères, he was more interested in the businesses and railroad ventures that sustained his Montreal law practice. As early as 1845, he invested in the railroad that would link Montreal to the ice-free harbour of Portland, Maine. "The prosperity of Montreal depends on its position as the emporium for the commerce of the west," he said in 1846. "We can only assure it by better means of transport from the waters of the west to the Atlantic."[4] By 1852, the Grand Trunk Railway had taken over the rail link to Portland and made it part of what was briefly the longest railroad in the world, all the way west to Sarnia in Canada West. Cartier was its key legal advisor. For Cartier, the political union of the Canadas was an economic union as well. He saw Montreal's prosperity tied to both.

By the mid-1850s, George Brown's Toronto newspaper was beating the drums for western expansion because the next generation of his southern Ontario farm supporters would soon be seeking to expand into new land and saw the prairie west as their birthright. Cartier was just as determined that when they did move west, Montreal would direct the process and reap the benefits. Happy though he was to gain tactical advantage from deriding George Brown to Catholic audiences in Canada East, Cartier's calculations of the security of French Canada still remained bound to LaFontaine's vision of cross-cultural partnership. Cartier saw Montreal and Canada East depending for their prosperity on a firm alliance with Canada West. If George Brown truly represented Canada West, Cartier would deal with him.

Commitment to a broad union with continental ambitions went deep for Cartier, and he had never seen himself taking a secondary place in that program. One of his memorable slogans, particularly when he was consulting with magnates and aristocrats in Britain, was "A French-Canadian is an Englishman who speaks French."[5] It seemed like a cringing plea from a self-abasing *Canadien* ashamed of his origins. Cartier, however, meant it as a challenge, almost a taunt. His British audiences of lords and gentlemen—and Queen Victoria herself—mostly understood hostility to France and all things French as part of the birthright of a true Englishman. They must have been taken aback to hear one who spoke French as his mother tongue dare to call himself an Englishman and their equal.

Cartier had a political point to make by his bold claim. In the British political tradition, the rights and liberties of citizens were rarely put forward as abstract universal or natural rights. Englishmen preferred to speak of "the rights of Englishmen." They understood these to have grown out of English soil and English history, and they boasted of such rights as the unique possession of Englishmen (and gradually, perhaps, Britons more generally). Cartier's political point was that as a citizen of British North America, he, a French Canadian, was entitled to all the political rights Englishmen considered uniquely theirs. Cartier's provocation expressed the radicalism that endured in the idea of responsible government. Cartier held to the principle of citizenship set down by his Reform mentor LaFontaine: British North Americans, English or French, were equal to Englishmen in their rights, their opportunities, and their share in running their own societies. They could manage their own affairs as Britons did theirs, and a French Canadian's claim, even to be prime minister, could be as good as any English Canadian's. As long as he held to this notion of equality, the parliamentary leader of francophone Canada East could never be absolutely conservative.

In the spring of 1864, in the unending parliamentary deadlock, with loss of power threatened with every vote, Cartier had reason to reconsider his opposition to George Brown, as useful as it had been. Cartier's bloc was strong in Canada East, but support for the positions Brown advocated grew and grew in Canada West. The 1861 census had shown that Canada West was far outstripping Canada East in population. Who there could continue to be elected while denying it the voting power appropriate to its population? For Cartier, the danger loomed that Brown's support in Canada West might become large enough to enable him to turn the tables and restore English domination in place of the "French domination" he attacked so relentlessly. Rep by pop might come, even if the Bleus stood against it.

Cartier's fundamental political task was to safeguard French Canada. The union had served that end by guaranteeing that Canada East always had as many votes as Canada West, but Canada East needed another strategy in reserve, in case rep by pop ever overcame that guarantee. For George Brown, federalism—splitting Canada West from Canada East—meant getting his province free of "French domination," but Cartier could also see the move's potential to shelter French Canada from anglophone domination. As early as 1858, Alexander Galt, another Quebec-based Reformer moving toward the centre and eager to preserve the economic benefits to be reaped by interprovincial cooperation, had floated a plan for federation as his price for joining Cartier's government. Cartier encouraged him. Met with incomprehension in Britain, that confederation project went nowhere. Since the status quo endured, Cartier did not need to pursue it, but he held the idea in reserve. In a federal union, French Canada could be a province of its own, where its vital concerns could be protected and safeguarded. In a federation, a partnership might still endure for railroads, commerce, intercolonial links, and all the other guarantors of progress so precious to Montreal and to George-Étienne Cartier. At the same time, French Canada's language, its schools and institutions, and its law codes could be entrusted to a provincial legislature; the French majority might be even more secure there than in the union.[6]

John A. Macdonald, with his eye for power and his sense that British North America needed strength at the centre, held out for a legislative union, uniting all the provinces under one government. Against the growing electoral advantage Brown's Reformers held in Canada West, Macdonald needed an ally in Canada East, and that could be lost in a federal arrangement. The only change in the union of the Canadas that Macdonald could wholeheartedly support was a change to more centralization. But Cartier, his usually unshakeable ally, had to disagree. If rep by pop had to come, or if more anglophone provinces and voters came into the union, then Canada East had to have federalism, more even than Brown's Canada West did.

Like Anne Brown, Hortense Cartier was absent during most of the conference in Quebec City, but there was no flood of letters between the Cartiers. They had been estranged for years, and Mme Cartier generally stayed in Montreal while Cartier was in Quebec City, sometimes with his mistress. When she did visit Quebec, Mme Cartier made little effort to curry favour with the English. "I hope Mme Cartier will not come again," Lady Monck, wife of the governor general, Viscount Monck, had written in April 1864 when the parliamentarians were returning to Quebec. Among the governor's circles she was not thought "presentable."[7] Lady Monck called Cartier himself a mountebank in the same letter, but that may merely have been aristocratic superiority, for Cartier was a regular guest at Spencer Wood.[8]

FIVE

September in Charlottetown: John A. Bounces Back

John A. Macdonald's activities and moods on the eve of the Quebec Conference are ill documented. In the midst of the conference itself, Governor General Monck's sister-in-law recorded that John A. Macdonald was "always drunk now.... When someone went to his room the other night, they found him in his nightshirt with a railway rug thrown over him, practising Hamlet before a looking glass."[1] There is no hint of what lines Macdonald might have favoured if he did in fact play the Prince of Denmark in the midst of debating the constitution of Canada,* but the story may not have been reliable. The governor's family did not hang about the corridors of the delegates' hotel, and this account may simply show the enduring legend of Macdonald's drinking finding its way into the gossip of a Spencer Wood community predisposed to find all the Canadians slightly inappropriate. No other sources suggest that Macdonald was incapacitated by drink during the conference, though every dinner and reception and ball would be fuelled by alcohol.

---

* There are other instances of Macdonald quoting Hamlet, right to the end of his life.

When her family was the governor general's guests at Spencer Wood, Mercy Coles noted how drunk D'Arcy McGee became, but she seems to have been charmed by Macdonald when he dined with her family later, perhaps even calculating his potential as a suitor. In his September and October letters to Anne Brown, George Brown made no accusations about his cabinet colleague's drinking habits.

Since the Canadian cabinet's return from the Maritimes on September 19, cabinet members and their handful of staff had been extremely busy. They attended cabinet meetings almost daily, catching up on work neglected during their trip to the Maritimes and laying down plans for the confederation conference.[2] There was routine business and official correspondence that had been neglected during three weeks' of travel. And as Brown noted with surprise, requests were received for interviews with the British and American journalists converging on Quebec for the constitutional conference. Once the conference began, the record suggests that Macdonald came punctually to every session, working hard every day, speaking constantly, presenting and defending motions, and then lobbying and coaxing long into the evenings. At the dinners and balls, he was as eager to tease and dance with the ladies or pay court to the governor's party as he was to whisper in the ears of rivals and allies, or, if required, even to give one of the many long speeches.[3]

If Macdonald was soberer during the conference than rumour suggested, it may have been more than the pressure of work that kept him away from the bottle. John A. Macdonald was an alcoholic, but one with a surprising degree of self-control.[4] For much of his career, he was capable of vanishing into what the press called "sprees," which left him unavailable to colleagues and family for days at a time. But the sprees often started when Macdonald needed to avoid an issue, or when he was losing on some issue and had no counter-attack. During the conference itself, Macdonald was presumably drinking along with many of the other delegates and guests. Brown, for all his Presbyterian rigour, was not a teetotaller, and Cartier drank sociably. Some of the delegates, notably Leonard Tilley of New Brunswick, were strict prohibitionists, and must have avoided the champagne somehow. More typical was Edward Whelan, who joked at one public banquet that the delegates had met in secret because they had dark sins to confess. "Behold how earnestly we are all doing penance," he finished, tapping the champagne glass and earning a laugh.[5] Macdonald presumably laughed and drank with the others, but he had put aside the irritated, negative, heavy-drinking hostility described by George Brown in late August. (Indeed, the matter of the Ottawa contractors that had been so contentious in August was dealt with as routine business—and to Brown's satisfaction—during a cabinet session in the midst of the constitutional conference.[6]) Since the meetings at Charlottetown, Macdonald had found reason for optimism, for action, and for disciplined sobriety. He now discerned a path to power.

All summer, Macdonald had been in the minority in the Canadian cabinet. He was greatly valued, certainly, for his political skills, his administrative abilities, and his grasp of what was possible—from local by-elections to discussions at Downing Street in London. But the federation policy was driven by its true believers: Cartier, Brown, and Alexander Galt. In the Canadian cabinet, Cartier and Brown had the votes. In a crunch, they could do without Macdonald, leaving him with only the unappetizing company of the anti-confederate minority. If a purely Canadian federation, involving only Canada East and West, went ahead, as seemed quite possible during the summer, Macdonald was likely to find himself and his supporters trapped in a permanent minority. The leader of the new federal government in the new buildings in Ottawa would be either Cartier or Brown, or both together in the shared premiership the old Province of Canada had had. As the Canadian cabinet spent the summer working out principles for the kind of federal union that Macdonald opposed, he worked with his colleagues, but he also drank and grumbled and set up irritants that might just send Brown stamping out in a fury of principle. After the Charlottetown meeting in September, that had changed.

Back in June, Macdonald had been one of those insisting that the first object of the confederation coalition must be to include the Atlantic provinces. At that moment, it seemed an impractical ambition, for plans to unite all of British North America had been collapsing for fifty years, and Brown had secured agreement that if the Maritimers proved uninterested, the smaller "Canadian" federation must go ahead. Still, a larger confederation—should it be possible—was acceptable to Brown. He was not immune to visions of a great northern nation, and in any case his rural farm supporters were eager to see a mechanism by which the prairie west might be annexed to Canada West. A larger confederation was agreeable to Cartier too, who favoured rail links between the provinces, saw Montreal as the future capital of those western territories, and was already looking with interest at the land controlled by the Hudson's Bay Company. So long as federalism guaranteed French Canada's control of the essential powers it needed to preserve its identity, Cartier welcomed the largest possible federation.

At Charlottetown, the Canadians, somewhat to their own surprise, found support for confederation. Macdonald found allies as well. The Canadians' presence at Charlottetown was informal, their confederation proposal one of broad principle only. The Maritimers quickly showed interest, but the serious work of determining the details of the union would be saved for a second conference, the one in Quebec City. When the Maritimers said yes to the confederation project, however, Macdonald's prospects were transformed at once. He may have been a skeptic about the confederation plan's airy idealism, its attempt to solve problems by pursuing constitutional dreams rather than employing the pragmatic "men and measures" politicking he preferred. But at Charlottetown he had a new and receptive audience, and he could count the numbers. To the Maritimers, he was less abrasive than the blunt, plain-spoken Canada West patriot George Brown. They were well aware that during his years in opposition, Brown had often opposed plans for interprovincial cooperation, at times denouncing them as plots by greedy

Maritimers to drain away the hard-earned prosperity of Canada West. Compared to Cartier, Macdonald was at least an anglophone. Cartier was clearly genial and effective and influential at Charlottetown, but unlike the Canadians, the Maritimers had not yet grown used to the power and influence of francophone politicians. Macdonald also quickly discovered that many of the Maritime politicians shared his views on strong central government. With no Acadians and few Catholics included among their political leadership, the Maritimers had never had to deal with the bicultural issues that made federal-style accommodations attractive to the Canadians. Britain, their model of parliamentary practice, was not federal, and the collapse of the American federation into civil war was no advertisement for federal unions. Although they represented small provinces that might seem instinctively supportive of local autonomy against the crushing majorities the Canadians would hold in a rep-by-pop national parliament, several of the leading Maritimers believed that power should be concentrated, not diffused. John A. Macdonald spoke their language.

Whatever his reservations about federalism, Macdonald spoke strongly and effectively in support of the Canadian proposal in the Charlottetown meetings. He applied his skill and charm and persuasion to convince the Maritimers that confederation was possible and worthwhile. A particular bond formed at Charlottetown between Macdonald and Charles Tupper of Nova Scotia. Six years younger than Macdonald and newly installed in the premier's office, Tupper had long been sympathetic to confederation. Raised in small-town Nova Scotia, but trained in medicine in Edinburgh, Scotland, Tupper looked for a big stage for his talents. The Maritimes, he said, "could never hope to occupy a position of influence or importance except in connection with their larger sister Canada." He looked ahead to the day when "British America, stretching from the Atlantic to the Pacific, would in a few years exhibit to the world a great and powerful organization." He had also hitched his political prospects to the plan for an intercolonial railway that would link Halifax to the eastern end of the Grand Trunk at Rivière-du-Loup in Canada East. Years of fruitless negotiations among the separate provinces had convinced him that only confederation could deliver the railroad.[7] No nostalgic conservative, Tupper was a blunt, hard-driving, combative politician. He shared Macdonald's acute sense of power. As the confederation talks proceeded, he would become Macdonald's consistent ally in advocating for a strong central government, confident that with strong men like himself in the new national government, Nova Scotia would be well represented even without guarantees of provincial autonomy.

Not every Maritimer Macdonald met at Charlottetown was as supportive as Tupper, however. Several of the Prince Edward Islanders in particular were deeply skeptical of any union and strongly committed to their island's autonomy. But Macdonald could calculate how having the Maritimers in the conferences—and in the future federation—changed the relationships. With them in the room, Macdonald no longer needed to accept being trapped between Cartier's supporters and Brown's; he could begin to recruit his own. The surly, uncooperative side of himself that Macdonald had exhibited just before the Canadians' departure for Charlottetown now vanished. Macdonald became one of the most active participants in the week of meetings, a leader of the Canadian team, and a genial, convivial, charming companion throughout the Maritime tour and throughout the Quebec City events. He surely drank. He may even have recited Shakespeare in his nightshirt. From the start of the Maritime excursion, however, there was no trace of the sulky, disruptive Macdonald that George Brown had confronted on August 29. Macdonald had a strategy and he had allies. He had no more time, and much less inclination, for sprees.

SIX

Monday, October 10: Étienne Taché in the Chair

By late morning on Monday, October 10, thirty-three delegates from five provinces* of British North America had managed to get themselves along Rue St-Louis, across the Place d'Armes, and down the steep slope of Rue du Fort to the Parliament House. No one recorded whether they slipped and slid on foot, or whether a line of one-horse *calèches* carried them from the hotel in groups through the slushy snow. George Brown rushed in late. He had spent the morning on a long letter, telling his wife, "We open our proceedings this forenoon and I am taking time by the forelock by writing to my Anne before the hurry begins."[1]

Quebec's Parliament House was an unimpressive building in a magnificent setting. Since the union of Upper and Lower Canada as the Province of Canada in 1841, Quebec had taken its turn along with Montreal, Toronto, and Kingston as host to the provincial government,

---

* New Brunswick, Nova Scotia, Prince Edward Island, and Newfoundland, plus Canada West and Canada East, which at this time were partners in the united Province of Canada.

pending completion of the new parliamentary complex in Ottawa. As long as the government met in Quebec City, "the government offices have to go a-begging up street and down street, wherever accommodation may be found," wrote a visiting journalist. Out-of-town politicians roomed where they could. Parliament House itself was "a paltry structure of brick," built a few years earlier to be the Quebec City post office and adapted as a parliamentary hall when the government returned to the city from Toronto in 1859.[2] But its site had once been graced by the palace of the bishops of New France and, though the building itself was plain, the view was magnificent. The Parliament stood right on the cliff's edge, high above Côte de la Montagne, the steep twisting path that led down to the waterfront warehouses and jetties of Lower Town.

For the constitutional conference, the Canadian government had set aside the second-floor reading room of the provincial upper house, with a panoramic view extending across the Quebec City basin, the Île d'Orléans, and the low hills beyond the ever-widening St. Lawrence. The sight was "wondrously varied yet unified into a harmonious picture…. hundreds of ships, large and small, some speeding with all canvas spread, some reposing as if in sleep on the translucent waters," wrote the correspondent of the Halifax *Morning Chronicle*.[3]

"The convention holds its meetings in the reading room of the Legislative Council," reported the Montreal newspaper *La Minerve*'s correspondent. "It goes without saying that the room has been completely transformed. The newspaper readers have been expelled." *La Minerve*'s English-language rival, *The Gazette*, gave its own account. "A long narrow table, covered with a crimson cloth and littered with stationery, statutes, pamphlets, and books of reference, ran down the centre of the room, leaving just space enough at the sides for the chairs of the delegates. The chairman occupied the centre, as at a dinner party."[4]

This man at the centre, as at a dinner party, was Étienne-Paschal Taché, "an old soldier and a refined gentleman" who had been pulled out from retirement to become prime minister of the province of Canada in March 1864, and then continued as premier in the newly formed coalition government. Taché held his position less because of his own ambition than because of the rivalries between Brown, Cartier, and Macdonald. The three party leaders had to work together, but joining in a coalition had not made them friends, and none was willing to see either of the others claim leadership of their coalition. Brown, Cartier, and Macdonald let Taché take the chair in order to pursue their larger ambitions. So Taché, at the age of sixty-nine, sat as titular leader of the Canadian government and host of the confederation conference.

The role suited Taché. Making his acquaintance at the start of the conference, the Prince Edward Island delegate Edward Whelan found him a venerable gentleman "of great business habits, and evidently of considerable ability." He also noted Taché's "most pleasing manners," and indeed it was the older man's affability that observers most often remarked upon. *The Gazette* compared Taché to Sir Roger de Coverley, the fat, cheery country squire, "more beloved than esteemed," of the still-popular eighteenth-century stories of the English journalists Addison and Steele.[5]

Still, Taché was not merely master of ceremonies. He was a living reminder of the political history that had made the conference possible. Few of the other delegates had been born at the time of the War of 1812, though several had fathers and uncles who had been shaped by it. Taché had fought in it. In 1813, at just eighteen, he served as an officer under Charles de Salaberry in the outnumbered force that won the Battle of Châteauguay and prevented an American attack on Montreal. After the war, Taché became a medical doctor in the south shore communities near Quebec City. He entered politics as a nationalist, close to many of the restive Patriots of the 1830s. When the defeated rebellions led to the forced union of Lower Canada with Upper Canada to form the Province of Canada in 1841, Taché sat in the first legislature of the newly united province of which he was now premier. He had been present at all the great moments in the political history of Canada West and Canada East.

In 1841, when the union of "the Canadas" was intended to assimilate the obstreperous French Canadians by submerging them in an anglophone majority, Taché became part of Louis-Hippolyte LaFontaine's campaign to subvert Britain's aim by allying with Reformers from the western half of the union, now called Canada West. The bond of this alliance was responsible government. Canada West's Reformers had long insisted that Canadian governments had to be accountable to elected Canadian legislatures, not to British appointees and their self-selected cliques of advisors. In that principle, LaFontaine perceived the best odds for the *survivance* of his people. If an elected legislature, even one with a large anglophone contingent, actually directed Canadian affairs, its bloc of Canada East francophones could ensure that assimilationist policies would never prevail. Self-government was the antidote to assimilation, he calculated, and alliance with Canada West the way to secure self-government.

With Robert Baldwin of Toronto, LaFontaine made responsible government into the great struggle of Canadian politics of the 1840s. Together they insisted on self-government as their right; as subjects of the British Crown, they were as much entitled to parliamentary government as any other Englishmen were, wherever they lived, whatever their mother tongue. LaFontaine and Baldwin were the leaders, but it was Étienne Taché, armoured in both his War of 1812 medals and his credentials as a proud francophone patriot, who gave the most memorable definition of what was at stake. French Canadians, said Taché in the Canadian legislature in April 1846, were British subjects, and they had the same rights as every other British subject. Let their right to govern themselves be guaranteed, he demanded. Then "the last cannon which is shot on this continent in defence of Great Britain will be fired by the hand of a French Canadian."[6]

Less than ten years after the rebellion that had shaken the Canadas in 1837 and 1838, this declaration turned aside the taunts of anglophone politicians who accused every francophone of being a rebel and a traitor. French Canadians would be Britain's great defenders *if*—for Taché's condition was vital. Francophone Reformers and their anglophone allies insisted loyalty and self-government had to go hand in hand. Within two years, Taché got what he demanded. LaFontaine and Baldwin's supporters swept the elections. They took office in February 1848, with Taché a cabinet minister. Sixteen years later, with LaFontaine and Baldwin passed from the scene, Taché had become a living symbol of all that had been achieved under their leadership. The transfer in 1848 of authority from autocratic colonial governors to the elected legislatures of the British North American provinces was what empowered the politicians of 1864. "There is no instance on record of a colony peacefully remodelling its own constitution," George Brown observed, "such changes having been always the work of the parent state and not of the colonists themselves. Canada is rightly setting the example of a new and better state of things."[7] The self-government Étienne Taché had seen achieved in 1848 made it possible for his younger colleagues of 1864 to consider how they might refashion all of British North America. Now representatives from all the colonial legislatures were gathered under Taché's direction to see if the job could be done.

At 11 A.M., Taché gavelled the conference to order and began establishing the authority of the gathering. "The several gentlemen representing the province of Canada," he declared, "were members of the executive council of Canada"—his cabinet, that is—and therefore self-evidently empowered to represent the province in the name of the governor general, Lord Monck. Taché then laid before the conference dispatches from the lieutenant-governors of Nova Scotia and Prince Edward Island that authorized the delegates of those provinces to represent their legislatures in discussing a federation of the British North American colonies. Premier Leonard Tilley of New Brunswick declared that he and his colleagues held the same authority from the lieutenant-governor of their province, even though delivery of the official dispatch had been delayed. "The conference stood accordingly convened," with just a nod to two Newfoundland legislators who were present. They had not been officially delegated, but came simply to observe and report.[8]

At the conference table, Taché was supported on his immediate left by his colleagues George-Étienne Cartier and Alexander Galt, and on his right by John A. Macdonald, Alexander Campbell, and Thomas D'Arcy McGee. Facing him across the table were the six remaining members of the Canadian cabinet: George Brown directly across from him, with William McDougall, Oliver Mowat, and James Cockburn of Canada West to his right and Hector-Louis Langevin and Jean-Charles Chapais of Canada East to his left. As Taché looked up and down the long table, reported the Halifax *Chronicle*, "at one extremity sat the astute leader of the New Brunswick delegation and at the other the gallant chief of the Prince Edward Island government." At New Brunswick's end of the table, Premier Tilley sat with his colleagues Attorney General James Mercer Johnson, William Steeves, Peter Mitchell, Edward Barron Chandler, John Hamilton Gray, and Charles Fisher. Adjacent to them sat the five Nova Scotians: Premier Charles Tupper with his attorney general, William Henry, and Robert Dickey, Jonathan McCully, and Adams Archibald. At the other end, Premier John Hamilton Gray of Prince Edward Island sat with fellow Islanders Edward Palmer, William Pope, Andrew Macdonald, George Coles, Thomas Heath Haviland, and Edward Whelan—who already had his notebook out and was busily scribbling shorthand notes. The two Newfoundlanders, Frederic Bowker Terrington Carter and Ambrose Shea, sat with them.

Thirty-three delegates. They made it a crowded room, almost too crowded for effective discussion up and down the long table. The group was numerous enough to have not only two Macdonalds (Canada West's John Alexander Macdonald and Prince Edward Islander Andrew Archibald Macdonald, generally called "A. A.") but two Grays as well— and both of the Grays were christened John Hamilton. John Hamilton Gray, an island-born retired colonel of the British army, was the premier of Prince Edward Island. Mr. John Hamilton Gray, a lawyer, was an ex-premier of New Brunswick, and a colonel of the New Brunswick militia as well, just to compound the opportunities for confusion.

Despite the crowd, those absent were significant. There were no officials of the British imperial government. The governor general of British North America lived at Quebec, and Lieutenant-Governor Sir Richard Graves MacDonnell of Nova Scotia had come to join the festivities, but neither man would be seen in the conference chamber. Governors took the advice of the cabinets the legislatures gave them, and did not participate directly in political discussion. Because the 1848 revolution had made the British North American colonies into self-governing entities, those at the table were representatives and delegates of their provincial legislatures. They still looked to Britain for military defence, foreign affairs, and much else, but they ran their internal and interprovincial affairs themselves—even to the point of rewriting their constitution to suit what they judged to be the needs of the provinces.

There were no women in the room. It was a profoundly patriarchal time, and in 1864, no elective legislature in the world allowed women either to vote or to be elected. British North America was no exception. The provinces broadly accepted what was sometimes called a "household" franchise: one vote per household, to be exercised by its male head on behalf of his wife, his children, his dependent employees, and anyone else under his roof. That legislators were accountable to voters was well entrenched, but the idea that voting was a citizen's right, not tied to property or gender, was barely considered. In the United States, the first proposals for woman's suffrage were barely a decade old in the 1860s. In 1885, Prime Minister John A. Macdonald would introduce a provision to allow female suffrage in Canada. He would claim he had always supported women's rights, and his bill would draw praise from suffragists worldwide, but after enjoying the fervent disagreements among his Liberal opponents over the proposal (at a time when Macdonald badly needed to divert Parliament's attention from several pressing issues), he would yield to the privately expressed views of his own caucus and remove the provision—as he had probably always intended.[9]

There were no Acadians from any of the Maritime provinces, few Roman Catholics, and only four francophones—Cartier, Langevin, and Chapais, plus Taché in the chair. Politically, however, the great absence was the Canada East Parti Rouge, which had refused to participate— and also been denied any chance to do so. The Rouges were the proof that Cartier was not the sole arbiter of Canada East's politics. Even when Cartier had been part of LaFontaine's Reform bloc, there had been a more radical group on their left, the heirs of Papineau's former Patriots, who looked to French and American republican ideas and disparaged responsible government as a mere tweaking of monarchy and empire. In 1864, when Cartier abandoned his support for preserving the union of the Canadas and his opposition to rep by pop, the Rouges occupied both his positions, defending the status quo and arguing that a federal union and rep by pop would lead to assimilation. The Rouge leader, Montreal lawyer Antoine-Aimé Dorion, had occasionally discussed federal arrangements with George Brown, and some of Brown's supporters regretted that Dorion had not joined the coalition to strengthen its Reform contingent.[10] Cartier, however, did not want Brown bringing any Rouges with him into the coalition government—and the Rouges were determined to oppose this federal project in any case. Since the Canadian delegation at the conference was the coalition government's cabinet, no Rouges participated, only members of the three parties that had formed the coalition in June.

The four Atlantic provinces all had party governments: Conservative ones in Newfoundland, Nova Scotia, and Prince Edward Island, a Reform one in New Brunswick. Yet each of them was represented not by a team of cabinet members, but by a legislative delegation with representation from opposition as well as government. This was why the reading room was crowded. Canada needed twelve delegates to adequately represent the three factions in its government, but to accommodate the multi-party rivalries in the Atlantic provinces there were another seven from New Brunswick, seven from Prince Edward

Island, five from Nova Scotia, and two from Newfoundland. The Conservative premiers of Nova Scotia and of Prince Edward Island, Charles Tupper and Colonel John Gray, each came with their Liberal opposition leaders, Adams Archibald and former premier George Coles. The Liberal premier of New Brunswick, Leonard Tilley, was accompanied by his Conservative rivals Edward Chandler and John Gray, both ex-premiers. Even the two Newfoundland observers were a matched pair: Conservative Frederic Carter from the governing party and mercantile St. John's and Reformer Ambrose Shea from the opposition and the outports.

The Quebec Conference was following the principle that in constitutional matters, legislatures, not cabinets or first ministers, hold the key to political legitimacy. If they were going to propose to refound each province with a new constitution as part of a new nation, the delegates needed to present more than a partisan initiative. They needed to represent a legislative consensus because British North American politics in the 1860s was rooted in the belief that only in the legislature were the whole people represented. The Quebec Conference would be a legislative conference, not an executive one, and since the delegates represented the legislature, not the government alone, nearly all elected factions and parties would participate.

Abstract principle was only part of what had induced the Canadians and the Maritime premiers to introduce their rivals into the discussion. Bipartisan constitution-making was also clever politics. Confederation would be hotly controversial. A narrow government measure put forward in the usual partisan fashion by a single governing party could never survive in the lively, independent legislatures of the provinces. As it was, confederation would cause a good deal of party-splitting in the coming months. If it were going to be challenged, some of the government leaders had already calculated, better that the opposition be inside and sharing the blame than outside pointing fingers. "Politicians are generally cunning fellows, and those in the several Maritime governments showed this quality to great advantage when they appointed members of the opposition to aid them in perfecting the great scheme of confederation," Edward Whelan would declare near the end of the conference, "because if the people of the several provinces should be so unwise as to complain ... the opposition would have to bear the censure as well as those in the administration."[11] The delegates knew they would have to sell their own legislatures on whatever they decided in the conference. If both parties had participated in the bargain, they might have a fighting chance.

With the delegates introduced and their authority to represent their provinces established, Taché was formally elected to chair the conference and delegates from each province were named as joint secretaries.* They agreed the conference would assemble from 11 A.M. to 4 P.M. every day except Sundays until their work was complete. A proposal on voting procedures was put over until the next day.

With these formalities completed, Etienne Taché opened the speech-making. He welcomed to Quebec and the conference "the leading statesmen of British America who are here assembled." George-Étienne Cartier followed with a long speech about the benefits of union. Leaders of the other provinces then responded with similar sentiments, at similar length. Finally Premier Tupper, perhaps growing bored with these rote speeches, proposed that "we should have a fuller exposition from the Canadian ministry of what was intended at the present." Then John A. Macdonald, seconded by Premier Tilley of New Brunswick, moved a resolution of the conference, one that restated the Charlottetown Conference's approval of a federation of all the British North American provinces if satisfactory terms could be arranged:

> That the best interests and present and future prosperity of British
> North America will be promoted by a federal union under the crown
> of Great Britain, provided such union can be effected on principles just
> to the several provinces.[12]

* Andrew Macdonald of Prince Edward Island understood that his fellow Islander William Pope was chosen as principal secretary, with delegates from the other provinces being merely additional secretaries. No conference record from Pope survives.

This resolution raised the first substantial issues of the constitutional conference, but soon after they began the discussion, Taché declared it was 4 P.M. They put the matter over to the next day, and adjourned.

Not that the work day was over. Government had not ceased while the constitutional conference proceeded. Many of the delegates—all of the Canadians—were provincial cabinet members, and during the conference they met frequently to review briefings from their civil servants and approve routine or urgent measures. On one such session, on October 22, the Canadian cabinet would approve the appropriation of an additional thousand dollars "to meet expenses connected with the visit of the delegates from the Maritime provinces to Quebec, the amount to be charged to unforeseen expenses of government."[13] On October 17, George Brown described how the days went: "We have had such a week. Council from 9 to 11, conference from 11 to 4, council again from 4 to 6 and sometimes till 7 every day, and then the letters and orders-in-council to write at night. It has been very hard work."[14] On the following day, the delegates would agree that during the conference sessions, there would be a break of just fifteen minutes for a light lunch in the room adjoining.

While the delegates worked, their wives and daughters had not been pining away at the hotel. On the morning of October 10, Mercy Coles went shopping with a daughter of William McDougall, one of the Canada West delegates, and bought an opera cloak. Then, anticipating lively times, she sewed trim on her velvet jacket. In the afternoon, young Charles Drinkwater, private secretary to John A. Macdonald, collected the young women and Mercy's mother for a drive. They toured the Catholic cathedral and the seminary chapel "where all the fine paintings are," and visited the "wonderful" library in the legislative building. Then it was time to prepare for the evening.[15]

"When the gentlemen came from conference," Mercy wrote, "they brought cards of invitation to Mrs. and Miss Tupper, Miss Gray, and Mrs. Alexander to dine at Government House. Ma and I have a card for

Wednesday. The governor general has committed to have all the delegates and their families to dinner over several days." This night, however, Mercy and her mother dined at the hotel, while Mr. Coles "and all the gentlemen who were not dining at Government House were dining at the Stadacona Club." The Stadacona, a private men's club on Rue d'Auteuil near the St-Louis gate, favoured by military officers and royal officials, had elected all the delegates as honorary members. Edward Whelan, who attended that evening, called it "a political society of great influence conducted in the best manner." The club constitution declared that "Politics and religious questions of every description shall be absolutely excluded from the objects of the club." Perhaps the rule was suspended for the duration of the conference.[16]

SEVEN

Monday, October 10: Viscount Monck's Dinner Party

While delegates joined their families or dispersed to clubs and private homes, the favoured few climbed into carriages for a five-kilometre drive westward, out though the St. Louis Gate and along the Grande Allée to Spencer Wood, a spacious estate of woods and gardens set high above the St. Lawrence. This had once been Bois-de-Coulonge, a summer retreat for governors of New France. Now Spencer Wood was the residence of Charles Monck, 4th Viscount Monck of the Irish peerage and governor general of British North America. Tonight's dinner would be the first of a long series during the conference. It was Monck's forty-fifth birthday, but he seems to have made no mention of that. Duty came first.

Viscount Monck was a lawyer by profession, and a politician. After losing his parliamentary seat in Britain, he had been offered the governor generalship by his prime ministerial mentor, Lord Palmerston, and he took the position largely because he needed the money. Monck was an Irish landlord, and the era when landed aristocrats could live in leisure on the rents their tenant farmers paid them was dying, killed in part by the flood of cheap food pouring onto world markets from North America's commercial farmers. Monck's imposing country home at Charleville, in Wicklow County south of Dublin, had become a drain on the family fortune, and he was glad to accept the generous ten-thousand-pound salary and other perks a governor general received.[1]

Fortunately for his hopes, competition for the post was not what it had been. In the 1840s, as British North America moved to responsible government, the governor general had been Lord Elgin, an earl from a family deeply involved in running Britain and its empire.* With responsible government established, however, governors had to defer to the colonial politicians, whom one of them denounced as the ignorant lumberer, the petty attorney, and the keeper of a village grog shop. Power in British North America had shifted, and the job of governing British North America no longer carried the same allure for British aristocrats. Elgin had gone on from Quebec City to occupy Canton, to invade Beijing, and to rule India in the name of the Queen, but his replacement in British North America was merely a baronet, Sir Edmund Walker Head, a minor bureaucrat in England. Monck, who succeeded Head in November 1861, was not much more grand.[2]

Monck was a skilful government servant, but personally modest and unpretentious, characteristics that served him well in governing British North America. He understood the political necessities Canadian politicians faced, and his own advice, whether directed to the British cabinet or to his Canadian ministers, was often perceptive. In June 1864, he had counselled a delay in the dissolution of the Canadian Parliament when the legislature deadlocked, and had thereby helped to nudge the rival politicians into the great confederation coalition. As governor, Monck reviewed decisions that needed his signature, but the government held its cabinet meetings without him, and no one expected him to take

---

* While in Constantinople as ambassador to the Ottoman Empire, Elgin's father, the 7th Earl, had acquired the "Elgin marbles," which he removed from the Parthenon in Athens to his personal collection at the family estate.

any non-ceremonial part in the confederation negotiations just down the road from his residence. The governor general understood it was his role to put the prestige of his office behind the actions of the government. Shortly after joining the coalition, for instance, George Brown was rewarded with an invitation to a social evening of singing folk songs at Spencer Wood. "He is to become a new minister and is very nice-looking, tall and greyish, with a Ponsonby face,"* one of the party wrote, noting that Mr. Cartier also attended; indeed, that he contributed some of his own songs. The evening both conveyed approval of the new minister and provided an opportunity for Brown and Cartier to add some personal rapport to their new political alliance.

Since June, Monck had been carefully advancing his ministers' confederation project. Colonial officials in Britain, he knew, were sometimes jealously protective of their role in planning for the Empire, and generally skeptical of any union of British North America other than a tightly centralized one. At first, Monck gave the Colonial Office only the good news: that a more broadly based ministry had been formed in Canada. He barely mentioned federalism until it was well established, and did not mention his ministers' departure for Charlottetown until they had sailed. There was a certain amount of harrumphing from the Colonial Office, but in August, the new colonial minister, Edward Cardwell, declared he had no objection to "a union of the whole of British North America in one great and important province." British officials sometimes objected to British North American assertiveness, but the British government and British public opinion mostly found the prospect of the colonists taking responsibility for themselves appealing. Having already accepted so much Canadian autonomy since the 1840s, the Colonial Office lacked grounds for refusing more. Monck understood that his British North America was not like his Ireland.

---

* Ashley Ponsonby was a British politician, a contemporary and ally of Monck's, and presumably known to the family. Photographs of the men of the Ponsonby family show long, serious faces that do resemble George Brown's.

At Spencer Wood, meanwhile, Monck could recreate much of the life he enjoyed on his Irish estate and in British court and political circles. "The Monck liveries and everything like home, and to think we are across the Atlantic at the other side of the world," wrote Feo Monck when she first arrived at Spencer Wood. The Moncks, devoted to horses and dogs and sport, appreciated the spacious gardens and grounds of Spencer Wood. The house itself, long and low and only a few years old, boasted more than sixty rooms and a separate servants' wing. Here the Moncks—Charles and his wife, Elizabeth (née Monck, for she was his cousin)—lived surrounded by family, which included their children, plus Lord Monck's brother and private secretary, Dick, and his wife, Frances "Feo" (sister to Elizabeth, so also a cousin to the governor), plus personal servants who had accompanied them. For dinners, cricket matches, and social evenings at Spencer Wood, they invited officers of the British regiments stationed at Quebec, aides-de-camp, Church of England clergymen, and distinguished visitors passing through. Canadians were often in the minority and suitably impressed, though Lord Monck's unpretentious style and dislike of ostentation helped set them at ease. His dinners for the conference delegates followed that pattern: the guests were selected at random, without much attention to status or precedence among them. Mercy Coles had been a little shocked to learn that Mrs. Alexander, the widowed sister of one Prince Edward Island delegate, had been invited ahead of Mrs. Pope, the wife of a cabinet minister. Only a handful of the British North Americans were invited each evening, along with the usual crowd of military officers and other members of the vice-regal entourage.[3]

As the local representative of the British government, Governor General Monck retained some significant responsibilities, principally in foreign and military matters. He was neither a professional diplomat nor a soldier, and there were both ambassadors and generals to handle these matters, but the British government, not the British North American provinces, still held authority over imperial foreign and military policy, and on these subjects Monck was accountable to it and not to his Canadian ministers. His focus was on one great foreign and military issue: relations with the United States. The American Civil War had begun in the spring of 1861, and Monck's arrival at Quebec in November of that year coincided with the first great crisis in British–American relations stemming from that war: the *Trent* Affair.

Relations between Britain, the old imperial power, and the United States, the fast-growing upstart that had broken away from King and Empire, had always been edgy, and Britain's response to the outbreak of civil war was mixed. Sympathy in Britain for the anti-slavery cause was widespread, but some Britons were attracted to the romance of the cause of the Confederate underdogs, who were imagined to be more aristo- cratic and gentlemanly than the crass commercial Yankees. A weak, divided United States appealed to British self-interest, and Britain's textile mills remained a large and eager market for the South's most important product—if the Confederacy could ship that precious cotton through the North's naval blockade. Early in the conflict, many in Britain did not believe that Americans would actually fight each other, so they assumed the independence of the southern Confederacy was assured. Upon the formal secession of the southern states, Britain had declared itself neutral and recognized the Confederacy as a belligerent, thereby conferring on it a degree of international legitimacy, to the fury of the northern Union.

In November 1861, the Union navy, struggling to blockade the Confederacy's seaports to keep cotton shipments in and armament supplies out, stopped the British merchant ship RMS *Trent*. Captain Wilkes of USS *San Jacinto* boarded the ship in international waters and seized from it two ambassadors whom the Confederacy hoped to see accredited to the governments of France and Britain. Captain Wilkes triumphantly delivered them to a prison in Boston, where their arrest was celebrated as a triumph for the Union cause. To the British government and the British public, however, an attack on a British ship on the high seas was an intolerable affront to British naval mastery. Prime Minister Palmerston declared that freedom of the seas was a cause worth war, and nothing short of an American apology and prompt release of the two Confederates would deter his government.

No one in the United States had done more to whip up hostility to Britain than President Lincoln's secretary of state, William Seward. Throughout his long career, Seward had found anti-British agitation a crowd-pleaser, and he even imagined he might prevent the civil war in his own nation by starting a war with Britain that would reunite North and South. Seward also knew that in such a conflict, the way to attack Britain was to invade and conquer British North America, just as had been attempted (not very successfully) in 1775 and 1812. When Palmerston's government sent its ultimatum over RMS *Trent*, it understood that war meant British North America could be faced with an American invasion. The threat was so serious that Britain ordered an urgent deployment of fourteen thousand additional troops to British North America, the largest troop movement there since the War of 1812. With the St. Lawrence closed by ice that winter, seven thousand of the soldiers marched across New Brunswick to the Grand Trunk railhead at Rivière-du-Loup. They were in position at Quebec and Montreal before the campaigning season opened in the spring of 1862.

By then the *Trent* Affair was over. For all the resentments on both sides, neither wanted war. Prime Minister Palmerston had spent his long career balancing Britain's rivals against each other; he could calculate that it was far better to have the United States divided and at war with itself than to have Britain engaged on either side. The Union's desire to avoid war with Britain was even stronger, given how much the South would have welcomed it. "One war at a time," President Lincoln told Seward, and by December most of the American press was saying the same. The United States freed the Confederacy's would-be ambassadors and allowed them to travel to Europe, though both Britain and France kept them at arm's length when they got there.[4]

As the world watched the South and the North committing every resource to an increasingly bloody and drawn-out war, the likelihood of the Union invading British North America faded almost to nothing, despite continued tensions along the border. The officers of the regiments garrisoning Quebec played cricket at Spencer Wood and ornamented the balls and receptions of the confederation conference. But concerns mounted again in the fall of 1864. General Sherman occupied Atlanta in September 1864, and General Grant continued his endless campaign against Robert E. Lee's armies defending Virginia. Anyone could see the end of the civil war was looming, and the North would defeat and occupy the South. Then, with another flashpoint like the *Trent* Affair, the vast and victorious American armies might yet roll across the border.

Britain and British North America had been arguing for years about the defence of British North America. Britain, reasonably enough, was unwilling to garrison North America forever. It felt that the growing and prosperous provinces of British North America should take responsibility for their own defence. The British government and public opinion were frequently aggrieved by the colonies' unwillingness to assume the cost of defending themselves. British North Americans, however, observed that it was Britain that held control of military and foreign affairs. The principal threat to Canada came from the danger of hostilities between Britain and the United States, in which British North America would not be the instigator but only the battlefield and prize in a great-power rivalry.

Early in 1864, the British military engineer Colonel William Jervois had submitted a report on the defence of British North America in an American war. He laid out a strategic plan in which Britain might eventually prevail through naval warfare against American coasts and commerce, and he recommended new fortifications in Montreal, Quebec, and Halifax. But he concluded bleakly that all of Canada west of Montreal would be abandoned, all the million and a half people of Canada West left to American conquest. The Jervois report caught attention not only in British North America, where the British guarantee of protection suddenly seemed hollow (in Canada West particularly), but also in Britain, where the bill for new fortifications had British MPs murmuring about the need to separate the greedy, ungrateful colonies from the Empire if they would not pay for their own defence. After the Jervois report, Prime Minister Palmerston had to rein in his chancellor of the exchequer, William Ewart Gladstone, who wondered how long the British treasury should continue paying for the defence of the British North Americans.[5] Colonel Jervois was sent back to Quebec to calm the colonial politicians with revisions to his report. He was scheduled to brief the Canadian cabinet, and particularly the agitated representatives of Canada West, on Wednesday, October 12.

The real problem of British North American defence was not one of taxation and resources, and who should be responsible for them. The real problem was that British North America was nearly indefensible. As Jervois had said, whatever forces were raised by the provinces, a war against the United States would require troops from Britain, combined with British naval action against the United States. It would be the War of 1812 refought, with the United States vastly stronger. All three sides—Britain, British North America, and the United States—had little desire to see that return.

The wish to turn that dangerous problem over to the British North Americans had helped make many British policy-makers into partisans for confederation. But in itself, confederation would do nothing to make British North America more defensible. Even with a national government and one unified militia force, the border would be just as long and just as difficult to defend against the Americans. There was only one way in which confederation could assist the defence of British North America. If the federated provinces began running their own affairs as a small, peaceable, and trade-minded new nation, while at the same time Britain withdrew its own forces and garrisons and disclaimed all future territorial interests and ambitions in North America, the United States might well come to accept that there was nothing on its northern borders worth a war. Confederation itself might safeguard British North America more effectively than even the most massive program of fortification and militia enrollments.

As a result, throughout the debates and discussions at Quebec, the delegates would hardly raise the subject of defence; the American threat was everyday politics, not a constitutional issue. When they talked of the United States, delegates compared its presidential constitution to the parliamentary one to which they were committed. Some argued that states' rights had caused the collapse of the American federation, and made that an argument for a strongly centralized union. Throughout, they were more engaged with these constitutional issues than with questions of armies or strategies of defence. In the end, the constitutional arrangements, by enabling the redcoats of one great power to be removed from the vicinity of the bluecoats of the other, would make an undefended border and a good-neighbour policy into Canada's most reliable defence.

So Governor General Monck, despite his responsibilities for military and foreign policy, could afford to leave his ministers alone to negotiate while, night after night, he entertained red-coated British officers and frock-coated provincial politicians. Monck and his ministers remained concerned, however, about one short-term risk. Another armed confrontation like the seizure of RMS *Trent* might bring back the spectre of Anglo-American war. On October 10, that crisis was only ten days away.

EIGHT

Tuesday, October 11: How to Run a Constitutional Conference

"I am willing provisionally to adopt the suggestion of Mr. Chandler, but I think the whole question should be carefully reconsidered at the eventual revise of the minutes," said John A. Macdonald during Tuesday's discussion.[1] Much of the morning of the second day of the conference, another cold day teeming with rain, was taken up with procedural matters like this brief exchange between Macdonald and the elderly and fastidious New Brunswick delegate Edward Chandler, who had raised a point about the recording of votes. The politicians spent the morning appointing secretaries, deciding how votes would be counted, and setting procedures for framing and debating motions. The delegates did not scorn these chores. As on the first day, with its punctilious reading of credentials, they gave the impression that they thoroughly enjoyed their mastery of the rules of order and were determined to follow all the niceties of parliamentary procedure.

They had to do all this themselves, to be sure. They had hardly any support staff and could not delegate to a civil service parliamentarian or a team of aides and advisors. But the British North American politicians of 1864 had no sense of shame or boredom about parliamentary democracy and representative government. It had been barely fifteen years since Canadian legislatures had taken charge of their own affairs and made it possible for elected representatives to make and break governments. In a world where no women and not all men voted, those male heads of household who did vote were proud to represent the others—one reason why they usually voted in public, not in the secrecy of a ballot booth. In the same way, the delegates were conscious of being "public men." All the procedural forms and every sub-amendment moved and ratified reminded them of the representative authority they wielded and the parliamentary tradition they proudly upheld.

The first procedural point the delegates took up that morning brought back the secretarial question: who would take notes and keep a record of their deliberations? The previous day they had named members of each delegation as "joint secretaries" to the conference. But now William McDougall, the Canadian joint secretary, declared that these secretaries had concluded quite sensibly that they could hardly participate fully in the deliberations while also keeping its record. McDougall proposed the appointment of Hewitt Bernard, chief clerk of the Crown law office of Canada West, as executive secretary. There was unanimous agreement. Bernard, who had evidently been forewarned, took up his pen. His notes of the conference began with the very next topic of discussion.

Bernard, thirty-nine and the Jamaica-born son of a plantation-owning family, had studied law in London. With the end of slavery eroding the prospects of the Jamaican planter class, he chose to practise in British North America. By 1864, Bernard was effectively deputy minister in the Canadian justice department, one of the handful of civil servants assisting the Canadian government at the conference. But he was an odd choice as secretary. As deputy minister, he was already busy advising on the conference's resolutions, a task likely to distract him from writing down every detail of the discussion. John A.'s own private secretary, young Charles Drinkwater, who frequently took shorthand dictation from Macdonald, was present at Quebec and might have kept a verbatim transcript. Drinkwater had little more to do during the days than drive Mercy Coles and her mother out to see the sights, but it was Bernard who got the notekeeping assignment.[2]

Bernard's appointment, however, was a small coup for Macdonald. Until his civil service appointment in 1864, Bernard had been Macdonald's private secretary. The two men had roomed together at Quebec and in Toronto, and Bernard had become a loyal friend and supporter. He had also introduced Macdonald to his younger sister, Agnes, who would become John A.'s second wife before the completion of the confederation the delegates were planning. Bernard had been at Charlottetown with the Canadian delegation and was known to all the delegates, but it was probably Macdonald's deft hint to the joint secretaries that had produced his name as the record keeper. The frequency with which Macdonald's contributions were included in the minutes suggests that Bernard had access to his speaking notes and an inclination to see his mentor well represented on the record. Bernard knew no shorthand, however, and as a deputy minister in the Canadian government had many pressing responsibilities throughout the conference. Of the seventy-two resolutions formally approved by the end of the conference, Bernard would manage to document the moving and passing of only fifty-six in his official conference minutes.[*] His summary of the discussion was not much better— frequently piecemeal and cryptic and not always agreeing with the even more limited notes other delegates kept. In his record, Macdonald's positions are usually made clear, but those of his rivals less so. Bernard's minutes and notes would survive as the most detailed record of the Quebec Conference, but also as the work of an unreliable narrator.

Macdonald had seen the potential power of the record keeper and ensured that his loyal ally would keep the minutes and control their final

* A separate and complete list of all seventy-two resolutions was kept, however.

polishing. When Edward Chandler raised his procedural point—he wanted to be sure that contrary votes and the individuals making them would be fully reported in the official record—Macdonald breezily assured him that such matters could be "carefully reconsidered" when the minutes were reviewed at the end of the conference. In the event, Macdonald and Bernard controlled the revisions, and Chandler's proposal would never be heard of again. For Macdonald, Bernard's selection was a small useful victory, just for ensuring his own contributions would be recorded with care. He was back in the game and playing for keeps.

With Bernard duly appointed, Taché led the conference through the rest of the procedural housekeeping. It was quickly agreed that each provincial delegation would have a single vote—but that Canada would be considered as two provinces, East and West, and have two votes. The delegates agreed that discussion would be free "as if in committee of the whole," allowing all of them to put their views forward, free of the stricter rules of parliamentary debate and of cabinet solidarity. If necessary, each delegation could retire in private to settle its position before it cast its vote.[3]

With these decisions made, the conference took up the previous day's resolution of principle in favour of a federal union. According to Bernard's notes of the discussion, Macdonald did much of the talking. Cartier, in his opening remarks the previous day (not recorded by Bernard), had underlined the advantages of a common legislature to "legislate more for the general advantage," but he had also affirmed that, "We thought that a federation scheme was the best because these provinces are peopled by different nations and peoples of different religions." Cartier airily used "we" throughout his speech, perhaps to imply all his propositions were generally accepted, but Macdonald was aware that several among the Maritimers had doubts about federalism and saw merit in a strong central government, and he played to their preference. He alluded to the "fatal weakness," the "primary error," of the United

States in affirming that individual states held sovereign rights, leaving, he said, the central government too weak to prevent dissolution and civil war. "We must reverse this process by strengthening the general government and conferring on the provincial bodies only such powers as may be required for local purposes." Macdonald seemed to be undermining his coalition partner on a point that had surely been discussed in great detail within the Canadian cabinet that summer, and indeed Macdonald soon hedged, acknowledging, "The people of each section must feel that they are protected, and by no overstraining of central authority should such guarantees be overridden."

Despite Macdonald's acquiescence to Cartier, and Brown's insistence on rep by pop and federalism when the coalition was formed, it may have seemed to the listeners that Cartier and Macdonald were still trying to square the circle of strong central government and powerful provinces. After all the discussions the Canadian cabinet had held during the hot Quebec City summer, the balance of power in the new nation still seemed up for debate. Macdonald continued with wide-ranging thoughts on railroad construction and an upper house for the new national legislature. George Brown, who had his own resolution on federalism ready to present, was irritated enough to say he "differed in many details, which he would discuss in other resolutions when they came up." Bernard did not record this intervention or others from the Maritimers; it was the Prince Edward Island delegate Andrew Macdonald who included them in his own personal notes of the proceedings. Macdonald concluded by urging, "We should keep before us the principles of the British constitution. It"—the constitution they were engaged in drafting—"should be a mere skeleton and framework that would not bind us down." He also stressed that this resolution was one of principle only; the whole conference would be devoted to settling the details of federal union. With that reassurance, the resolution was passed unanimously.[4]

At the lunch break, Taché announced he had to meet the governor general, and he yielded the chair to Premier Gray of Prince Edward

Island. Then George Brown, seconded by his fellow reformer Adams Archibald of Nova Scotia, moved a resolution that began to turn the conference from matters of procedure and principle toward the big issues that would have to be faced. This resolution declared that there should be

> a general government charged with matters of common interest to the whole country and local governments for each of the Canadas and for the Maritime provinces, charged with the control of local matters in their respective sections, provision being made for admitting into the federation the North-West Territory, British Columbia, and Vancouver Island.[5]

During what remained of Tuesday's sessions, it was the great territorial ambition at the end of this resolution that sparked debate. Had the five provinces really got the authority to annex an empire to the confederation they had come to build? They agreed they had, but before they could get to federalism and the division of powers, it was 4 P.M. Federalism would wait for tomorrow. It was time to adjourn the conference's second day, in order to prepare for the day's other order of business, the first grand social event of the conference: the governor general's reception. "We have had nothing here for the last fortnight but feasting and dancing in honour of the delegates from the 'Sister Provinces' who have come here to consider whether they might not all be united into one province," Lady Monck would write home on October 21, and these ceremonies were about to begin.[6]

"While waiting for the result of the intercolonial conference, the ladies have been plundering the shops of Quebec of their ribbons and flowers, to prepare their finery for tonight," wrote *La Minerve*'s correspondent. Tonight was the governor general's "drawing room," where the visiting delegates and their families would be formally presented to him in the council chamber at the parliament building. Some eight hundred guests were expected, "including almost every person of note or influence in the naval, military, volunteer, and civil services of the province together with the leading members of the best society."[7]

"The ladies looked very well and were quite a credit to the lower provinces," wrote Mercy Coles, who wore her best blue. The ladies were not dressed quite so formally as they might have been, she noted: "There were only two or three trains." Mercy declined offers from half a dozen gentlemen eager to escort her in, she wrote, so she could be presented with her father. In the legislative council chamber, Governor General Monck took the centre of the room, encircled by a long line of guests waiting to be presented. The governor general's private secretary, Denis Godley— "Almighty Godley" to the Canadians who felt he was sometimes too protective of access to Monck—made the presentation. The governor general spoke briefly to each guest, and the line advanced. "Mr. Tilley took charge of me and walked about with me," wrote Mercy, and the courtship, if it was such, continued. This event, however, was centred on the presentations, and with eight hundred people lined up to be presented to the governor general, it was a long and, in Mercy's telling, a tedious and tiring process. She looked forward more eagerly to the ball later in the week.[8]

Edward Whelan, the Prince Edward Island delegate, admired how "silks and satins blazed with jewels and precious gems," but he was not ready to surrender to the charms of the local ladies, at least not in his dispatches home. "I have seen more pretty girls at a Government House ball in Charlottetown," he wrote, declaring that the women of Quebec seemed to run to "corpulency." Still, he admired their "easy manners" and finally declared that "the Quebec ladies, and particularly those of French origin—appear to be the most healthy vigorous and good natured daughters of Eve whom I have ever had the pleasure to meet."[9]

NINE

Wednesday, October 12: What Federalism Means

The third day of the conference, as rain-lashed as the previous ones, began with approval of the previous day's minutes and continued with a flurry of letters and invitations. Perhaps the governor general's levee the night before, with its demonstration of vice-regal patronage for the conference, had stimulated the city's awareness that the conference and its delegates constituted a power worth cultivating. Suddenly, the delegates were being inundated with invitations to dinners and balls. They were invited to tour the university and the historic buildings of the Catholic diocese and invited to private clubs and institutions throughout the town. Most of these offers would be accepted.

Another letter came from the members of the press who had come to cover the conference. The press corps at Quebec for the conference was substantial and impressive. The leading British North American newspapers, from Halifax to Toronto, had correspondents on the scene. The prominent international journalist George Sala of London's *Daily Telegraph* had come, taking time away from his vigorously pro-Southern coverage of the American war. Feo Monck, impressed despite herself by this celebrity, declared him "not pretty but amusing." There were correspondents for *The Economist*, *Punch*, *The New York Herald*, and other leading journals on both continents. By Wednesday, the newspapermen were growing tired of writing about the weather and the dinners. They wanted news. Their letter, signed by Phillips Day, Charles Lindsay, and B. Chamberlin, was a demand for press access, declaring, "It would be impossible for them satisfactorily to discharge their duties if an injunction of secrecy be imposed on the conference and stringently carried into effect." The journalists acknowledged that discussion within the conference had to be unconstrained and therefore secret. Still, they suggested, the "propositions made and the treatment they meet with" should be made public. Day, Lindsay, and Chamberlin wanted regular press briefings: "a kind of compromise between absolute secrecy and unlimited publicity." Such a course, they said with perhaps a hint of menace, "would have the further advantage of preventing ill-founded and mischievous rumours."[1]

The conference was not swayed. Indeed, the proposal seems to have been barely discussed before a resolution was passed "declining the proposition made." The next day, the conference approved a written reply declaring it was "inexpedient," at the present stage of the proceedings, to furnish information "that must of necessity be incomplete." No communication to the press of their proceedings could properly be made, they said, before a formal report had been made by the delegates to their own legislatures. In rejecting even the cautious half measure the journalists proposed, the delegates were expressing the vast confidence they had in themselves as authorized representatives of the people. They, and not the press, represented the public. So long as they were in the room, they confidently believed, the exclusion of the press did not mean the public went unrepresented. Publicity could wait.

The delegates had concluded they needed to talk freely among themselves. They wanted no public declaration of positions that, once taken, might be difficult to abandon. Perhaps they were also growing aware of the difficulties yet to be resolved. Until they had successes they were ready to share with the world, they offered nothing up to potential critics and opponents. Even Edward Whelan, whose livelihood depended on the Charlottetown *Examiner* of which he was publisher, editor, and principal writer, approved of confidentiality. As long as "there is great diversity of opinion touching the details" of confederation, he thought, secrecy was essential.[2] The press would remain close enough to the conference room that sometimes it could report on the uproar of voices coming from inside, but little specific news would come out. Several of the delegates were themselves working journalists or owners of newspapers, but their papers did not leak much beyond what the delegates made public in after-dinner speeches. Some newspapers grumbled that the Toronto *Globe* was getting inside information from its owner and editor, George Brown. The *Globe*'s correspondent did publish some good guesses about the discussions, but Brown was not leaking much, for his paper did not really have any inside scoops. Whelan wrote almost daily reports for his Charlottetown *Examiner*, but he included nuggets from the delegates' deliberations only if he was sure they had already been leaked elsewhere.

With the press petition dismissed, the delegates resumed the interrupted topic from the previous day: George Brown's motion about federalism and westward expansion. The initial discussion had been mostly about how to incorporate the west into the new nation, not about dividing power between a central government and several provinces. Indeed, linking federation to western expansion was vitally important to George Brown. The bedrock of his support in Canada West, its farming population, was growing so fast that the rural counties of southwestern Ontario were rapidly being filled; soon there would be no new farmland for the next generation. Already, Manitoba and the golden west had been identified as the outlet for that population and therefore as Canada West's vital colonization project.[3] So long as the Canadas remained locked in a single province, Canada East could not look very favourably on expansion by the Province of Canada if that meant the western section became ever larger than Canada East. But if federalism released Canada East and Canada West from each other's crushing embrace, George Brown's constituents could be freed to seize the bright prospects of the west. The welcome the delegations gave to the prospect of adding all the territory out to the Pacific Ocean was good news for Brown. This new confederation might be costly for Canada West, with its wealth taxed by the new national government to be spent by the demanding east, but in recompense it was promised a new empire in the northwest.

Westward expansion was as appealing to George-Étienne Cartier as it was to Brown. Montreal was Cartier's power base, railroads his livelihood. From the days of the fur trade, Montreal had always been a gateway to the west, and Cartier intended to see Montreal continue in that role: as the hub of the new regions' railroads and their link to the Atlantic and to the American seaboard. Cartier could foresee some of Quebec's farmers, also squeezed for space, joining the francophone communities already established around Red River and farther west, but he wanted the west in confederation primarily for his railroad and business clients on Saint James Street in Montreal. It made sense to both Brown and Cartier to link westward expansion and federalism. Questions of ethnicity and language in the new western territories did not come up, and neither did a guarantee that when settled they could accede to provincial status. Later in the conference, there would be one brief, glancing consideration of the existing inhabitants of the northwest, the First Nations.

Neither man had to struggle to see his case for westward expansion made. The idea of a new nation stretching out to the Pacific had evidently captured most of the delegates. Edward Palmer, a skeptical Islander, objected that the conference had no mandate to consider territorial annexations. Newfoundland's Frederic Carter was inclined to agree on the technical point, but he liked "the grandeur and magnificence of the scheme." Palmer's fellow Islander—and political rival—Edward Whelan was inspired by the "great and glorious principle" behind "a constitution for a country larger than Europe." Most of the Maritimers seemed to share his nation-building ambitions. With approval from the provinces assured, Cartier sat quiet and satisfied as Brown's resolution went roaring through. As long as Quebec controlled its vital interests—its language, its religion, and its laws, in the parlance of the day—the expansion of Canada promised nothing but benefits to Cartier.

Hewitt Bernard's records do not make clear whether Brown's resolution, now approved by all the provinces, was understood as a challenge to Macdonald's previous resolution. Brown's referred specifically to local governments charged with control of local powers, whereas Macdonald's had warned sternly against a weak, decentralized federation like the Americans'. Brown's resolution was approved, just as Macdonald's had been, but the crucial part of federalism, the balance of powers between the national and the provincial governments, was yet to be discussed. On the specific constitutional powers to be given to the two levels of government, federal and provincial, Brown's resolution was hardly more specific than Macdonald's. Had Brown introduced his local-governments motion on his own initiative, simply to contend with Macdonald's more ambiguous position and his warnings against disunity? There is nothing in the record to say so specifically, but after the vote, Ambrose Shea, the veteran reformer from the Newfoundland delegation, offered a procedural suggestion: "It would tend to the dispatch of business before the conference if the several resolutions intended to be moved were prepared in advance by a committee composed of the delegates of Canada." Get your act together, Shea seemed to be saying to the Canadians wavering between Macdonald and Brown.

In endorsing this suggestion, the Maritimers were explicitly surrendering the direction of the conference to the Canadians. In effect, they had already accepted that situation. Even at Charlottetown, the Maritimers had discussed abstract principles while the Canadians had presented a well-prepared outline for a federal union. What drove Shea's suggestion may have been a concern that the Canadians were losing their way, with Brown and Macdonald wasting the conference's precious time on overlapping resolutions and conflicting and imprecise views of how federalism would work. If that was the rebuke behind Shea's suggestion, the Canadians accepted it. The conference adjourned early so that the Canadians could caucus together and return the next day better organized, with coherent and complementary resolutions for the conference to consider.

Hewitt Bernard, presumably needed in the Canadians' private session, recorded nothing about what the Maritimers talked about as the Canadians withdrew. Andrew Macdonald of Prince Edward Island did, however, and the Maritimers' talk became a problem for the conference and particularly for George Brown. According to Andrew Macdonald, the Maritimers, who stayed in the council chamber while the Canadians caucused, discussed a suggestion they attributed to Brown "that the Lower Provinces be admitted as one." The Maritimers were concerned that despite their clear decision at Charlottetown, Maritime union might be returning to the agenda. Brown's resolution proposed "local governments for each of the Canadas and for the Maritime provinces." Though they had voted for it, the Maritimers evidently feared this meant the Canadians, or Brown at least, still expected Nova Scotia, New Brunswick, and Prince Edward Island (and Newfoundland too, perhaps) to enter confederation as a single province. They would take up this issue the next morning.[4]

Adjourning early on its third day, the conference was developing a leisured and disorganized quality. There was a lot of talk, and the delegates were setting out procedures and sizing each other up, but resolutions seemed to come forward randomly from whoever was moved to present one. None of them had moved the confederation plan much beyond what had been settled at Charlottetown.

On Wednesday night, Lord Monck renewed his program of nightly dinners with small groups of the delegates and their families. The guests included the Coles family. That day, Mercy and her mother had been for a long carriage drive despite the cold rain. The day's highlight, however, was the dinner at Spencer Wood, "a very pleasant party," in Mercy's opinion, and marred only by D'Arcy McGee, "who got so drunk he was obliged to leave the table." She ignored him and was praised for her dignified behaviour by Premier Gray himself.[5] Hosting groups of delegates every night, Lord Monck was making a good impression on them. Edward Whelan, who would attend the next night, declared the party lacked for nothing in the department of cuisine and vintage, and even less in "the ease, affability, and good humour" of the guests. Whelan gave the credit to his host. He found in Viscount Monck a man who had a sense of humour and who "converses in a free and easy matter-of-fact style, same as any sensible man would," hardly at all like the lordly figure some of the delegates and their families had expected. "If his companion in conversation is not a born fool, he need not be oppressed by any of that stupid awe which fools sometimes feel in the presence of a live Lord."[6] It was a bold egalitarian statement from an Irish Catholic raised poor and largely self-educated.

TEN

Thursday, October 13: Nations and Empires

"The sun has not shone for two hours ever since we have been here," complained Mercy Coles to her diary. The sore throat she was developing after her day out in the cold and rain would not respond to the homeopathic medicine Premier Gray offered her. Indeed, Gray was under the weather himself. He missed the Wednesday session of the conference and would miss the Friday one as well "through indisposition."

After the Wednesday afternoon Canadian caucus, George Brown must have heard about the Maritimers' discontent with his motion on federalism and western expansion. Thursday morning, with the conference assembled in the reading room again, he acted immediately to mend fences. According to Hewitt Bernard's notes, he moved, seconded by Nova Scotia attorney general William Henry, that "the union shall presently embrace the following provinces: Upper Canada, Lower Canada, Nova Scotia, New Brunswick, Newfoundland, and Prince Edward Island."[1] Whatever Brown had actually said or implied the previous day about a single Maritime province coming into confederation, he was now publicly disavowing the whole idea. The conference endorsed the new motion, apparently without further debate.

But the Island delegate Andrew Macdonald, who had been part of the Maritimers' discussion on Wednesday afternoon, recalled this Maritime union incident differently. In his notes, he recorded that on Wednesday Brown had actually presented a motion providing for just three provinces in the new confederation: Canada East, Canada West, and the "lower provinces." Apparently Brown would have included Newfoundland with the three Maritime provinces. According to Andrew Macdonald, what Brown did on Thursday morning was to withdraw these motions entirely. Just to complicate the matter further, Edward Whelan, who would also have been part of the Maritimers' discussions on Wednesday afternoon, recalled that the Maritimers had mostly discussed not the preservation of the separate Maritime provinces, but how many seats the Maritimers could command in the new federal parliament.[2]

The details are lost beyond recovery, but deliberately or inadvertently, Brown had reinforced Maritime suspicions that insensitive Canadians were planning the future of the Maritimes without much concern for the expressed preferences of the Maritime delegates. Indeed, Brown's heart did lie with Canada West, and he did fear that if permitted, the smaller provinces would become a permanent drain on Canada West's resources. The Maritimers' concerns were not groundless. Whatever he had done or implied, Brown had managed to raise Atlantic-Canadian hackles against Canadian arrogance. John A. Macdonald's well-known preference for a very centralized union had not been nearly so offensive—indeed, several Maritimers shared his doubts about federal systems and were inclined to agree that the new nation should have just one national government. Brown risked alienating those Maritimers more sympathetic to his federalist vision as well as those inclined toward a strong central government.

Still, for all the offence he had given, the firm assertion by the Maritimers that produced Brown's new resolution reinforced the agreement that the new union must be a federal one. When even the small provinces would not consider combining into one, Macdonald's chances of selling the Maritimers a legislative union of all the provinces were bleak indeed, whatever the doubts some of them raised about divided authority. Again, Cartier kept his own counsel and let Canada West and the Maritimes bicker.

The Canadian cabinet session of Wednesday, which was supposed to put some organization into the conference's resolutions, had not yet borne fruit. With the separate existence of the Maritime provinces confirmed, the next resolution came not from the Canadians but from Charles Fisher, an independent-minded reform delegate from New Brunswick. With the support of Nova Scotia's Robert Dickey, a Conservative, he raised a matter barely raised in Charlottetown and apparently not foreseen in the Canadians' planning. His resolution read

> That the constitution of the general and local governments shall be framed upon the British model so far as is consistent with our colonial condition and with a view to the perpetuation of our connection with the mother country.[3]

Was this simply a rote affirmation of loyalty, a demand that all present affirm their commitment to the British Empire? Or did Fisher have some specific concern that the Canadians might harbour ideas of a different system of government—or even of independence? Nothing in the record specifies, but Fisher's motion was not accepted as some uncontroversial affirmation of loyalty. Debate arose, along with denials that anyone was contemplating separation from the Empire. Premier Charles Tupper, with support from Peter Mitchell—another Nova Scotia–New Brunswick alliance, another Conservative–Reform partnering—quickly proposed an amendment that was really an argument against Fisher's motion:

That while it is the avowed desire of this conference to perpetuate the connection with the parent state by every means in our power, it is not judicious to fetter our actions by the passage of a resolution of a simple declaratory character, and which may embarrass our action in the selection of the best means of providing for the general and local government of the country.[4]

Again the record keepers provided little explanation of the thinking behind this counter-proposal, with its bold suggestion that a constitution "framed upon the British model" and the "perpetuation of our connection with the parent state" might somehow "fetter the actions" of the conference. If Fisher's motion could be read as a loyalty oath, Tupper's could be interpreted as a declaration of autonomy, if not precisely independence. The crossfire of motions was not yet done. A third Nova Scotia–New Brunswick duo, Leonard Tilley and Adams Archibald, both Reformers this time, weighed in with another amendment that was once again more like a contrary motion:

That in framing a constitution for the general government, the conference, with a view to the perpetuation of our connection with the mother country and to the promotion of the best interests of these provinces, desire to follow the model of the British constitution as far as our circumstances will permit.[5]

Andrew Macdonald found no whiff of revolution here. In his notes, he suggested the point of this last motion lay in its specification that this question concerned only "the general government." Tilley and Archibald may have been aware that Brown, for the sake of efficiency and cost savings, and John A. Macdonald, to strengthen central authority, had indeed been musing about provincial administrations that might be something less than fully autonomous bicameral parliaments on the Westminster model. Perhaps this resolution was intended merely to preserve freedom to experiment in provincial governments, for it linked only the form of "the general government" to the British constitutional model. Edward Whelan, however, thought the point of the resolution lay in the words "as far as possible," meaning that the conference would "not be trammeled by too close an adherence to the forms of the British constitution."[6]

There was "a long discussion" on the topic raised by these three resolutions, and the debate was "characterized by much warmth," said Whelan. Hewitt Bernard's official record of resolutions suggests only the third version, the Tilley–Archibald resolution, went to a vote. The delegates took it seriously enough that the conference had its first divided vote. Canada (that is, the Canadian cabinet, wielding two votes), New Brunswick, and Newfoundland all supported Tilley's motion, but Prince Edward Island and Nova Scotia were both opposed. It passed four votes to two. The easy consensus of Charlottetown and the first days of Quebec was ruptured.

Was there a hinting at independence in the motion that was passed? The conference had affirmed the British connection, but by the third and successful resolution the "colonial" condition lauded in the first motion had become "the interests of the provinces." The delegates had declared that the degree to which British forms of government prevailed, even for the general government, would be determined not by colonial subservience but by British North American needs. "The best interests of these provinces" would prevail over "our colonial condition." British constitution usage, even the perpetuation of the British connection, would be preserved only "as far as our circumstances will permit."

This was bold language. But ever since 1848, these British North American politicians and their predecessors and mentors had had wind in their sails. As soon as they had secured control of colonial politics from the old autocratic governors, the provincial legislatures and governments had pursued ambitious programs of nation building and social and economic reform, and as long as the provinces were paying, the British colonial authorities had rarely been much involved. No longer was there an impasse in British North America between legislatures that had the taxing power and governors who controlled the spending power. The most evident example of this shift was the way the provinces had laid the groundwork for the great railroad boom and the industrial expansion that went with it, but vigorous use of the new machinery of government went much further. Canada East abolished its seigneurial landholding regime in the 1850s and wrote a new civil law code in the 1860s, boldly reinterpreting traditional bulwarks of francophone identity to which an insecure, defensive political community would have clung protectively. Canada West, the fastest growing of all the provinces, renewed many of its institutions and built handsome courthouses, city halls, and other public buildings across the province. In 1854, the Province of Canada negotiated the Reciprocity Treaty, a bold move toward freer trade with the United States that proved profitable for Canadian producers.[7] Across the Maritimes, where merchants and shipowners thrived in the late days of sail and invested their profits in universities and other cultural endowments, governments looked eagerly at railroad and canal projects, and grew concerned at how their small size and lack of political heft limited more ambitious projects.

Amid all this confident expansion, no successful British North American politician advocated a rupture with Britain. The American Civil War had given the U.S. North the largest, most battle-hardened army in the world, and against that threat British North Americans valued the British military guarantee behind them. They needed British investment as well. All those long railroads were mostly being paid for by British investors and financed through British banks. Still, British North American leaders of the 1860s knew that Britain was not besotted with its colonies. Britain had adopted free trade in the 1840s, sacrificing Canadian access to British markets for the sake of cheaper goods from elsewhere, even at the risk of seeing colonial loyalty erode. The British North American reformers who had been campaigning for more self-government since the 1820s found by 1848 that they were knocking on an open door, for Britain was positively eager to divest itself of most of its responsibilities for colonies such as British North America. When George Brown went to Britain immediately after the Quebec Conference, in fact, he was disconcerted to discover a widespread opinion that British North Americans should "shift for themselves" and a regret "that we did not immediately declare for independence."[8]

By the 1860s, Britain was pushing hard for British North America not to be more subservient but to take on more responsibility. In leading British circles, it was widely assumed that before long the "white" colonies would gradually go their own way, leaving Britain to focus on India, the part of the Empire that really mattered. The delegates recalled how, in his wide-ranging speech on Tuesday morning, John A. Macdonald had argued that, as it was, British North America's weakness was an embarrassment to Great Britain, but "if organized as a confederacy, our increased importance would soon become manifest."[9] That is, a fervent avowal of colonial submission might gain less respect in Britain than a bold claim to autonomy. Alexander Galt, an anglophone delegate from Quebec, had long experience with British financiers and investors, and he believed Britain was pushing British North America toward an independence for which it should be prepared.[10]

Only three of the thirty-three men around the conference table had been born in Britain: George Brown and John A. Macdonald, both Scots who had emigrated as boys in families escaping difficult circumstances at home, and Alexander Galt, who had also been raised and educated in British North America. Macdonald, who was comfortable with authority, skilled in deferentially coercing British officials, and better than most Canadian politicians at charming and coercing British opinion, visited Britain often, typically making such trips an escape from his burdens in local politics. Brown went there only on government business or for his wife's sake. Edward Whelan, frustrated with British interference on behalf of Prince Edward Island absentee landlords, had often heaped abuse on Britain and its aristocratically led governments, and Alexander Galt had long been convinced that Britain mostly wanted rid of British North America. Most of the delegates, anglophone as well as francophone, were generations away from British or French roots. Those who had grown up in the fight to establish responsible government and political accountability in the British North American provinces had lived for years with the accusation that they were disloyal to Britain and the Crown. As early as the 1830s, when Robert Baldwin, a hero to many of the delegates, visited Britain, he observed that Britons "seemed rarely to have the fact of the existence of [Canada] present to their minds" and was glad to return to Upper Canada, "my own, my native land."[11]

Baldwin and his political heirs around the conference table at Quebec City could imagine British North Americans running their own affairs. Building on the vital transfer of authority achieved in 1848, confederation would be a new assertion of autonomy, truly a new nation rather than a collection of isolated and dependent colonies. "The best interests of these provinces" was no idle phrase for many of the delegates; it was and had to be the lodestone to which their political compasses aimed.

Still, this was a narrow line for the delegates to walk. To maintain the British alliance, to secure British investment and British protection, and yet to run their own affairs, was the double-edged policy that would bedevil Canadian politicians for many years. Having found a compromise, at least for the day, between the equally troubling alternatives of too much national assertion and too much deferential loyalty, the delegates moved on to a new issue, really the first in which they would get to grips with the serious choices to be made in the drafting of a constitution. John A. Macdonald moved, with the support of Premier Gray of Prince Edward Island,

That there shall be a general legislature for the federated provinces composed of a Legislative Council and Legislative Assembly.[12]

Despite the turmoil they had just had, this resolution was uncompromising about adhering to a British constitutional model. The new nation would have a bicameral parliament, a parliament with two chambers. As Britain had its House of Commons and its House of Lords, the parliament of the federated provinces would have a lower house and an upper house. After all the earlier disagreements, this resolution seemed to generate no heat at all. There was discussion, but the resolution was quickly passed, setting the stage for another resolution on the upper house. This time both mover and seconder were Canadians. John A. Macdonald moved, with the support of a fellow Canadian, the Reformer Oliver Mowat,

> That for the purposes of forming the Legislative Council, the federated provinces shall be considered as consisting of three divisions: 1st, Upper Canada, 2nd Lower Canada, and 3rd, the four Maritime provinces, and each division shall be represented in the Legislative Council by an equal number of members.[13]

The Legislative Council was to be the upper house of the parliament of the new nation—eventually it would be named the Senate of Canada. But the resolution was also finally getting down to real constitutional choices. Since Monday they had been quibbling over procedures, or reaffirming decisions made at Charlottetown—federation, westward expansion—or debating large affirmations about loyalty and independence. Now they were beginning to define the structures of government. The fight over "our colonial condition" turned out to be only a warm-up.

This motion was evidently the first to come out of the Canadian delegation acting as the organizing committee for the preparation and presentation of motions, as Newfoundland's Ambrose Shea had proposed. Atlantic Canadians might be coming into the federation in four separate provinces, but for the purposes of the upper house, this resolution was lumping them together again: one region with one block of seats equal to that of the future Ontario and the future Quebec. The proposal drew an immediate riposte from the Maritimers. Premier Tilley of New Brunswick, supported by Robert Dickey of Nova Scotia, countered with a resolution to give the Maritime provinces thirty-two seats against the twenty-four of Quebec and Ontario. But it was 4 P.M., and there the day ended, with the matter put over until the next morning.

Working long days and moving between the hotel, the parliament building, and the dinners and private sessions in the evenings, the delegates were probably largely oblivious of doings in the city outside—except for the constant rain at the windows. Mercy Coles, however, went for a walk with her mother that afternoon, along the cliffside terrace above Lower Town. "While there, a large piece of rock fell," she wrote in her diary.[14] After eight days of endless rain combined with the weekend snow and frost, the steep cliff between the densely developed Upper Town and the equally crowded Lower Town was vulnerable to erosion. Mercy had witnessed a massive collapse. "Opposite the old customs house a rockslide came down," reported *Le Courrier du Canada*, a local paper. "Two houses of Rue Champlain were completely destroyed by the avalanche of stone and earth. They were left a ruined mass." Crowds gathered to rip desperately at the rubble. All they could do was bring out the bodies. The householder, labourer John Hayden, his wife, Mary Scanlan, their nine-year-old daughter, also named Mary, and Sarah McCann, eight, the child of a tenant in the house, had all been killed.[15]

Quebec was a divided city: wealthy, prosperous, and secure in the Upper Town, poor and insecure below. A decade earlier, Isabella Bird had written that "the little world in the upper part of the city is probably the most brilliant to be found anywhere in so small a compass." But she found another world below, "another nation, seldom mentioned in the aristocratic quarter of St. Louis, where vice, crime, poverty, and misery jostle each other, as pleasure and politics do in the upper town."[16] These were not nations defined by language, however. The influx of immigrants from the British

Isles had brought many poor labourers like the Haydens, Scanlans, and McCanns to crowded vulnerable homes in the lower town they shared with the older francophone population.

Mercy happened to see the tragedy occur, but she said little more about it. The local newspapers covered the story for several days, but nowhere did they mention that the politicians gathered for the constitutional congress took note of the disaster. No politician spoke to the press about accident prevention, the need to shore up the cliffs, or the townspeople's right to secure housing.

ELEVEN

Friday, October 14:
An Upper House

Mercy Coles gave the weather report as usual on Friday. "Rain again. Will it ever be fine?" *Le Courrier du Canada* provided more coverage of the rockfall and the grim search for bodies on Rue Champlain. It noted the rain had been ceaseless for six weeks: "Again, today there is pounding rain. This season of rain has done much damage to the potato crop."[1] It was stormy in the conference room at the parliament building, too. Thursday afternoon's late resolution and its amendment, on the allocation of seats in the Legislative Council, became the sole item of business for Friday's session—though Hewitt Bernard kept no notes of the discussion, Andrew Macdonald covered it only briefly, and Edward Whelan had only a single sentence about it in his dispatches home. "The resolution regarding representation in the Upper House of the confederate Parliament was debated all day with considerable warmth and ability but no agreement," Whelan said.[2] There seem to have been several amendments offered, but most were withdrawn.

The debate was driven by the demand of the Maritimers, or at least some of them, for more seats in the upper house than either Ontario or

Quebec would have. "Well, their population is more than double that of the whole of them put together," wrote Whelan, who could see grounds for the Canadian position. But it was precisely because the rep-by-pop principle at the heart of the Cartier–Brown bargain meant the Maritimers would have only a minority of seats in the lower house, that the Maritimers contended for more representation in the upper house, where regions or perhaps provinces, rather than the population at large, would be represented.

These arguments met a brick wall erected by the Canadian delegates. What counter-arguments the Canadians offered on Friday were never coherently recorded, but they did not concede any significant change in the proposal for equality among the three regions they had identified: Canada West, Canada East, and Atlantic Canada. The disagreement continued all day. At 4 P.M., the delegates were as unresolved as ever, and the question was put over until the next day. Drafting a quick message for his newspaper in Charlottetown, Whelan feared the collapse of the conference was imminent. Whelan was one of the strongest Maritime supporters of confederation; his discouragement came from knowing how his fellow Island delegates were coming to feel not only about the upper house but about the whole subject of union. The upper-house question had come close on the heels of the clumsy offence given to the Maritimers over the merger of their three provinces. At the same time, the Maritime delegates were coming to grips with how much the Canadians intended to dominate the conference and how much they had already mapped out the confederation they wanted. In the upper-house debate, they were learning that the Canadians would resist changes on important matters.[3]

The upper house debate, important in itself, was also about power in the conference, about whether the Maritimers could find common ground for their priorities and, if they could, whether they could shift the Canadians from their predetermined positions. At four o'clock, the frustrated delegates adjourned to prepare for the grand ball being given that evening by the government of Canada in honour of the delegates from the Maritime provinces.

Mercy Coles, who had been anticipating the grand ball all week, did not get to go. Her sore throat had become compounded with a painful headache. At the hotel, as she and her mother were dressing for the great event, she fainted. Then, to her embarrassment, she burst into tears. They called in Charles Tupper, who, though a premier, never went anywhere without his medical bag. Dr. Tupper diagnosed a high fever and prescribed medicines and bed rest—no dancing. A family friend stayed with Mercy, and her parents went off late "in wind and rain" to join the ball.[4]

A thousand people, perhaps even more, had been invited. "It was a stunning and crushing affair as regards numbers, gorgeous dress, lavish expenditure on the part of the government, and indeed everything that was calculated to make a sensational sacrifice at the shrine of pleasure," wrote Edward Whelan the next day.[5] At least eight hundred of the favoured people attended, and every room on two floors of the parliament building was in use. The band of the 17th Regiment was installed in the visitors' gallery of the Legislative Council chamber, and the band of the 25th in the gallery of the Assembly. There were card tables in the Speaker's room, and refreshments in the Assembly reading room. The reading room of the Legislative Council, where the delegates had been arguing a few hours earlier, was laid out with the supper prepared for Governor General Monck, Premier Taché, and their special guests.

Some confusion about introductions and presentations started the evening off awkwardly. In her sickbed the next day, Mercy Coles was told "the Quebec people never introduced the ladies or gentlemen to any partners" or even helped them to supper. Hearing that Colonel and Mrs. Gray came away "rather indignant at the way their daughters were treated," she concluded the ball had been "rather a failure." But Edward Whelan rhapsodized about the ball for his readers in Charlottetown. He even retracted his earlier ungallant comments about the local women. "Beautiful women and gay officers in uniform ... grace, loveliness, and politeness at every step." The bands, playing lancers, quadrilles, polkas, and waltzes, were "not allowed to have any time on their hands," and "grave and venerable ministers of state contended with the youngest and gayest votaries of fashion for the possession of the floor."[6]

Another guest at the ball took a more reserved view than Whelan. This was Frances Elizabeth Owen Monck—"Feo" to her family—wife to the governor general's brother Richard, who had sailed from Ireland in May 1864 to spend the year with her husband in Quebec City. They had been travelling during the month before the conference, and had missed the arrival of the politicians "who are come here to arrange about a united kingdom of Canada." The Moncks had just come down from Montreal by steamboat that morning, sharing the crowded ship with Montrealers eager to be part of the festivities. Confident in her place in the Anglo-Irish ascendency, Feo had a keen sardonic eye for the lack of deference and the assumption of equality she saw everywhere in the United States and British North America. She had a habit of laughing about anything that was foreign to her, and she was not easily impressed.

Feo, as the governor general's particular guest, was to be escorted into the ball by Premier Taché, immediately behind Lord and Lady Monck, and the four would lead the first quadrille of the evening. But she discovered that "Sir E is so very old that he can't dance, and he would not take me in for fear of having to dance." John A. Macdonald, unabashed, stepped into Taché's place, and Feo soon concluded Sir Étienne was "the only non-dancing old man—wigs, gray hair, and spectacles don't hinder people from dancing." At the buffet table, she pointedly observed, Taché served himself to several dishes with a single knife. Even Lieutenant-Governor Richard MacDonnell of Nova Scotia, considered by many among the British North Americans as one of the grandees of the event, failed to impress her. "He wore a red riband and order but otherwise looked nothing much…. I wonder how they could entrust any government to him." Feo preferred events at Spencer Wood, where the company was mostly British and the guests carefully selected.

The Moncks left early, but Feo heard that the end of the ball, at around 4 A.M., "was most amusing—such drunkenness, pushing, kicking, and tearing … the supper room floor was covered with meat, drink and broken bottles."[7]

Whelan admitted to no such drunkenness and disorder. Though he was annoyed by a grey-haired Cockney fop, a railroad promoter whom Whelan found too forward with the wives of premiers he was lobbying, he declared the event took place "without interruption and without an incident to mar the harmony of the occasion, until nearly 3 o'clock." In particular, Whelan was moved and excited by the unique mixing of anglophone and francophone Canadians that Quebec City was showing to him. It charmed him with a sudden vision of the future country. "There is no fun in seeing two persons from the same country in conversation," he observed, "but to see those who are foreigners in language and race striving to communicate their thoughts to each other, is an incident particularly charming. Here is the gay, garrulous, and polite Frenchman (or Frenchwoman, if you will) gesticulating with hands and head, striving to make the Englishman, or Irishman, or Scotchman who does not know a word of French any more than he knows Sanscrit, comprehend a strange jumble of French and excessively bad English. The French ladies here give a delightful tone to society."[8]

"It went off very well," wrote George Brown to his wife on coming back to his hotel room around midnight, "but to me it was an insufferable bore, and I have come to my quarters weary and worn and with a shocking headache."[9]

TWELVE

Saturday, October 15 to Sunday, October 16: The Work to Be Done

The hired help must have been busy overnight. The ball had gone on until either 3 A.M. (per Edward Whelan) or 4 A.M. (per Feo Monck), but at eleven the next morning the constitutional conference reassembled in the reading room. Evidently the staff had cleared whatever meat, drink, and broken glass had been strewn about, and had covered the table with a fresh cloth and restored the conference's constitutional texts and records. A long evening of dancing and drinking with the fair ladies had not kept any delegates from returning to the fight over the upper house. Hewitt Bernard had spent the evening welcoming guests as they arrived at the ball, but he was in his place at 11 A.M. and he recorded perfect attendance as the debate resumed.

First, however, the delegates reorganized their hours of meeting. With a week of meetings behind them, they had done little more than to recapitulate what had been settled in a few days at Charlottetown before falling into rancorous and inconclusive debate about the upper house.

None of the fundamental details of the constitution had been addressed, let alone settled. At this rate, the conference could take forever. When he had sent his wife and daughter to Britain in June, George Brown had expected to follow them in a few days. Caught up days later in the political whirlwind of confederation, he had been postponing his departure ever since. Just before sailing for Charlottetown at the end of August, he promised Anne that he would leave for Britain on October 5, noting, "I cannot tell you how this happy thought affects me." Back from Charlottetown, with the conference scheduled for October 10, he still expected he could get away on October 19. Writing his midnight letter after returning from the ball, however, he conceded he could not sail before November 2. "The probability is that at least another week will be consumed," he wrote. "I am very sorry at the long separations these political matters have caused us, but it was not to be helped, and we must not repine, my dear Anne, at doing our duty."[1]

Other delegates were making similar calculations about when they might return home. Even if they did not have a baby daughter and a much-loved wife awaiting them, they had businesses, law practices, and political obligations at home. They could see the volume of work the conference still had to face, and perhaps they had been discussing it between the lancers and the waltzes the previous evening. That morning, John A. Macdonald proposed they revise their schedule, and they all agreed to put more hours into the constitutional conference. Instead of meeting from 11 A.M. to 4 P.M., leaving the rest of the day for government business and private caucusing among the delegates, they endorsed Macdonald's motion "That on and after Monday next, the conference commence its sittings at ten o'clock A.M. and sit until two o'clock P.M. and that it reassemble at 7.30 P.M., and sit until adjourned on motion."[2]

With these extended hours agreed on, they returned to the question of seat distribution in the upper house—and to deadlock once more. More than just the matter of a few seats seems to have been at stake, for Andrew Macdonald noted that "the general subject of federation was discussed in connection with this resolution." The delegates were perhaps beginning to consider just what this resolution said about power sharing in this federal state. "Nearly all of the delegates expressed their views at some length," Andrew Macdonald wrote, but the only recorded motion of the day, from Charles Fisher of New Brunswick, proposed a 30-30-30 division of seats, including Newfoundland in the Atlantic provinces' bloc of 30. This was hardly a radical revision of the original Canadian proposal of 24-24-24. They gave up at 2:30 P.M., and adjourned until Monday at ten.[3]

That night, the Board of Trade of Quebec City hosted a dinner at the banqueting room of the Russell Hotel on Côte du Palais, a few blocks from the parliament building and the Hotel St-Louis on the north-facing slope of the Upper Town, looking toward the mountains rather than the river. Attendance at the dinner was very numerous (about 125, in fact), according to Edward Whelan, who emphasized the presence of the leading members of the mercantile community along with the governor's courtiers, politicians, and public servants—and this time no women. Leading off the toasts and speeches, President Joseph of the Board of Trade said the merchants of Quebec had no opinion on federation itself, but hoped to see progress on a commercial union, an end to tariffs among the provinces, and "the iron ties of the inter-colonial railway." Premier Tupper, evidently a little miffed at this coolness to the nation-building ambition of the conference, replied that he thought the circumstances would have justified the president "in giving a little more encouragement to the project," though indeed the secrecy of the conference meant the Board of Trade probably had little idea of just what "the project" entailed. There would be little likelihood of the merchants seeing any tariff adjustments, Tupper declared pointedly, "while we are separate." Confederation, however, "would place them upon the exchanges of the world in a far better position than we can hope for in our present divided state." One after another, delegates from the Canadas and from the Maritime provinces gave long speeches about the warm welcome they were enjoying and about the great wealth and prosperity of the provinces they represented. No delegate, however, revealed anything significant about the matters with which the conference was beginning to engage. Certainly no one mentioned the delegates' long, rancorous, and still unsettled disagreement over the upper house.[4]

On Sunday, Whelan gratefully noted, "A quiet day. No invitations, for which I heartily console myself." He attended mass at St. Patrick's, the cathedral of the town's Irish Catholics, and walked out to visit the monument to Wolfe and Montcalm and to "take a cursory view of the great battlefields of the last century." Earlier, he had promised that once he had learned "to thread with some degree of accuracy its mazy, crooked, narrow and bewildering streets," he would give his newspaper readers his impressions of "this ancient and historic city"—and, he would later add, "the great monuments of skill, industry, art and enterprise which abound in every street." But not yet. After the endless demands of the week passed, he preferred now to return to his quiet room "to think and dream."[5]

With the first week of the conference ended, and the day of rest providing contemplation, Whelan was not at all confident. "With so much diversity of opinion," he had written on Friday, "it is very difficult to say whether the convention will not be compelled to break up prematurely. Matters do not certainly look very promising.... I have grave doubts respecting a satisfactory result."[6] George Brown was much more confident. "There is no appearance yet of any insurmountable obstacle," he wrote to his wife while the deadlock over the upper house raged on. Was this just a line tossed off in a family letter, or were the Canadian delegates confident in holding firm while the Maritimers talked themselves out? The Canadians had not come casually to their plan for the upper house. Their design for it was deeply integrated into their idea of the parliament they wanted. No one left records of what private meetings, caucuses, dinners, and drinking sessions the delegates held in search of consensus during their day off, but the issue would be joined again on Monday.

THIRTEEN

Monday, October 17: Representing the Regions

The delegates had taken Sunday off, but some review of the week's progress must have been going on. When Premier Taché gavelled the meeting to order at 10 A.M. on another grim, cold, rainy morning, the delegates immediately disinterred a matter that had seemed settled the previous week. On Wednesday, George Brown's resolution on federalism and western expansion had caused some Maritimers to complain that he was pushing Maritime union on them. On Thursday, the conference had passed a resolution declaring there would be six provinces,* not three or four, but some dissatisfaction must have lingered, no doubt compounded by the disagreements about the upper house. Wednesday's resolution endorsing provincial governments for local matters and a federal government for common matters of common interest was now formally exhumed and amended, with the words "Maritime Provinces" removed and "Nova Scotia, New Brunswick, and Prince Edward Island"

---

* Assuming all agreed to join, the six would be Newfoundland, Prince Edward Island, Nova Scotia, New Brunswick, Quebec, and Ontario (the last two still without those names).

substituted. No one was going to be able to claim from the resolutions of the conference that the Maritime delegates had given approval, even inadvertently, to Maritime union.[1]

With that confirmed, the delegates returned to the issue of the upper house seats. Suddenly, the problem they had been fighting over since Thursday was settled, done, and behind them. The Islander Andrew Macdonald reported that he himself launched Monday's discussion by arguing for provincial equality in the upper house: "While the lower house should have its numbers of members based on population," he asserted, "the upper house should be more representative of the smaller provinces as it was to be the guardian of their rights and privileges." Macdonald went on to threaten that Prince Edward Island was "not specially desirous" of changing its situation, and the Canadians would need to sweeten their offers if they wanted to entice the smallest province into the federation. But his proposal for an upper house in which the provinces were equally represented, as states were in the American Senate, was, in his own words, "not entertained."[2] The Canadians flatly rejected it, and they were able to carry most of the Maritimers with them. Hewitt Bernard did not even make a note of this argument. During the Sunday break, the tide had turned in the Maritime caucuses. A broad consensus in favour of accepting the Canadian upper house plan had emerged. Charles Fisher withdrew his compromise proposal for a ninety-member upper house—thirty from each of the three regions. Before they broke for the afternoon, the question of seat allocation was settled by the passage of three motions in quick succession.

The delegates agreed there would be three equal blocs in the upper house: Canada West, Canada East, and a Maritime bloc for the three provinces—much as the Canadians had proposed the previous week. Next, they agreed there would be twenty-four members from each bloc, with the Maritime representation divided into ten for each of Nova Scotia and New Brunswick and four for Prince Edward Island—again, the original Canadian proposal in essence, even if the detailed regional subdivision was new. In the third resolution, the delegates made an allowance for Newfoundland, whose place had been left unspecified in the first upper house proposals. During the summer of 1864, there had been no certainty that Newfoundland would be represented in the constitutional talks, and the Canadian cabinet's summertime planning for the upper house had apparently made no allowance for Newfoundland. Frederic Carter and Ambrose Shea, the two Newfoundland delegates, had been present and voting all week just like the other delegates, but now a new motion formally invited Newfoundland to join the federation and promised it four seats in the upper house, separate from the Maritime provinces' allocation of twenty-four. Hewitt Bernard's record of motions affirms that these resolutions met unanimous agreement, but Andrew Macdonald reported—plausibly, in light of his arguments that morning—that the Prince Edward Island delegation was split. The Island's single vote was cast in favour of the motions, but Macdonald knew that not all its delegates approved.

After having argued about seats in the upper house from Thursday until Saturday morning, the Maritime delegates were giving the Canadians almost precisely what they had proposed at the start: regional, not provincial, equality in the upper house, though now with a commitment for additional seats to be allocated when new regions came into the federation. How and why the Canadians had succeeded in defusing the Maritime arguments for a larger representation—indeed, for a different kind of upper house—was hardly explained by any of the participants and commentators. An explanation would start to emerge, however, from the next issue the conference took up: how members of the upper house would be appointed.

Working with the new schedule they had adopted on Saturday, the delegates had convened (after an early cabinet meeting, at least for the Canadians) at 10 A.M. instead of eleven, and they broke for the afternoon at two, as soon as the upper house seat allocation resolutions had been approved. After two more hours in yet another Canadian cabinet session,

George Brown prevailed on his cabinet colleagues to adjourn that meeting at four. A mail boat was due to sail, and he was determined to have a letter ready to go.

"The conference proceedings go along very well," he wrote from his room at the St-Louis, "considering we have a great deal of talkee-talkee and not very much practical administrative talent among our Maritime friends. We were very near broken up on the question of the distribution of members in the upper chamber of the federal legislature, but fortunately we have this morning got the matter amicably compromised after a delay of three days. We have eight or ten other points of great difficulty yet to be got over." This letter was his first leisure activity all week, he declared. Even so, he was interrupted several times while writing it "by people pestering me about one thing or another." He was still hoping to take ship for Britain before the end of the month but, should the conference grind on, he admitted it would be impossible for him "to ruin himself" with his political friends and "abandon the great scheme at the very moment when a firm hand was most needful." Brown concluded the last page with the dinner bell about to ring. As a Canadian minister resident in the hotel, he hosted the Maritime guests at their reserved table—"a company dinner of the first class!"[3]

Dinner done, the delegates gathered again in the parliament building at 7:30 in the evening for the first of the new night sittings. John A. Macdonald moved the resolution that would make the Senate of Canada infamous for 150 years:

> That the members of the Legislative Council shall be appointed by the crown under the great seal of the General Government and shall hold office during life.[4]

The delegates debated this resolution all of Monday evening, not adjourning until midnight. Andrew Macdonald noted that John A. Macdonald, George Brown, Charles Tupper, "and others" spoke, but no one kept notes of what arguments they offered. At midnight, a motion to adjourn was offered, and they went to bed with the question still pending.

Even more than the decision for regional equality, the resolution on appointment, rather than election, of the upper house reflected the Canadian vision for that chamber, indeed, for the parliament of the new nation. A provincially equal upper house, with each province having the same voting power regardless of population, could have been a significant factor in the federal parliament and in national politics. This body might have established itself as the true representative of the sea-trading Maritimes, the francophone farmers of Quebec, and the commercial interests of Ontario. Like senators in the American upper house, members of the upper house might have claimed to express the interests of their provinces, despite the disparity in the provincial populations they represented.* That kind of upper house might have become a vital player in the politics of the new nation, centralizing power in the new national capital, putting the local governments in the shade, and even challenging the dominance of the rep-by-pop lower house as well. Had they provided an upper house with that kind of authority, the delegates might also have planned for provincial governments that were weak and dependent, with power centralized and the real contest being between the upper and the lower houses.

Power centralized in a national capital was the political system against which George-Étienne Cartier and George Brown had placed a veto as soon as they began to talk in June 1864, and their design for the Senate was not a whim. The Canadian cabinet delegates were acting on a plan they had negotiated in the long cabinet sessions in Quebec City during the hot, humid summer of 1864. Even their willingness to concede additional seats to Newfoundland, as a fourth region rather than part of

* Even today, Wyoming and South Dakota, with barely two million people between them, have the same representation in the United States Senate as California and New York, where almost sixty million Americans live.

the Maritimes, suggests their outline of the upper house had been fixed early, before the participation of Newfoundland. The powerlessness of the upper house was a key feature of confederation that the Canadian politicians had agreed on during their own constitutional negotiations. It was an integral part, not an error, in the political system to which they were committed.

George Brown had no faith in upper houses. In a few days, he would propose that once confederation was achieved, each province should abolish its own upper house and govern with a single legislative chamber. The constitution for the new province of Ontario, which he had a large part in shaping, provided no upper house, and though initially Ontario was the only Canadian province without one, eventually every other province followed its example. Brown was a thoroughgoing parliamentary democrat and an uncompromising rep-by-pop man. He wanted the national government accountable to a legislature that was accountable to the voters, and he wanted no unrepresentative upper house to be able to block the will of the representative legislature. He was also a thoroughgoing federalist: his alliance with Cartier had been born from his determination to get his cherished Canada West out from under the interference of Canada East, able to run its own local affairs unimpeded. The place to secure that kind of provincial power was in the provincial legislatures. It was not to be diluted away in the upper house of a central government. George Brown's one requirement for the upper house was that it be weak.

George-Étienne Cartier's position was identical. In leading francophone Quebec into confederation, he was calculating that the Quebec voting bloc—*his* voting bloc—would be large and cohesive enough to continue to wield substantial influence in a national legislature based on rep by pop. He was also determined to ensure that the vital cultural powers that seemed essential to the flourishing of the francophone society—language, education, social services, the law—would be entrusted to the new province of Quebec, not to the national government. A powerful, confident upper house in which Quebec was just one bloc among several, and always in a minority regardless of its population, held no attraction for Cartier. The prospect of protection for Quebec's vital interests shifting from a Quebec legislature dominated by representatives of its francophone population to a national upper house sure to be dominated by anglophone Canadians had to be abhorrent to him.

This shared interest of Cartier and Brown had surely been decisive during the Canadian cabinet's summertime deliberations on constitutional policy. In his speech on the conference's opening day, John A. Macdonald claimed "an open mind" regarding the election or appointment of upper house members. A week later, the Canadian cabinet must have stiffened his resolve, for on this matter there were no more of the internal disagreements the Canadians had exposed in the conference's first days. The confidence with which the Canadian delegation withstood the Maritime onslaught on the upper house issue from Thursday through Monday suggests their position was a deeply held part of a coherent constitutional package, based on a rep-by-pop lower house being the essential element of the national government. The longer the debate went on, the more the Canadian principle began to sell itself to the Maritime delegations.

The Maritimers had begun, in effect, with horse trading. They were not attempting to design an upper house fundamentally different from the Canadian proposal, but simply bargaining for more seats. Even as they resisted these demands, the Canadians, who could have been outvoted four to two by the Atlantic provinces at any time, had been gradually convincing most of the Maritimers that the Canadian constitutional vision—strong provinces, power entrusted to rep-by-pop legislatures, and a weak upper house—best suited the interests of all. After three days of squabbles about seat allocation, Brown commented sourly about the administrative talents of the Maritimers. But he was also beginning to find kindred souls there. "Mrs. Archibald is a very nice person," he told Anne in his letter, referring to the wife of the leader of Nova Scotia's

Reform opposition, Adams Archibald, "and so is her husband. If the confederation goes on he will be a political ally of ours in Nova Scotia, and so will Mr. Tilley be in New Brunswick." Brown was not only gaining what he needed for Canada West. He was beginning to see a progressive alliance across the provinces, one that could one day make George Brown or some other Reform leader the head of government.[5]

Several of the Prince Edward Islanders were still refusing to go along with the appointed-upper-house proposal, unable to accept that their very small share in the rep-by-pop legislature would not be balanced by a larger place in the upper house. By Monday afternoon, however, most of the Maritimers had come around to the Canadian position. They were beginning to adopt the Cartier–Brown argument: they did not need more upper house seats because the upper house was not going to be—should not be—where power would truly lie. Now, with gaslights burning in the reading room against the October darkness, the Maritimers struggled to come to terms with the other part of the Canadian plan: to have the upper house members not merely appointed, but appointed by the national government. They would settle that question on Tuesday morning.

FOURTEEN

Tuesday, October 18:
The Senate Defined

"I am sure I shall know the shape of every shingle on the roof of the old house opposite," Mercy Coles told her diary resignedly on Tuesday afternoon. After her collapse on Friday night, she had been laid low all weekend, and had barely lifted her head from her pillow, except to accept Dr. Tupper's treatments. On Tuesday she made her first venture downstairs to the hotel drawing room, but she quickly staggered back to bed. Mrs. Tupper, who visited, told her she had almost certainly had a bout of diphtheria. Diphtheria had killed one of the Tuppers' own children some years previously, and their daughter Emma, another of the delegates' daughters enjoying the Quebec City festivities, would come down with a milder case a few days later. Even after a stream of visitors bearing gossip and newspapers, Mercy was miserable, and she vented her fury about all she was missing on Quebec City. "I shall get quite well whenever we leave Quebec. It is the most miserable place to live in one can fancy. We have not had one fine day since we came. It has been pouring." Mrs. Coles, however, was having a much better time, except that her social commitments were relentless. "Ma is going to have a new black silk waist made," Mercy noted. "She has only the one evening dress and finds it rather awkward." Mercy was still hoping to be well enough for Wednesday's ball, but Mrs. Coles was not going to miss it.[1]

When the delegates gathered on Tuesday morning, John A. Macdonald's resolution on an upper house appointed by the federal government headed the agenda. In his opening remarks to the conference's first meeting, Macdonald had airily said, "Some are in favour of the elective principle. More are in favour of appointment by the Crown. I will keep my own mind open upon that point as if it were a new question to me altogether." He joked that whatever the form, an upper house would surely be necessary because it was necessary to protect minorities—"and the rich are always fewer than the poor."[2] But the plan for the upper house worked out by the Canadian cabinet allowed for no such alternatives. Macdonald, now pulled firmly into line, presented as his own the key resolution that would ensure the powerlessness of the upper house.*

The weak upper house being urged by the Canadian cabinet was probably congenial enough to Macdonald. As a Conservative, inclined to support the familiar and the traditional, he was determined that the new national legislature should grow to the stature and dignity for which Britain's Westminster parliament was the model, so he wanted an upper house that lent dignity to the new Canadian parliament. But Macdonald's eye was always on power. He would have preferred—and frequently said so—a centralized union in which power would lie with the national government. He could be glad of a chamber the national government could use to reward its friends and dispose of those no longer useful to it. But he had no reason to want a powerful, representative, authoritative upper house. As a young politician in the 1840s, Macdonald had opposed

---

* Long after confederation, Canada West delegate William McDougall claimed he had supported an elective Senate during the Quebec Conference with Oliver Mowat's support. Possibly he proposed it to the Canadian cabinet and was overruled. Possibly both Hewitt Bernard and Andrew Macdonald ignored him. There is no other evidence of any of the Canadians ever supporting the elective principle.

the responsible government revolution that made the governor's cabinet fully accountable to the elected legislature. But in the following years, he had helped bring his Liberal-Conservative Party around to full support of responsible government, and he had become a parliamentary man to his fingertips, one who preferred that the lower house, the representative and governing house, not be trammelled and constrained by an interfering upper chamber. So on Monday morning, in a string of resolutions, he threaded his way carefully, presenting the upper house as a dignified and respectable chamber, a Canadian House of Lords almost, while at the same time ensuring that it had little likelihood of ever seriously challenging the government that was accountable to the lower house.

As their first order of business, the conference took up Macdonald's resolution from the night before: the upper house would be appointive, not elected, and appointments to it would be made by "the Crown under the Great Seal of the General Government"—that is, by the governor general acting on advice of the federal cabinet. Hewitt Bernard's record is thin on this point, but this profound choice had surely been debated and defended during the conference's long allocation-of-seats wrangle in which the Canadians had gradually made the case for their kind of upper house. This morning, the resolution went through almost without debate, without even a pause for the provincial caucuses to withdraw and consult on how to vote. Support was unanimous, according to Hewitt Bernard, and this time Andrew Macdonald's notes did not contradict him.[3]

More than almost any other decision of the Quebec Conference, the decision to have an appointed upper house was mocked and attacked from the day it was announced. The opponents of confederation denounced it as evidence of the autocratic and anti-democratic tendencies of the confederation makers, as if their intention was to create an aristocratic upper chamber from which the chosen creatures of the colonial ascendency would thwart the will of the Canadian people forever. Those in the conference, however, were coming to understand it meant precisely the opposite. An appointed house, particularly one appointed by the central government, would always be dignified, ceremonial, advisory—and largely without power. It might be clothed with theoretical authority, like the British House of Lords, to veto anything that came before it. But in the reality of Canadian political culture in the 1860s, and ever after, an appointed chamber could never stand up in a real and concerted way to the will of the lower house, the one given legitimate power by being elected by Canadian voters in proportion to their numbers on a broad electoral franchise. That was what the conference delegates had come to believe was required. On Tuesday morning, October 18, 1864, they settled that such would be their advice to their legislatures.

In defending the upper house during the Province of Canada's legislative debate on confederation that followed the conference, Alexander Mackenzie, a friend and supporter of Brown's and a future prime minister, declared, "It is my opinion that we would be better without an upper house." Mackenzie had not been a delegate at Quebec City, but he acknowledged that the question there had been "not what is the best possible form of government," but only "what is the best that can be framed for a community holding different views on the subject." On that basis, he was prepared to accept an upper house, so long as it was a mere "court of revision," not an independent chamber. "Hear, hear!" called Brown, "and therefore I accepted as a fair compromise, a second chamber nominated by the [federal cabinet]." The Canadians had insisted on appointment not to make the upper house independently powerful, but to ensure its dependence on the government and subservience to the lower house. It seems to have been understood that it might be awkward for the delegates to declare too frankly that the principal quality they sought in an upper house was its weakness vis-à-vis the elected lower house. During the debates on confederation, a good deal of effort would be expended to demonstrate the dignity and importance the upper house would have. John A. Macdonald liked to argue that since it was impossible to have a hereditary body as in Britain, "the only mode of adapting the English system to the upper house is by conferring the power of appointment on the crown," which he called "the system most in accordance with the British constitution."[4]

Still, Macdonald was careful to dispel suggestions that the upper house might threaten the authority of the lower. He pointed to the fixed numbers of members in the upper house, a rule that would prevent the government of the day from packing it with supporters in order to have its way in a crisis. The upper house must maintain some distance from the lower house, he continued, "for it is only valuable as being a regulating body, calmly considering the legislation initiated by the popular branch." Nevertheless, he continued, "it will never set itself in opposition against the deliberate and understood wishes of the people.... There is an infinitely greater chance of a deadlock between the two branches of the legislature, should the elective principle be adopted." By making the upper house an appointed one, the delegates had deliberately prevented that.[5]

With Crown appointment confirmed as the way upper house members would be chosen, Macdonald next presented the conference with a resolution proposing that the dignity and status of the upper house would be guaranteed by requirements that members to be appointed to it had to be British subjects, at least thirty years of age, and possessing real property worth four thousand dollars. No such age limits or property requirements would apply to elected members of the lower house, who would need only the votes of the electorate. With that rule endorsed unanimously, the conference adjourned for the afternoon.[6]

When the delegates met again at 7 P.M., they fell into a long wrangle about how to appoint the first block of seventy-six members of the upper house. This would consume their time and attention until midnight, and again the next day until the afternoon break. Since they had already agreed that appointments would be the prerogative of the federal cabinet, it was an odd issue upon which to lavish another day of their tight schedule, but there were three issues at stake. First, the conference was a multi-party one, and all the delegates wanted to ensure that their own party members had a share in the first distribution of seats in the new federal upper house. Second, the delegates were aware that for confederation to be ratified, support in the upper house of each province would be required, so a proposal that was attractive to the existing provincial councillors would be useful. Third, seven of the thirty-three men in the conference were themselves legislative council-lors, and most of them saw themselves ornamenting the new upper house of the new national parliament.* As a result, there were many proposals for earmarking seats in the first federal upper house for members of the existing provincial ones. George Coles was one of the few who argued that all citizens should be eligible for appointment. He denounced as corrupt the attempt to buy the provincial upper house members with these first federal appointments, but he got little support. The delegates agreed that priority for appointments to the first upper house would go to existing provincial councillors. In a nod to the bipartisan unity that had brought opposition as well as government members to the constitutional conference, they agreed that in the first distribution of seats, government and opposition councillors would be appointed in proportion to their existing numbers in the provincial upper houses. The first Senate of the new Dominion of Canada, in other words, would be appointed on a bipartisan basis—but only the first one.[7] They fought over this problem until midnight, and again for most of the next day before they had it sorted out.

---

* Taché was the only upper house councillor from Canada, but three of the six delegates from New Brunswick (Edward Chandler, Peter Mitchell, and William Steeves), two of Nova Scotia's five (Robert Dickey and Jonathan McCully), and Andrew Macdonald from Prince Edward Island were legislative councillors.

FIFTEEN

Wednesday, October 19: Were the Confederation Makers Democrats?

Seven-thirty P.M. on Wednesday evening, October 19, and finally the conference was done with the upper house. By ensuring that it would never challenge the representative lower house of the new federation, the delegates had laid in place a cornerstone of Canadian parliamentary democracy. Yet their choice would sustain a long-lived legend to the contrary: that by proposing an appointed upper house, they were indulging in fear and hatred of democracy itself. "They were not democrats" would become a much-repeated dismissal of confederation itself.[1]

If democracy is measured simply by how many people vote, the delegates certainly fell short of the democratic standard. They did not want an elected upper house. They looked skeptically at referendums and plebiscites, certain that it was in legislative debate, not in mass votes on yes/no questions, that the needs of the people could best be determined. The "household franchise" that they mostly upheld, while it gave British North America one of the broadest electorates in the world of the 1860s, certainly fell short of the concept of voting as the right of all adult citizens. Leaders of the confederation movement sometimes rejected the very word *democracy* itself, though only when they took it to mean mob rule or used it to describe governments that, once elected, could rule tyrannically, accountable to no one.

The confederation makers put less emphasis on how many voted than on who was accountable to whom. They were determined that the governments of their new federation should be accountable, not just to occasional elections but constantly, held accountable by lively independent legislatures that they believed to be representative of the people. They were parliamentary democrats, and their choices about the upper house were proof of that commitment.

Already the delegates had talked through almost nine days. They had reviewed some fundamental principles and learned to work with each other. They had skirmished for position and influence. They had partied lavishly. But apart from spending most of a week to hem in the upper house of the new nation's parliament, they had hardly addressed any of the fundamental mechanics of a constitution. Now they were ready to move. George Brown rose with the resolution he had been waiting fifteen years to present: representation by population, rep by pop:

> The basis of representation in the House of Commons shall be population, as determined by the official census every ten years.[2]

Brown's resolution continued on through several more clauses. The resolution proposed an elected House of Commons with two hundred seats. Sixty-five of these were allocated to Canada East, which would become the baseline province. Every other province would have seats that reflected quite precisely how its population related to Canada East's. Canada West, with 36 percent more people, would have eighty-nine seats to Canada East's sixty-five: 36 percent more. The same yardstick gave Nova Scotia nineteen seats, New Brunswick fifteen, Newfoundland seven, and Prince Edward Island just five: two hundred altogether. After each ten-year census, Canada East's seat allocation would remain at sixty-five, and other provinces' seat totals would grow or shrink as their population changed in comparison to Quebec's. This detailed proposal could not have been thrown up in the midst of discussion or sorted out on the back of an envelope. It reflected a program and a policy worked out and scrutinized in detail. It had been among the questions the cabinet of the Province of Canada struggled with during their summertime deliberations of 1864, and was now put forward as their settled position.

"Representation by population" had been Brown's campaign slogan ever since he entered elective politics in the early 1850s. In 1841, when Britain jammed Canada East and Canada West together in the wake of the rebellions of 1837, the idea had been to make the francophone population a permanent minority so as to ensure their rapid assimilation into British ways, British ideas, and the English language. Canada West, then significantly smaller in population than Canada East, was given an equality of seats with Canada East in the regions' new shared legislature, so that Canada West, joined with the anglophones of Canada East, could not be outvoted by the larger French population.

In the following years, Canada West grew rapidly. Immigrants who poured in from the British Isles soon made Canada West much larger in population than Canada East, and the gerrymandered equality of the two parts suddenly came to favour Canada East. The united bloc of French-Canadian representatives, with more seats than Canada East's population size would warrant, needed only a handful of Canada West allies—first Baldwin's Reformers, later Macdonald's Conservatives—to hold a permanent advantage over the divided forces of Canada West. Brown, stuck in the legislative minority for most of the 1850s and early 1860s, had come to call this reality "French Canadianism"—the ability of French Canada to impose policies on the union, and even on Canada West itself, that the people of Canada West did not support but for which the more prosperous economy of Canada West had to pay.

The demand for rep by pop had begun as a regional grievance of Canada West, an attempt to rebalance power in the Province of Canada. But with confederation, Canada West and Canada East would become Ontario and Quebec, each with its own government to manage its own affairs. The political problem that Brown had ridden to political success—Canada East's interference in Canada West's local affairs—would evaporate. In the planning for confederation, however, rep by pop had come to mean something notably different. It meant a radical commitment to equality of voting in the lower, elected house: throughout the new nation, every voting citizen's vote would be the equal of every other's. The unequal upper house, where smaller regions had the same representation as larger ones, had just been rendered weak and secondary. Rep by pop meant the new government would be held accountable by a fundamentally representative Assembly.

In the conference room that evening, Brown's victory should have been assured. Rep by pop had been fundamental to his bargain with Cartier and Macdonald in June 1864. Cartier had calculated that with a strong provincial government, his people would not be threatened by a genuinely representative federal legislature. Macdonald, whatever his doubts about federalism, never resisted rep by pop in the confederation plan. The Canadians had brought the rep-by-pop principle with them to Charlottetown and laid it out plainly. There had been no disagreement there.

Tonight, however, there was disagreement. If Hewitt Bernard's record can be relied on, it developed slowly. At first, the discussion turned on technical details about the censuses and on considerations of larger legislatures. Then, suddenly, the Prince Edward Islanders launched a revolt. Heath Haviland upended the discussion with a blunt declaration: "Prince Edward Island would rather be out of the confederation than consent to this motion. We should have no status." Edward Palmer backed him up: "Representation by population is not applicable when a certain number of provinces are throwing their resources into one confederation and giving up their own self-government and individuality."

Andrew Macdonald agreed: "We are not bound by the principle of representation by population." Even Edward Whelan, an enthusiast for confederation and a longtime foe of Palmer in Island politics, spoke against the motion, though mostly from calculation of the electoral risk it would cause back home: "Our people would not be content to give up their present benefits for five members." Only the Island's premier, Colonel Gray, and former premier George Coles held back from the attack. Gray had been blindsided by the defection of Palmer, his attorney general, and he lacked the support of his provincial secretary, William Pope, who missed this session. Premier Gray had come to Quebec committed to representation by population but was now outvoted in his own delegation, and he declared his position "humiliating." Coles seems to have enjoyed the split between Gray and Palmer. "I understood the matter to have been settled," he said, suggesting that if Palmer could not stick to his own government's policy, he should withdraw from the conference, and perhaps from the provincial cabinet.[3]

The other provinces' support for rep by pop, however, was rapid, apparently unanimous, and bluntly confrontational. "This is rather a singular ground of objection," said New Brunswick's Leonard Tilley as soon as Haviland had spoken. "It was fully understood at Charlottetown that those who came to the conference expected representation by population." Newfoundland's Ambrose Shea backed Tilley, Charles Fisher of New Brunswick noted that he "came here convinced that representation by population was settled," and Jonathan McCully of Nova Scotia declared that the rule of representation by population "must be rigid and unyielding." The Canadians let the Maritimers lead the charge against Prince Edward Island's position, though the Anglo-Quebecker Alexander Galt said, "It would be a matter of reproach to us that the smallest colony should leave." His remedy was for the Islanders to reconsider.[4]

The Prince Edward Island delegates' sudden, unexpected, and visceral rejection of rep by pop came from other discontents more than from a fundamental dislike of equality of representation. The Island had a tradition of progressive politics, citizen engagement, and representative government. It had pioneered free public education and universal manhood suffrage, and the Island's vigorous political culture had long produced lively debates among parties that regularly traded places in power. It was one of the two provinces of British North America that elected the members of its provincial upper house.* But Island nationalism was strong. Islanders thought of themselves as prosperous, self-contained, and living in a debt-free province with thriving agriculture and successful ocean trades. For every Islander attracted to the national vision of a transcontinental nation, there were others who preferred to stand on their own. All the more so if their small size would render them powerless within confederation.

An appropriate answer to that concern from the advocates of rep by pop might have emphasized federalism: the Island would have few representatives in the federal parliament, but it would continue to have its own provincial government. The likeliest way to assuage Island concerns about lack of influence in Ottawa was to emphasize that most of the matters run from Province House in Charlottetown before confederation would continue to be run from Province House after confederation. But the conference had not yet taken up the powers of the provincial governments. Perhaps no one was ready to take up that contentious subject. In any case, another topic altogether was alienating the Island delegates.

Alone among the provinces of British North America, Prince Edward Island was a society of a few great landlords and many tenants. When Britain set up the separate colony of Prince Edward Island in the wake of the conquest of New France, it divided almost all the island into sixty-seven great estates and gave them to friends of the British government and officers of the British army. Most rural Islanders had been paying rent to those landlords ever since. The thirst of ordinary Prince Edward

* The Province of Canada had begun electing its upper house in 1856, against the will of Brown and others, but the process was incomplete, and many life-appointed councillors remained in office there.

Island farmers to throw off tenancy and break the power of the absentee landlords living in London had been the critical issue in Island politics for years. The Conservatives—the party of Premier Gray, William Pope, Edward Palmer, and Heath Haviland—had often included landlords or their local agents. Reformers such as George Coles, Edward Whelan, and Andrew Macdonald supported the tenant cause. But the problem was insolvable: the Island could not afford to buy out the landlords on behalf of the tenants, and when reform governments had moved in that direction, the government of Britain vetoed the project, since Britain was also a society of great landlords (and one where tenants did not vote, as they did in Prince Edward Island). Lord Palmerston himself, the British prime minister, was a great landowner and, like many leading British statesmen, a personal friend of Island landlords.

At Charlottetown it had been tacitly agreed that confederation would place the new national government between the Island and the British government, and that Canada would help the tenants buy out the landlords. Delegate John Gray of New Brunswick, who had led an inquiry into the Island's landholding issue, promised as much at a public meeting during the Charlottetown meetings.[5] If confederation would end landlordism while providing a fair purchase price to the landlords, one Island observer wrote, "the islanders almost to a man will hold up both hands for the union."[6] The prospect of defeating landlordism had instantly converted Reformers George Coles and Edward Whelan from skepticism to support of the confederation project. But somewhere between Charlottetown and Quebec City, the delegates from the other provinces lost interest in the Islanders' landlord problem. There were no more promises to help the tenants. On Saturday, October 15, when the Island delegation was making its doomed case for more upper house seats in the new confederation, Andrew Macdonald apologized for not taking detailed notes of the argument "because he was engaged in compiling statistics of P.E.I. in dollars and cents."[7] Was this perhaps a reference to some otherwise-unnoted negotiations about the tenancies of the Island farmers and the cost of a fund to assist them in buying out the landlords? It is unclear whether the Islanders' dissident votes and their threats to withdraw from the confederation project provoked the other provinces to abandon their Charlottetown commitment, or whether it was the other way round. But the Islanders' fruitless, self-defeating effort to reject rep by pop, a principle they generally believed in themselves and which was one of the fundamental conditions of confederation, must surely have had some deeper cause.

The result of the rep-by-pop vote, taken before 10 P.M. on Wednesday, was a foregone conclusion: Prince Edward Island opposed, all the other provinces in favour. Discussion on this vote would flow over into Thursday morning, but for now discussion had to be postponed. They would not sit until midnight tonight. There was another ball.

Ulric Tessier was a business lawyer, a law lecturer at the university, and also a banker, financier, and railroad executive—very much a pillar of the francophone urban bourgeoisie of Quebec City. He was also the Speaker of the Legislative Council of the Province of Canada, and in that capacity he and his wife, Marguerite, herself an heiress, offered the next grand ball in honour of the constitutional conference and its delegates. This time, the site was not at the parliament building but at the Tessiers' substantial house on Rue Ste-Ursule, just inside the western walls of the Upper Town. Apart from the delegates and the governor general's party, the guest list was "chiefly French," with only a handful of the uniformed military officers who had ornamented previous events. "Bad and broken English" was much in vogue, reported Edward Whelan, who claimed that by now the delegates were all promising to study French. "Indeed vendors of French dictionaries and grammars are beginning to find a considerable number of customers among the people from the lower provinces." He joked that the Maritimers would "go back to their Down East homes forgetting most of their mother tongue and talking a strange conglomeration of English and excessively bad French."[8]

Linguistic divisions were not the only ones on display at the Tessiers' ball; different views on social decorum also arose. Feo Monck, who came with the governor general's party and opened the dancing with M. Tessier, was amused to find that at parties hosted by the francophone elite, there were only quadrilles and lancers, which were danced in groups rather than by couples. Archbishop Baillargeon, she was told, frowned on "round" dances like the waltz. "I never suffered so in my life from suppressed laughter," she wrote. "So many old people I never saw, and the older they were the more they danced." Among the old people who insisted on dancing with her was Mercy Coles's father, George. He told Feo about his daughter, still afflicted with diphtheria and forced to miss yet another ball. The next day, Feo described him in her letters as "a retired butcher and oh, so vulgar," and derided his accent, his conversation, and his dance steps. Mme Gingras she also found vulgar, noting that her husband, though a member of Parliament, "is going to make our sleigh—he is a coachmaker." (Edouard Gingras, a Rue Ste-Ursule neighbour of the well-to-do Tessiers, ran a carriage-making business with twenty employees.) "I shall not cry when these delegates are gone—it is a bore dancing with them," she wrote.[9]

Feo Monck's aristocratic disdain for the British North Americans was in sharp contrast to how they themselves saw the event. Whelan thought the Tessiers' ball was "gay and brilliant" and told his readers he found it "advisable to be somewhat reticent hereafter regarding the social parties in which the delegates engage in this stupendously hospitable city, lest it should be supposed they do nothing else but frolic." Whelan was being seduced by the bilingual society of "this fast city" and "the gushing and overwhelming hospitality of its generous-hearted people." He was discovering more than the joys of language. Before the end of the conference, this unilingual Irish-born Islander would report to his readers back home that "the French desire most ardently to be left to the undisturbed enjoyment of their ancient privileges—their French institutions, civil law, literature and language. It is utterly impossible to anglicize them—the attempt to do so would outrage their most deeply rooted prejudices and lead to insurrection." After a conversation with Étienne Taché, Whelan was persuaded that "Lower Canada will, most especially, be the firm and fast friend of the Maritime provinces," allying with them to resist "the grasping ambition of Upper or Western Canada."[10]

The conference delegates might be at loggerheads, but Quebec City seemed to be working on their sentiments. Mercy Coles, at home in her sickbed, reported that her father "came home with every stitch of clothes wringing wet with perspiration. He says he never had such a time. The French ladies are the very mischief for flying round." And the confrontation over rep by pop had been left in the conference chamber. At the close of the ball, he and John A. Macdonald had sociably escorted a party of ladies home.[11]

SIXTEEN

Thursday, October 20: The Mechanics of Democracy

George-Étienne Cartier and other members of the Canadian cabinet may have been distracted when the constitutional conference met at ten o'clock on the morning after the Tessiers' ball. Overnight, telegrams had alerted the government to a military crisis. The American Civil War was erupting across the border.

The day the confederation conference began in Quebec City, a young Confederate Army officer, Lt. Bennett Young, had travelled in civilian clothes from Montreal, crossed the American border, and checked into a hotel in the Lake Champlain village of St. Albans, Vermont. Over the next week, twenty more men, all Confederate soldiers in disguise, drifted into town, telling locals they had come for "a sporting vacation." Young had been captured earlier in the Civil War but had escaped from a prisoner of war camp and fled to Canada. He had persuaded the Confederate government that stirring up conflict along the British North American border could usefully divert Union troops from their assault on the Confederacy, and perhaps stir new hostilities between the Union and

Britain. The Confederate government had assigned him to lead that mission. St. Albans was the first target.

On Wednesday afternoon, October 19, Young and his men brought out their weapons and seized all of the town's three banks, plundering them of a sum estimated at $208,000. They rounded up everyone in the town and held them at gunpoint. To slow down pursuit, they commandeered every horse in the livery stable. When the stable owner resisted, waving a six-shooter that would not shoot, the rebels fired at him, and a bystander became the only casualty of the raid. Young ordered the town put to the torch with the aid of "Greek fire" they had brought with them, but the same endless rain that Quebec City had endured doomed their efforts. Only a shed went up in flames. By nightfall on Wednesday, the raiders had crossed back into Canada with their plunder and begun trying to blend into the populace of the Eastern Townships. Behind them, the telegraph lines began to buzz.[1]

In Quebec City early on Thursday morning, Governor General Monck came hotfoot down to the parliament buildings to sign urgent cabinet orders putting the Canadian militia and police on an emergency footing. In the next few days, local police in Frelighsburg, Farnham, and other small towns on the Canadian side of the border put Lt. Young and most of his raiders in custody. With close assistance from Americans who had pursued Young's men over the border, the Canadian forces brought the Confederate campaign in Canada to an abrupt and permanent halt. By Sunday, Feo Monck could write that her brother-in-law was no longer "in a fuss" about the raiders: "They have been caught and the Yankee papers praise him much for his prompt conduct." Feo evidently shared the assumption of the American journalists about Canadian politics: that decisions of the governor-in-council reflected Lord Monck's personal will, not that of his cabinet.[2]

There was a brief moment of crisis soon after, when the American military commander for Vermont went on to authorize his troops to engage in unrestricted military operations in British North America should there be more raids—a violation of British North American neutrality and of territorial integrity. After the prompt action of the Canadian authorities, however, President Lincoln countermanded those provocative orders. With the raiders securely held in Montreal pending trial, the likelihood of conflict between British troops and Union forces, never large, faded. "The likelihood," declared *The New York Times* on October 24, "is that these rebels will altogether fail in their efforts to involve us in a foreign war."[3] The red-coated British officers who had been entertaining Feo Monck at the soirees of the great confederation conference would not be flung into the defence of the Richelieu River corridor against an American invasion.[4]

Still, the American Civil War loomed over the conference. In Canadian papers, war news sometimes crowded the constitutional talks out of the headlines. As the Union moved toward a nearly inevitable conquest of the South, the future promised a vastly more powerful reunited United States, with large and battle-hardened military forces and no great fondness for the northern neighbour that had stayed out of the war. At the start of the conference, John A. Macdonald had made military defence one of his arguments for union, suggesting "our present isolated and defenceless position is, no doubt, a source of embarrassment to Britain."[5] Steering his way carefully through these delicate issues at one of the conference dinners, Charles Tupper of Nova Scotia declared that never in their lifetimes would they see Britain abandon British North America, although "the sentiment of the British Empire, instead of rendering us supine and indifferent, should nerve us with increased vigour to place ourselves in the position in which we can best cooperate with the brave army and gallant navy of Great Britain for the defence of this portion of the British Empire."[6] Defending the Quebec Resolutions some months later, George-Étienne Cartier would be more blunt, asking whether British North Americans could expect Britain to defend them if they would not organize to defend themselves.[7]

In the conference itself, American issues rarely impinged—except as a constitutional model to avoid. Cartier deprecated the reckless democracy he professed to see in American political institutions. Macdonald cited the American founders' choice to grant all unspecified powers to the individual states as an example not to be followed. He criticized the constitution that made American presidents at once the impartial head of state and the partisan leader of one faction.[8] The confederation makers were parliamentary democrats and constitutional monarchists. They believed in the form of self-government that had developed in Great Britain, and they took pride in having built their own version of it in the self-governing British North American colonies. The news of the St. Albans raid was a reminder of the provinces' vulnerabilities, and news of the prompt arrests must have been reassuring, but there is little to suggest the small and unsuccessful Confederate sally had much impact on the work of the conference. In December, however, the St. Albans raiders would come to trial, and the matter would flare up more dangerously than ever.

On Thursday morning, meanwhile, George Brown asked the Prince Edward Islanders for an explanation of their vote the previous evening, and the conference heard out the rest of the rep-by-pop confrontation. William Pope, who had been absent the previous evening, acknowledged the Islanders had no "right" to more than their share of seats, but he urged the conference to consider extra seats as a measure of expediency. The other provinces, however, had no inclination to make a peace offering. George Coles was the first to grasp that reality and draw out the consequence. "Whatever may be the result of this matter, Prince Edward Island should submit," he said. "Let us go on with the business and let Prince Edward Island settle for themselves when the question comes before them."[9] He surely meant his province would "settle" on remaining out of confederation, and saw no profit in continuing the debate. The business that they would "go on with," meanwhile, concerned the constitutional mechanics of parliamentary democracy, and the Canadians let John A. Macdonald lead for them:

The legislature of each province shall divide such province into the proper number of constituencies and define the boundaries of each of them.[10]

Some political thinkers in the 1860s were alive to the idea of proportional representation—that is, of allocating seats in legislatures to parties rather than individual representatives. The British philosopher John Stuart Mill had worked out much of the theory of it in his *Representative Government*, published in 1861. In 1867, he would introduce an unsuccessful motion in the House of Commons to implement it in Britain. In Canada, Sandford Fleming, the engineer and railroad surveyor, would propose his own system of proportional voting in the 1890s. But such ideas had little traction: the British North American provinces had long adopted the British system of geographical constituencies and a voting system in which, no matter how many candidates stood, whoever received the most votes was elected. What was striking about Macdonald's proposal was that it allowed the provinces, not the central government, to lay out the constituencies, and only the word "proper" gave any kind of reassurance against efforts to gerrymander constituency boundaries for political advantage. This morning, the resolution passed without any recorded discussion. Macdonald would later declare that allowing provinces to control federal constituency boundaries was an obvious error, though the motion was his own and must have been planned in advance in the Canadian cabinet. Macdonald would arrange to revise the conference minutes to that effect. In the end the final text of the British North America Act would shuffle control of constituency boundaries to the federal government:

There shall be a session of the legislative council and assembly at least once in every year, so that a period of twelve calendar months shall not intervene between the last sitting ... in one session and the first sitting ... in the next. And every legislative assembly shall continue for five years.[11]

Pausing briefly to make the case that five years was an appropriate life for a parliament, even though at that time a British parliament had statutory authority to continue for seven years, Macdonald received the conference's approval.

Macdonald continued with a motion, quickly approved, that provincial laws regarding elections and eligibility to vote would apply in federal elections as well, unless and until the new national parliament took steps to establish its own criteria for federal elections. In 1864, some provinces allowed all adult males to vote. Others set property qualifications. Macdonald was proposing that, for the time being at least, rules governing who voted in a federal election would be different in, say, Canada West and Nova Scotia. This seems to have been a pragmatic accommodation, one that would allow the first federal election to be held without the need for an entirely new set of electoral rules even before there was a federal parliament to write them. It was passed without debate, but, in its granting to the provincial governments a certain control over the election of federal governments, it would come back to haunt Macdonald, the future prime minister. He moved on, however, to lay down a larger principle:

> The executive authority or government shall be vested in the sovereignty of the United Kingdom of Great Britain and Ireland and be administered according to the well-understood principles of the British constitution by the Sovereign personally or by representative duly authorized.[12]

There was discussion following this resolution, seemingly on peripheral matters, but the motion was soon passed. Indeed, all these resolutions were confirmed well before the daytime session concluded. In these technical questions, the delegates were actually taking stands on some of the most fundamental matters of how a parliamentary democracy operates. Since all the delegates were already members of their provincial parliaments, they understood the mechanisms well—in practice, but also in theory.

They were declaring that a parliament, federal and provincial, must meet at least once a year, whether it seemed necessary or not, because an elected parliament was the fundamental bulwark of the liberties of the Crown's subjects. In the mid-nineteenth century, British North American provincial legislatures generally met for only a few weeks, usually in late winter or spring. (Even after confederation, one Canadian parliament stood prorogued for 362 days.[13]) But at Quebec it was constitutionally affirmed that government was barred from using arguments about lack of important business or about cost-cutting to avoid legislative review. Once a year at least, it had to face Parliament and account for its actions.

Macdonald's second resolution concerned the cabinet, and the only control it placed on executive authority was "the well-understood principles of the British constitution." The delegates, and the legislators they answered to, understood parliamentary principles. They knew that the sovereign administered the state, not on his or her own inclinations, but exclusively on the advice of the politically accountable cabinet. The authority of cabinet depended on maintaining the confidence and support of a majority of the people's elected representatives in the legislature. The delegates passed this resolution, but in fact they did not leave this bulwark of responsible government to depend merely on "well-understood principles." In the next few days, they would return to the subject and spell out the subtle mechanics that bound the Crown to the cabinet and the cabinet to Parliament's will:

> All bills for appropriating any part of the public revenue or for imposing any new tax or impost shall originate in the House of Commons or the legislative assembly, as the case may be.[14]

Here, in a deceptively bland formulation, was the rule that made the Crown a constitutional monarchy—and made the cabinet responsible to the people's elected representatives. The delegates could speak airily about the authority of the sovereign, but that sovereign could not raise or spend a dollar. Only the federal House of Commons* and the provincial legislatures could authorize the spending of public money or the levying of any kind of tax or revenue measure. Parliamentarians could be as lyrically deferential to Queen Victoria and the royal family as they wished. They knew well that a monarch without money was a figurehead, and a cabinet without money had nothing to do. Elected parliamentarians would both authorize the raising of money and review how it was spent—and therefore control both the monarch and the monarch's advisors.

A linked resolution, passed at the same time, put shackles on the House of Commons as well:

> The House of Commons or legislative assembly shall not originate or pass any vote, resolution, address, or bill for the appropriation of any part of the public revenue, or of any tax or impost to any purpose, not first recommended to the House or Assembly by message of the governor-general, during the session in which such vote, resolution, address or bill is passed.[15]

The conference had just agreed that only the legislature could pass "money bills." But the legislature's money power was fettered. Although only the legislature could *pass* a money bill, only the Crown's agents and advisors—the governor-in-council, meaning the cabinet—could propose any bill that proposed to raise or spend public money. The cabinet had to take its requests for money to the legislature, but the legislature had to entrust the work of budgeting to the cabinet. There would be no random money bills—neither new spending nor taxation measures—being put forward by a member of Parliament who could gather a momentary popularity for himself or his pet spending project. Instead, there had to

---

* Macdonald used that term here, and told the conference he wanted the new national legislature to take that name, though he warned the British authorities might seek to restrict it for the exclusive use of their own parliament.

be a central organizing body, the cabinet. It sorted out priorities, matched spending against revenues, and presented to the legislature a comprehensive plan for raising and spending. Here was the constitutional basis of the "confidence motion." If the people's representatives did not approve of the money bills that the government put forward, then the Crown, in order to get and spend, had to find a new government who would command the legislature's support.

These resolutions reinforced the easy platitude of "the well-understood principles of the British constitution" with very specific conditions. The resolutions put into constitutional form the bedrock requirements of parliamentary government in Canada and the provinces. To have the sinews of power—money—the Crown was obliged to rely on a cabinet of ministers drawn from and able to work with the popularly elected legislature. The cabinet in turn could not work without legislative support, because only the legislature could authorize the raising and spending of money. Finally, the legislature was constitutionally obliged to entrust the cabinet with the authority to organize that raising and spending, which is to say, the authority to run on a daily basis the business of the nation (or province, for the rules applied at each level). The cabinet could call and prorogue Parliament as it wished, but, because it needed money, it could not irritate or ignore elected members to the point that they began to consider deploying their own ultimate weapon: the power to withhold the money and bring down the government.

These were "well-understood principles," as the first resolution said. They were not merely conventions, however, if conventions suggest a set of gentlemanly agreements dependent on the honour and goodwill of those entrusted with power. These resolutions passed at Quebec City on Thursday, October 20, 1864 (and completed the following Tuesday, October 25), made responsible government principles constitutional bedrock and embedded them permanently in the constitution of Canada. Since Britain had no written constitution, there was no model ready to hand from which to draw these resolutions, though they had been discussed in the British North American context back to the Durham Report of 1839. That the delegates to the Quebec Conference could draft, review, and approve these stipulations without much drama or difficulty undermined the charge sometimes made, even at the time, that the political leaders of British North America were backwoods hicks without much political sophistication, moving ahead on a tide of champagne and strict instructions from their colonial masters.[16]

These resolutions, covering such fundamental matters so precisely, had been carefully drafted and considered in advance. Certainly the Canadian cabinet had reviewed them closely during its summertime preparations. It was John A. Macdonald, however, who presented them and offered explanations of them. Macdonald was a parliamentarian to his fingertips. In 1848, he had actually opposed responsible government; with his acute sense for power and reluctance to see it diluted, he had been comfortable with the pre-1848 situation where the British governor retained autocratic powers and independent financial resources but took advice from chosen advisors, generally ones with the kind of conservative temperament Macdonald himself possessed. Yet when responsible government triumphed, Macdonald adapted swiftly to the new environment. By 1861, he could describe a fellow Conservative who looked back nostalgically to pre-1848 times as one who "belonged to the old fossil party—a Tory of the old Family Compact."[17] The old fossil was James Cockburn, a member of the Canadian coalition cabinet and a delegate there in the room, but one who knew he was there to support his leader and who never said one recorded word during the whole sixteen days of the Quebec City conference. Macdonald, meanwhile, had the floor most of the day to put forward, with a nice combination of persuasive charm and legal precision, the constitutional fundamentals of the new order.

In November, when he told a friend of his own contributions to the drafting of the Quebec Resolutions—"I must do it all alone, as there is not one person connected with the government who has the slightest idea of the nature of the work"—Macdonald was not telling the whole truth by any means.[18] There were other constitutional law experts at the conferences, and any Macdonald proposal had been subject to veto from Cartier and Brown all summer. Indeed, while Macdonald presented the "well-understood principles" resolution on Thursday, it would be Oliver Mowat, another lawyer skilled in constitutional and administrative law, whom the Canadians chose to present the more specific resolutions the following Tuesday. Mowat was later saluted, by his own followers at least, as the one chiefly responsible for putting the Quebec Resolutions "into constitutional and legal shape."[19] But on this Thursday, Macdonald might have felt it was close to being true; he probably had helped draft these particular resolutions. Taking the conference through the fundamentals of constitutional democracy and parliamentary democracy in a few hours, with almost no dissent and with unanimous agreement even from the Prince Edward Islanders, was a very substantial success. And the delegates doubtless noticed Macdonald's easy confidence and his command of all the constitutional technicalities.*

Macdonald had taken the conference through these matters so smoothly, in fact, that there was time, even before the afternoon break, for what seems to have been a spontaneous proposal from George Brown. Brown moved "That in the local government there shall be but one legislative chamber."[20] Brown had reason to be pleased by the successful passage, earlier on, of his resolution on federalism and westward expansion, two key commitments his Canada West supporters would require in any confederation settlement. He was delighted with the outcome of the long fight to keep the federal upper house weak and ceremonial. He was proud of the conference's affirmation of rep by pop, for which he had waged a lonely, seemingly hopeless campaign for years.

* In 1866, D'Arcy McGee declared that Macdonald alone had drafted fifty of the seventy-two Quebec Resolutions. Tracking down the source of the claim, Macdonald's rivals found it came in a speech at a testimonial dinner for Macdonald in his Kingston constituency. The claim was hotly denied, and the sobriety of all concerned in making it was strongly questioned.

But each victory had had its price. His federalism resolution had managed to rouse Maritimer suspicions that he wanted to force them into a Maritime union. The senate fight had raised the spectre of Ontario using its population advantage to dictate terms to the rest of the country forever. Even the rep-by-pop resolution, which should have been uncontroversial, had provoked the Prince Edward Islanders into the bluntest threats yet to repudiate confederation altogether, with the smallest province confronting the largest. Now Brown was making another undiplomatic move.

As a believer in the British parliamentary system—his early immigrant years in New York City with his father had left both men appalled by American republicanism—Brown should have cheered on John A.'s skilful, lawyerly presentation of the constitutional underpinnings of responsible government. But now he wanted to push that initiative further with a bold proposal for the provinces. If the federal upper house was to be weak, what about dispensing with upper houses entirely in the new provincial governments? Brown was probably riding his own hobby horse here; he got little support from the Canadian delegation, which by now was united on most points. And the proposal had risks. All the British North American provinces had existing legislative councils and might regret dispensing with their air of dignity and their opportunities for rewarding friends. The delegates around the table who were members of upper houses—including Taché, Brown's own nominal leader—could not have been flattered to see Brown cavalierly abolishing their seats and their chambers. Some delegates probably calculated how difficult it would be to get confederation approved if the legislative councils of every province had to consent to their own extinction.

If Hewitt Bernard's notes can be relied on, Brown made the situation worse with his arguments in support of the motion, going far beyond the abolition of provincial upper houses to propose a radical rethinking of their legislatures as well. "We desire in Upper Canada that they should not be expensive, and should not take up political matters," Bernard quoted Brown as saying about provincial governments. Brown seems to have gone on to propose real executive authority for the lieutenant-governor, and heads of government departments who would be elected separately and would sit in the legislature with a right to speak but not to vote, and provincial elections that would be held every three years. In short, Bernard's notes have Brown floating the idea, not simply of a unicameral legislature in each province, but one that distinctly diverged from the responsible government principles he had fought for since the 1840s.[21]

Years before, Brown had taken up federalism as the best way to get Canada West free of the suffocating merger with Canada East, free to run its own affairs. It seems impossible that he ever would have expected the Canada West government not to take up "political matters." The view Bernard ascribes to Brown sound more like the views of the radical faction called the Clear Grits, a republican-leaning faction in Canada West that Brown had long since neutralized and absorbed into his parliamentary Reform caucus. Was Bernard trying to tar John A.'s old rival by ascribing to him all the radical views to which the Conservatives had long since tried to link him?

That cannot be completely the case. Brown certainly said enough to provoke the responses Bernard attributes to the speakers who followed him, and indeed Brown would again argue for simple, inexpensive provincial administrations in 1866, when the last parliament of the Province of Canada was settling the details of governments for the new province of Ontario.[22] At Quebec, some of the delegates were plainly shocked by Brown's proposals, which seemed to undermine the fundamental principles of responsible government they had been cementing into the constitution that afternoon. Even George-Étienne Cartier, for all his disdain for getting into wrangles in the conference, abruptly weighed in against his own coalition ally. "I entirely differ with Mr. Brown," said the man who controlled the largest of the voting blocs required to ratify confederation. "It introduces into our local bodies republican institutions." Taché, generally a neutral chairman of the discussions, intervened too, saying hastily, "This motion is made merely to elicit opinion of conference"—meaning presumably it was not the settled policy of the Canadian government. Brown was freelancing.

Some delegates from the other provinces shared Brown's concern about keeping costs down in the new nation where, for the first time, citizens in each province could be taxed to support both a federal and a provincial government. But several speakers urged that the provinces should "keep the existing things as they are, so far as is consistent with expense." Charles Tupper, a Conservative, expressed some sympathy for Brown's proposals, but with a caution. "The government should be as simple and inexpensive as possible," he said, declaring that provincial governments might indeed be simplified, "but we must not shock too largely the prejudices of the people in that respect."[23] Tupper's fellow Nova Scotian and political rival, the newspaperman (and upper house member) Jonathan McCully, seems to have put forward what was constitutional bedrock, particularly for the Reformers: "We must have miniature responsible governments [in the provinces]," he declared.[24] There might be a new national government in Ottawa, that is, but even if the provinces were smaller in scale and in some theoretical sense subordinate to it, they had to run on the same parliamentary principles that existed in any Westminster parliament.

The idea that the provinces would not take up political matters was absurd. In order to discuss political matters, particularly the raising and spending of money, there had to be a cabinet accountable to the legislature, and a legislature accountable to the voters. Brown was prevailed upon to withdraw his proposals. McCully made a proposal that both soothed his vanity and put the issue nicely aside. "With a view to reducing the expenses of the local governments," he suggested, with a gesture to Brown's concern for cost savings, "it should be left to each provincial legislature to design its own constitution, so that provinces could preserve or abolish their upper house as they saw fit." This became the decision of the conference: within the limits of responsible government, every province would be free to tinker with its own constitution.

Ontario would indeed come into confederation without an upper house, and in time all the other provinces would follow its lead.*

The conference then took its usual afternoon break from two o'clock until seven-thirty. The delegates had accepted one of the many invitations they had been given from local institutions. That afternoon they went to visit Laval University, then housed in a cluster of historic buildings not far from the parliament building in Upper Town. The rector there was much more effusive about the work of the delegates than the Board of Trade had been at its dinner. He declared that "history will hand down to posterity the names of all those to whom the confidence of their fellow-citizens has entrusted with this great mission of examining the basis of our political constitutions." The seminary band serenaded the delegates on the roof terrace of the main building "whence a magnificent view of the city, harbour, and surrounding country was obtained." Then they toured the library, the schools of law and medicine, and other parts of the university.[25]

After this interlude, the delegates gathered again for the evening session. Macdonald took the lead again, moving

> That for each of the provinces there shall be an executive officer styled the Lieutenant-Governor, who shall be appointed by the Governor General in Council.[26]

The lieutenant-governor "shall be a very high officer," said Macdonald, and once appointed could not be removed for five years, so that "he should not be removable by any new political party." In effect, the resolution was confirming what McCully had said before the break: the provinces, like the federal government, would indeed be responsible governments, almost constitutional monarchies in miniature, with a

---

* The last provinces to abolish their legislative councils were Nova Scotia in 1926 and Quebec in 1960. Newfoundland had an upper house until the 1930s, but came into confederation without one.

governor as local head of government, but guided by advisors accountable to the elected legislature. Since the provinces could not interfere with the office of lieutenant-governor, a federal nominee, this resolution safe-guarded the whole structure of responsible government in each province. The lieutenant-governor needed a cabinet, and the cabinet had to be responsible to the legislature, so the provinces' freedom to amend their constitutions hardly went further than permitting them to tinker with constituency boundaries and voting procedures or to abolish their upper houses. Brown's notion, if indeed he had proposed it, of directly elected cabinet members and legislatures that did not play a political role, had been very firmly knocked on the head. It was never mentioned again.

After the lieutenant-governor's resolution was passed, Macdonald read out "his several proposed resolutions as to the powers of the federal and local governments." That would be material for the next day's debates—and for many decades afterwards.

SEVENTEEN

Friday, October 21 to Monday, October 24: Ottawa and the Provinces

The Quebec Conference had spent its first week and more passing nothing very substantial. In their second week at Quebec, the delegates had begun to work with greater speed. On Wednesday and Thursday of that week, their resolutions on rep by pop and on the details of parliamentary relations in the new federal regime had established how governments and legislatures would run in Canada for the foreseeable future. Finally, near the end of the week, they took up the great and fundamental question they had been sidling toward for ten days: the division of powers between the new central government and the enduring provinces. On Friday morning, October 21, they had in front of them detailed resolutions for both federal and provincial powers. Taché kept Friday's discussion focused on the federal rather than the provincial side, but the two matters were inseparable. The debate flowed over into Monday's discussions, when the provincial powers came to the agenda, and would continue into Tuesday's sessions as well.

On Friday morning, to present the motion on federal powers in the new confederation, the Canadians once again relied on John A. Macdonald. His resolution began

> That it shall be competent for the general legislature to make laws for the peace, welfare and good government of the federated provinces.

and continued through thirty-two headings that set out the long list of matters that would be the responsibility of the new national government. It was by far the longest, most detailed resolution the conference had yet taken up. The powers it listed were imposing. The new national government would hold authority over trade and commerce; customs and excise; taxation of all kinds; money, banking, and financial matters; ocean navigation, lighthouses, and sea fisheries; the militia, military and naval service, and defence; immigration and naturalization; railways and other works connecting any two or more of the provinces; the criminal law and the appointment of judges; and a long list of administrative responsibilities such as the postal service, patents and copyrights, weights and measures, and the census; and finally

> all matters of a general character, not specially and exclusively reserved for the local governments and legislatures.[1]

Presenting detailed and complex resolutions such as this had become John A. Macdonald's role in the conference. He always knew the details, always knew how to smooth or divert the discussion. By now he seemed to have won the confidence of the conference delegates, more than the silent Cartier or the sometimes maladroit Brown. But in this case, responsibility was a double-edged sword for Macdonald. His colleagues and rivals in the Canadian cabinet, indeed, may have delegated this resolution to him in order to bind him more firmly to it. Fundamentally,

Macdonald believed in the concentration of power, not its diffusion among half a dozen governments, as these resolutions were going to propose. Obliged to compromise by the force of numbers represented by Brown's Reformers and Cartier's Bleus, he had yielded during the summer's negotiations on his preference for legislative union. Still, the resolution he was presenting, for all the federal powers it proposed, hardly reflected his own view of proper national authority. As soon as he had moved the resolution, Macdonald yielded the floor to a cabinet colleague who was surely one of its principal authors.

Alexander Tilloch Galt, a forty-seven-year-old businessman and financier from Sherbrooke in the Eastern Townships, was the finance man in the Canadian cabinet—and a forceful constitutional thinker who had been engaged with the idea of federalism as long as anyone in the room. British-born, Galt had come to Canada as a youth. After the collapse of the land development projects his father John Galt had come to manage in Canada West, young Alexander persevered in Canadian development projects. In the 1840s, he brought into being an industrial empire—woolen mills, flour mills, cotton mills—in Sherbrooke, Quebec, where he made his home. Then he raised financing for the first railroad in British North America, running from the south shore of the St. Lawrence opposite Montreal, through Sherbrooke, southeast toward the American border. As railroad projects soon began to blossom across the Province of Canada, Galt sold his own line profitably to the Grand Trunk—this was the line that in 1864 would bring the Coles family and other Maritime delegates to Canada from Portland, Maine—but continued in railroad construction. Like many railroad entrepreneurs of the time, he found it useful to get himself a seat in the Canadian legislature.[2]

As an anglophone in Canada East, Galt stood a little aside from the main political factions there, Cartier's Bleus and the more radical Rouges. He looked back to the cooperative cross-cultural alliance of Baldwin and LaFontaine and had been identified as a Reformer. He particularly shared the Reform view that Canadians ought to take responsibility for their own affairs—a view only strengthened as he observed his British business contacts grumbling about the costs of empire. Galt was one of the few politicians of his generation willing to talk frankly about "independence," by which he meant facing the separation from Britain and its empire that he thought both inevitable and necessary. He was no friend of George Brown's, but Galt, like Brown, could see in the 1850s that the rapid growth of Canada West was going to require changes to the union of the Canadas. Galt soon concluded that a shared parliament with an equal distribution of seats between East and West could not endure and, even before Brown, he identified federalism as the solution. He argued that "irreconcilable difficulties present themselves" against any effort to maintain equality of representation in the united Province of Canada, and he was vital in persuading George-Étienne Cartier to see the issue as he did.

George Brown, the champion of Canada West, presented federalism as a demand of his surging region—and provoked mostly resistance from the political leaders of Canada East. Galt, who lived in Canada East, maintained much better relations with the francophone leaders. They saw the threat to francophone society in Brown's plan to diminish Canada East's place in the legislature, but Galt urged them to see federalism as their solution. Cartier, at least, began to see reason in Galt's thinking: in a federal system, his people could have a continuing share in the economic progress of the union, but a separation on the divisive questions of culture and language. Cartier began to calculate that French Canada's vital interests could be preserved, even if the legislative union between the two Canadas had to be surrendered. In 1858, when Cartier urgently needed Galt's help to put together a government, the two struck a bargain. Galt would put aside his Reform affiliation—as Cartier had done earlier—and join the Cartier-Macdonald government that was forming. In exchange, Cartier promised that the new government would investigate Galt's proposal for a British North American union. With Cartier's support, Galt drafted a proposal for a national parliament to manage the great economic issues that were his vital interest, and for local governments in each section to hive off the incompatible cultures of Canada East and Canada West. A federal system, Galt observed in 1858, would also make possible the entry of the Maritime provinces and eventually the northwest as well, creating a truly national economic space as Britain (inevitably, in Galt's view) withdrew its interests and support from the former colonies.[3]

Galt's and Cartier's confederation proposal of 1858, which John A. Macdonald, though their government partner, declined to sign, proved a non-starter. British colonial officials were irritated that the project had been started by the colonials, not by them. Politicians in the Maritimes, unconsulted and taken by surprise, barely responded. The idea that railroads would bind the British provinces into an economic union still seemed utopian in 1858, and there was no American Civil War yet to get British North Americans thinking about external threats and mutual defence. Galt's 1858 confederation proposal had taken him away from his reform inclinations and into government with Cartier and Macdonald, but it went no further than that.

The 1858 proposal had included a detailed plan for dividing powers between a central government and the provinces. With Galt back in the coalition cabinet, that proposal had become the basis of the division-of-powers plan the Canadian government agreed to endorse during the summer of 1864. The federal powers Galt was now advocating to the conference in Quebec City were almost identical to those he had drafted in 1858, from the fine details ("the confederation might include the constitution of a federal court of appeal," he wrote in 1858; it was repeated in 1864) to its affirmation of federal supremacy ("the local legislatures," he declared in 1858, "would not be in a position to claim the exercise of the same sovereign powers which have frequently been the cause of difference between the American states and their general government").[4]

John A. Macdonald had not associated himself with their confederation project. Federal union was no part of his program in 1858. He made no secret of his preference for preserving the legislative union that prevailed in the Province of Canada. In the spring of 1864, when Galt voted with George Brown and George-Étienne Cartier in favour of exploring federalism anew, Macdonald stood opposed. In June, Macdonald yielded to the force of numbers and agreed to join the confederation coalition, swallowing his disagreement with the coalition's federalist policy for the sake of his hold on power. During the summer of 1864, as Cartier, Galt, and Brown determined that a federal union, not a legislative union, was the government's policy, Macdonald was compelled to agree. It was broadly their plan, not his own preference, that he had put forward on Friday morning.

The discussion during Friday's session was mostly technical, and led by Galt more than Macdonald. Questions were raised about New Brunswick's timber export levies—a crucial revenue source for the province but now to be surrendered to the new federal government. Control over Nova Scotia's coal was raised, as was the handling of banking licences during the transitional period. Amid these urgent but specialized matters, the only place where the delegates raised larger principles was in relation to agriculture. In the draft resolution, agriculture was specified as a federal power, but the delegates had clearly seen the list of provincial powers as well, and they knew that agriculture was also a provincial matter—a "concurrent" power. "Such an arrangement will be found to be unworkable," said the Nova Scotian reformer Jonathan McCully. "It will lead to a conflict between the two jurisdictions." Oliver Mowat of Canada West, a fellow reformer, disagreed, arguing, "Danger often arises where there is exclusive jurisdiction, and not so often in cases of concurrent jurisdiction." "I take another view," replied McCully. "Concurrent jurisdiction is the ground of the difficulties in the United States." He moved that agriculture be struck from the list of federal powers. The vote by provinces was unanimous against him.[5]

The delegates were just beginning to warm to the intricacies of federal–provincial powers. Bernard's notes of Friday's discussion went no further, but McCully and Mowat were touching on one of the essential problems of a federal state: defining the boundaries between federal and local governments. Clearly neither was intimidated by the constitutional intricacies involved. This was a matter that they would take up in more detail on Monday, when the provincial side of the division of powers was introduced into the discussion. There would be no sitting until midnight on Friday evening, however. The delegates adjourned at 4:30 P.M., for there was yet another ball to attend. The "bachelors of Quebec," a group of the younger well-to-do gentlemen of the city ("lumberers and merchants," wrote Feo Monck), were this night's hosts, once again host- ing more than six hundred guests at the parliament building.

"It is pretty certain that unless they leave Quebec soon," the Toronto *Globe*'s correspondent told its readers after the bachelors' ball, the delegates "will be so wearied out with dinners and balls" that they would decline all invitations when they visited other cities. *The Globe* found the company at the bachelors' ball brilliant. The officers in their scarlet and blue regimentals floated "like butterflies." With the French and English women rivalling each other in beauty, "The bachelors of Quebec must be hard to please if they remain bachelors long."[6] Whelan was once more greatly impressed, and even Feo Monck restrained her pen: "There were several pretty people at the ball, and the dresses were some of them very good." She danced with George-Étienne Cartier, whose wife was not among the party, and with John A. Macdonald, whom she declared "very agreeable." Mercy Coles, still too weak to go out, heard it was a grand affair. Her consolation, now that she could leave her room and even visit the hotel drawing rooms, came in visits from unmarried delegates and their aides. Leonard Tilley gave her "such a nice carte of himself," but no hint that their relationship was progressing. All the delegates had been having their photographs taken, she wrote. "Papa's is only tolerable."[7]

"The cabinet ministers, the leading ones especially, are the most inveterate dancers I have ever seen," wrote Edward Whelan after the bachelors' ball. He joked it was proof of their political cunning. "They know if they can dance themselves into the affections of the wives and daughters of the country, the men will certainly become an easy conquest." Indeed, the ball was so successful that the conference started at noon instead of 10 the next morning, and they would adjourn at 6 P.M.[8]

Saturday, the delegates talked money.* It was on Monday, October 24, that they returned to the other half of the division-of-powers question: the powers that would remain with the provinces, and how that arrangement would affect the balancing of sovereign authority between the national and provincial governments. The provincial-powers motion was another long list. To present it, the Canadian cabinet turned to a delegate whose role in the conference had so far been slight. The forty-four-year-old Oliver Mowat was a successful Toronto lawyer who had once been John A. Macdonald's law student but had become George Brown's strong right arm in the reform caucus. He was among the conference's experts on questions of administrative and constitutional law, and they were in new territory here. British North American politicians were used to testing their own legislatures' powers against imperial supervision from London, but to have a federal division of powers within a parliamentary regime was unprecedented. Even the Cartier–Galt proposal of 1858 had not attempted to define provincial powers in any detail. What Mowat now read was a substantial list: the provinces were to retain responsibility for agriculture; education; Crown lands; property and civil rights; municipal institutions; penitentiaries; hospitals and charities; local works; the administration of justice; local offices and officers; direct taxation; retail licensing; and "private and local matters." This last phrase was soon revised to read "generally all matters of a private or local nature," presumably to invite comparison with the "all matters of a general character" assigned to the federal authority.[9]

Mowat's list suggested that under the new confederation, the provinces would retain substantial authority; indeed, Leonard Tilley would

---

* In order to group related matters that flowed from Friday into the following week, I diverge here from strict chronological order. Saturday's financial issues are taken up in a later chapter.

later say that five of six matters dealt with by the pre-confederation legislature of New Brunswick would remain within its purview after confederation.[10] All the vast and valuable Crown lands of the new nation would be conveyed to the ownership of the provinces, as would matters of property and local business, everything to do with local and municipal government, and even the running of the courts and prisons. The assignment of education, hospitals, and charities to provincial authority followed the principle that "cultural" matters should be local rather than national. In Canada East, it was the Roman Catholic Church that directed most schools, most hospitals, and most charitable agencies; the assignment of these powers to the provinces was in effect a guarantee for the distinctly Catholic culture of French-Canadian society, so long as Quebec chose to delegate those responsibilities to the Church. It would have been impossible for Canada East's delegates to have yielded up these powers. Instead, every province received them.

Nevertheless, the first criticisms of Mowat's list came from the other direction, urging more provincial power. "I object to the proposed system," declared Edward Chandler of New Brunswick. "You are adopting a legislative union instead of a federal." Chandler, a lawyer and at sixty-four one of the older delegates, came from a well-to-do Loyalist family long established in New Brunswick, and he was respected for his paternal, noblesse-oblige concern for the humbler classes of New Brunswick, including its Catholic Acadians.† Since 1836, he had held an appointed seat in New Brunswick's upper house. In the 1850s, he had led the provincial government. Chandler favoured confederation—indeed, he had also favoured Maritime union—but from long political experience, he believed that the strongly local and even parochial politics of the Maritimes would never accept a closely centralized union. Chandler thought it essential to defend the rights and powers of the existing provincial legislatures. On that score, he found Mowat's proposal fundamentally inadequate.

† Chandler's paternalism ran deep. He told Feo Monck that American slaves loved their masters and were miserable when emancipated.

Chandler's complaint was that Mowat's long list of provincial powers would, paradoxically, produce a legislative union—one with no real provinces, he said, "merely large municipal corporations" firmly under the thumb of the national government. His opposition was rooted in the fact that the resolution listed the provincial powers, indeed laid them out in specific detail. For Chandler, what was important in a federal constitution was the *unspecified* powers. In his opinion, any power that was not specifically listed was likely to default to the senior government. He was sure that many essential powers would eventually be found to lie outside the two lists, and that these would all become federal powers. Inexorably the federal government would become all-powerful. The provincial legislatures should not have their powers listed at all, he argued. List only the federal powers, Chandler argued, and let all remaining powers accrue to the provinces. "This is a vital question, which decides the question between a federal and legislative union," he declared. "It will be fatal to the success of confederation in the lower provinces" to hem the provinces in with a specific list of their powers. "The local legislatures should not have their powers specified, but should have all the powers not specified to the federal government, and only the powers to be given to the federal government should be specified."[11]

Edward Chandler's intervention—a sophisticated constitutional analysis, for all that it came from a small-town lawyer in one of the smaller provinces—shifted the discussion from quibbles about particular powers to a debate on the principles of federalism. The other delegates proved up to his challenge. The first to respond was a fellow Maritimer and fellow Conservative, Premier Tupper of Nova Scotia. Tupper agreed that powers left unspecified would gradually accrue to the federal government and expand its power, but he declared that was a good thing: "Mr. Chandler says it gives a legislative instead of a federal union. I think that a benefit." Tupper rejected Chandler's argument that the people of the Maritime provinces would never surrender their provincial autonomy to a faraway government dominated by the Canadians.

"Powers undefined must rest somewhere," Tupper insisted. "Those who were at Charlottetown will remember that it was fully specified there that all the powers not given to local should be reserved for the federal government." They had agreed, he said, that it was desirable to have a plan contrary to the constitutional principle adopted by the United States, "where all powers not given to Washington, D.C. became states' powers."[12]

Tupper alluded to the cost of the national government they were creating. Was it to be a government with nothing to do, "to be one of mere delegates" of the provincial governments? In the national government," he said, "we have provided ... for the representation of every section of all the provinces." Indeed, it might be easier for citizens in remote parts of Nova Scotia and New Brunswick to reach the national legislature than their provincial one, he claimed. Tupper acknowledged Canada East's need for a local government, but suggested the Maritimes required provincial government only because municipalities barely existed there and provincial administrations would be needed to maintain the local services.

In any case, Tupper said, this deliberately circumscribed role for provincial governments "was stated as a prominent feature of the Canadian scheme" at the Charlottetown meeting. Chandler said tartly, "My argument is met not as to merits but as to what was laid down at Charlottetown," but George Brown intervened to confirm that "this matter received close attention of the Canadian government. I should agree with Mr. Chandler, were it not that we have done all we can to settle the matter." Brown seemed to be hinting that while he himself was a provincial rights man like Chandler, Mowat's resolution incorporated a hard-fought compromise between centralizers and federalists in the Canadian cabinet, one he had decided to accept and was loath to see reopened.[13]

Mowat himself did not take up Chandler's challenge to the resolution, and discussion moved to a comparison of the Canadian plan with the constitution of New Zealand, where local governments had been abolished in favour of a unitary state. This enabled John A. Macdonald, not often an advocate for provincial rights, to insist that under the Canadian plan, local governments would not erode away: "That is just what we do not want. Lower Canada and the lower provinces would not have such a thing." Perhaps Macdonald had accepted the compromise the Canadian delegates had made during the summer and was now defending federalism against his own inclinations, much as Brown defended limits to provincial powers. But Macdonald also defended the centralizing tendency attacked by Chandler: "We should concentrate the power in the federal government, and not adopt the decentralization of the United States. Mr. Chandler would give sovereign power to the local legislatures, just where the United States failed."[14]

Chandler, protesting that his plan was not precisely the same as in the United States, raised another point. "If my plan is not adopted, I should have elective legislative councillors." During the previous week's debates on the upper house, Chandler had accepted that the upper house of the new confederation would be weak, almost ceremonial—but only because he had assumed that the interests of less populous regions would be safeguarded by powerful provincial governments. Strong provinces, he was saying, would render a strong upper house unnecessary. But if the provinces were going to be as weak as he now feared, then to withstand the Canadian majority in the rep-by-pop national legislature, Chandler believed there had to be a powerful upper house in the national parliament to represent regional interests. To have such power, the upper house would have to be elected.[15]

Chandler was a member of the old Loyalist ascendency of New Brunswick and a longtime member of the appointive upper house in that province. In the 1850s, as premier, he had defended autocratic, elite rule until responsible government was finally forced upon him. Chandler's understanding that only an elected upper house could defend the regions if the provincial governments were to be as weak as he feared was the plainest statement possible that the confederation makers had not made the Senate appointive because they wanted to put power in the hands of a reactionary, autocratic upper house of appointed gentlemen, empowered to restrain the democratic impulses of the elected representatives of the people. The upper house they had designed would be appointive *and* weak. Chandler had accepted that because he had expected the provinces would be strong enough to defend regional interests. Only if that were not to be the case did he want a powerful—and therefore elected—federal upper house.

Chandler still had allies. Robert Dickey of Nova Scotia was Tupper's cabinet colleague in Nova Scotia, but he saw Chandler's point, stating, "I am rather inclined to agree with Mr. Chandler. Immense interests [are] omitted in Mr. Mowat's motion." George Coles of Prince Edward Island and Adams Archibald of Nova Scotia, both reformers, offered amendments to leave the powers of the provinces unspecified—and therefore unlimited. But the Canadians did not move, and when it came to a vote the critics lacked support even in their own delegations: every province opposed their motions. Then it was 11 P.M., and they put the rest of the discussion over until the next day.[16]

There were two particularly notable non-participants in Monday's discussions on federal versus provincial powers. One was Oliver Mowat, who had moved the motion listing provincial powers but said nothing as the provincial power advocates and the central power advocates made their arguments. In later years, as premier of Ontario, Mowat would become the first provincial premier to advocate forcefully for provincial rights and powers against Ottawa's claims. From the 1870s through the 1890s, he was the most articulate defender of the idea that the provinces were sovereign powers within their own realm. At the conference table at Quebec, however, he seems to have held to George Brown's position that the compromise worked out within the Canadian cabinet was sufficient protection for the provinces, and that it should not be tinkered with, or even talked about.

The other silent witness to Chandler's argument that the provinces were too weak, and to Tupper's reply that such weakness was a good thing, was George-Étienne Cartier. Cartier had built his whole parliamentary career and that of the Bleus on establishing the party as the defender of French Canada's interests—*notre langue, nos institutions, et nos lois.* Cartier had taken a bold and risky step in going into coalition with Brown and agreeing to put an end to the Canadian union—in exchange for the promise that federalism would permit the new province of Quebec to retain control of French Canada's vital affairs. Cartier, like Mowat, apparently held his tongue during the discussion in Quebec. Perhaps both felt it was best to stand by the intricate compromises made in the Canadian cabinet sessions. Perhaps they felt that with the conference racing to a close, they had the votes they needed and should not get caught in wrangles about the philosophy of federalism. In any case, Tuesday's session would bring forth an even more fundamental aspect of the rivalry between federal and provincial powers: disallowance.

EIGHTEEN

Sunday, October 23: The Work Still to Be Done

Friday night's ball hosted by the bachelors of Quebec was the last of the great entertainments of the constitutional conference. Mercy Coles, stuck in her sickroom, never got to attend one. The following morning, she pronounced herself "heartily sick of Quebec" and hoping to leave by Wednesday. Lord Monck had completed his series of small dinners for delegates and their families at Spencer Wood. No further dinners and "drawing rooms" had been planned, though the dining room at the Hotel St-Louis was as busy as ever, and delegates and lobbyists doubtless continued to gather at the Stadacona Club and other congenial places for private negotiations. Mercy described in her diary how John A. Macdonald dined with her family on Sunday evening. Macdonald had good reason to court George Coles, who might yet influence Prince Edward Island's response to confederation, but he entertained her "with any amount of small talk" before leaving for Mme Duval's regular Sunday night political soiree. When he paid particular attention to her in the hotel drawing room a couple of nights later, she may have been considering what his interest in her was; he was, after all, a widower. "What an old humbug he is," she would write a few days later. "He brought me my dessert into the drawing room. The conundrum." After this second weekend of the conference, however, the official events were pretty much done. No one had expected the conference to last so long.

On October 18, *The Globe*'s correspondent reported that he still had no idea when the conference might be over. At its opening on October 10, George Brown had imagined—or at least promised his wife—that he could attend the post-conference events and still sail for Britain on October 26. Even at the end of the conference's first week, he told her the meetings might last only another week. He would have to stay no matter how long the conference continued, but not every delegate was so committed. Peter Mitchell had been called back to New Brunswick on private business on the second Wednesday, and some of the others had less than perfect attendance. After the sessions of October 20, the press reported that the Newfoundland delegates, Shea and Carter, were obliged to take ship for home, though Shea at least remained for some days. The next day, Sir Richard MacDonnell, lieutenant-governor of Nova Scotia— the only provincial lieutenant-governor visiting Quebec City during the conference—went off with Lady MacDonnell to Montreal, on their way to see Niagara Falls. On October 24, William McDougall, one of Brown's Canada West delegates in the Canadian coalition, left to campaign for his re-election in the North Lanark constituency of Canada West. McDougall had managed to get himself defeated in a by-election during the summer— his inept campaigning had infuriated Brown—and the North Lanark seat had been opened for him.[1]

The end was in sight, however. At the end of the conference's second week, newspapers began to predict that the delegates' ten-hour days might enable them to wrap up in one more week—by October 28, roughly. During the weekend, the conference organizers would inform the city of Montreal that the delegates would attend a ball being prepared for them there on Friday evening, October 28. That meant that if the conference was to complete its work in Quebec City, only four working days remained. Possibly the Canadian cabinet had done some vote counting and concluded that urgency would be no bad thing. If there was barely time to discuss the resolutions, they would simply get them through faster. Still, it was going to be a very busy week. The weather was improving a little.

NINETEEN

Tuesday, October 25 to Wednesday, October 26: What Quebec Needed

Of the thirty-three men who participated in the conference at the parliament building in Quebec City that October, some said nothing that was recorded, and several more said little. The Canadian delegation in particular deferred to its leaders. Macdonald, Brown, and Cartier, all party leaders, spoke when they wished, and Oliver Mowat and Alexander Galt spoke on their areas of particular expertise. The rest of the Canadian delegates mostly kept their mouths shut. Brown's supporter, William McDougall, a lawyer-journalist and political veteran, and a man strongly convinced of his own importance, went unrecorded during the discussions, as did Macdonald's more docile supporters, Alexander Campbell and James Cockburn. The Maritimers were either less deferential or less organized, for a wider range of them spoke out, frequently to disagree with each other. But no delegation was more disciplined than the Bleus of Canada East. Cartier's three allies, Étienne Taché, Jean-Charles Chapais, and Hector Langevin, went almost completely unrecorded in the notes on the conference. Taché was held back by his role as chair, and

Chapais was a minor figure, recently added to the Canadian cabinet for internal party reasons. But Hector Langevin, though just thirty-eight, was a powerful political actor, Quebec City's man in the cabinet and its former mayor as well as a shrewd politician well connected to the political and clerical hierarchy. Yet his recorded interventions in the discussions are scarce. Even Cartier, one of the dominating figures of the confederation process, spoke less often than many minor participants.

The Bleus, of course, had been relieved of the necessity of arguing their cause at the conference table. They expected to get what they wanted anyway. Cartier's alliance with Brown and Macdonald, and the indispensable place of the Bleu parliamentary bloc in delivering the votes that sustained the Canadian coalition, meant that their requirements were sure to be respected. The small group of francophone delegates—just four among thirty-three, and therefore getting a taste of their future minority status in a rep-by-pop federal parliament—secured their victories in the backrooms and did not have to argue or plead for their causes around the conference table. Yet it remains puzzling that at several points in the discussions, neither Cartier nor Langevin seized opportunities to make the case for French Canada. They often allowed Macdonald or one of the others to say that a particular choice was required "on account of Lower Canada" or must be rejected because "Lower Canada would not have such a thing."[1] Either of them could have made the case for Lower Canada directly, and been attended to.

Even without raising their voices in the conference, Cartier's caucus got most of what they required. To begin with, they got a province. This was Canada East's great and fundamental requirement, and the essence of Cartier's bargain with Brown in June 1864. In the Union, Canada East had been protected by its half share of the legislative seats, which insured it could not be outvoted on its vital concerns. To surrender that guarantee for a federal union based on rep by pop, there had to be a new, separate province able to protect and encourage French Canada's unique cultural, religious, and linguistic situation.

That was the essence of the federal union. "Confederation," wrote the Quebec City journalist and politician Joseph Cauchon in a critical but mostly supportive account of the Quebec Resolutions soon after they were published,

> in giving us a local constitution that safeguards the privileges, the inherited rights, and the institutions of the minority, certainly offers protection, no matter how large the union, since from a minority we will become and remain forever the national majority and the religious majority [in the new province]. We do not demand the exclusion of other races and religions, nor special privileges for ourselves. All we require is that ours does not disappear. It is not a lot to ask.[2]

Brown and Cartier had promised each other that, in the new confederation, Canada West and Canada East could run their own essential local affairs and still draw the benefits of an economic union. As Brown's *Globe* had said before the Charlottetown meeting, Canada East and Canada West were each to acquire a provincial legislature "beyond the control of the central power, set apart from it, untouchable by it."[3] Soon after the Quebec meeting, Joseph Cauchon would conclude they had delivered.

On Tuesday and Wednesday, October 25 and 26, the francophone caucus in the conference saw several fundamental requirements ratified without their having to speak. On Monday, control of education had been established as one of the long list of powers conferred on the provinces. On Tuesday morning, D'Arcy McGee offered an amendment that would add to the education clause the words

> ... saving the rights and privileges which the Protestant or Catholic minority in both Canadas may possess as to their denominational schools when the constitutional act goes into action.[4]

McGee represented the Irish-Catholic community of Montreal and Canada East, yet his resolution was not directed at the needs of Irish Catholics in Canada East. It was the *Protestant* minority of Canada East that would be protected—and also the Catholic minority of Canada West. In effect, the resolution would limit the authority of the new province of Quebec to restrict the education of Protestants within the province, and that of Ontario to restrict Catholic education. It was a constitutional recognition of religious minorities. Only the future Ontario and Quebec were covered. No one spoke up for the francophone Acadians of the Maritime provinces or Catholic minorities elsewhere, or contemplated future schools in the west. Still there was an affirmation that some Protestants in Quebec and some Catholics outside Quebec would have their right to an education safeguarded. Catholic culture, whether Irish or French, would have a recognized status within the new confederation, even beyond the province of Quebec. While the francophone delegates were close-mouthed about this topic in the conference record, Joseph Cauchon understood its importance. "Education is the whole society rearing its young," he wrote. "It is the morals, the sentiments, the inclinations and the strivings of the generations on the doorstep of the future."[5] Cauchon was proud that Canada East had a thriving educational system that served the Protestant minority alongside the Church-run system for the Catholic majority. He saluted McGee's amendment, but it was axiomatic that French Canada had to control its own education system. The list of provincial powers introduced by Oliver Mowat had ensured that would be so, and McGee's amendment would extend protection to Ontario's Catholics as well, without Quebec giving to its Protestants anything not already granted them.

In French Canada, what might be called community services or social welfare were, like education, almost entirely provided by the Roman Catholic Church. These were an essential part of the Catholic Church's institutional role in French-Canadian society. The guarantee of provincial authority over "the construction, maintenance, and management of hospitals, asylums, charities, and eleemosynary (that is, 'pertaining to charity or almsgiving') institutions," as well as provincial control over municipal institutions of all kinds, made it certain that these community services would be provincial responsibilities. No religious guarantee was required; few foresaw a time when a government of an autonomous province of Quebec would challenge the authority of the Roman Catholic Church over all these matters, though indeed nothing in the conference's seventy-two resolutions prevented secular rather than clerical control over education and community services.

Another matter of profound importance to French Canada was the civil law. A legal code seems a narrow and technical subject to become one of the talismans of national identity, but in Canada East the Civil Code of Lower Canada had achieved that status. At the time of the British conquest, English criminal law—with the jury system, the presumption of innocence, and the adversarial system that pitted defence counsel against the Crown's prosecutors before an impartial judge—had replaced the old French system, in which powerful investigating magistrates took charge of criminal investigations and trials, and trial lawyers had been virtually unknown. Civil law, however, was entirely different. To replace the system of marriage and family law in the conquered society of New France, or to restructure how land was held and contracts enforced, would have required a massive disruption that would have reached down to every household in French Canada. Britain soon declared that the old civil law code that had prevailed in New France would continue under British rule. In the 1850s and 1860s, soon after responsible government was achieved, anglophone and francophone lawyers and politicians of Canada East collaborated on a massive intellectual, social, and political achievement, the overhaul of the now-antiquated civil code preserved from the French regime. They created in its place the new Civil Code of Lower Canada, which was better adapted to modern legal realities, particularly commercial ones, but still sustained the traditional legal processes upon which property transactions, wills and inheritances, marriage agreements, and other familiar aspects of life in Canada East were based. That work was still going on during the confederation conferences; the new civil code would be passed into law in 1866.[6]

For decades, the civil law had been understood in French Canada as one of the bulwarks of French-Canadian civilization, and the massive renovation being achieved simultaneously with confederation had only enhanced that status. "Lower Canada has its own civil code, entirely its own," wrote Joseph Cauchon, "which it will not abandon for anything in the world ... because it is in our habits and our affections and we believe we find there more than anywhere, protection for our property and our families."[7] The Quebec Conference ratified the continued existence of the civil code in two ways. It confided "property and civil rights" to the provinces (civil rights generally meaning matters of civil law, rather than the broad freedoms and liberties implied by the term today). A more indirect protection was given in a resolution that permitted "rendering uniform all and any of the laws relative to property and civil rights in Upper Canada, Nova Scotia, New Brunswick, Newfoundland and Prince Edward Island," after confederation, if those provinces wished to do so.* Only one province was not part of this option. Property and civil rights law for Quebec could not under any circumstances be amalgamated with that of the other provinces because those provinces all followed the common law tradition inherited from Britain. Quebec was set apart by its own unique civil code.[8]

Perhaps the only topic more precious to French Canada than provincial autonomy and the civil code was language. "Everyone knows," wrote Cauchon, how the union that Britain imposed on Upper and Lower Canada in 1841 had made English the only official language of government and the legislature, as part of Britain's plan for the rapid assimilation of French Canada into English-speaking norms. Every francophone, he continued, also knew of the resistance of the people of

---

* They never have. The provinces continue to make their own laws in these areas, consulting only informally.

Canada East that had prevented the assimilation plan from becoming a reality—and how only the partnership of anglophone and francophone reformers had established French as one of the working languages of the Province of Canada's legislature. In Canada East, this reminder of the vulnerability in its own homeland of the French language—and French culture with it—was recent history, stark and ominous.[9] Securing a constitutional affirmation of the equal status of the French language, in the new legislature and government of Quebec, and in the new federal parliament, was a vital necessity for the delegates of Canada East. On that point, the Bleu caucus in the Canadian government would have tolerated no dissent. On Wednesday morning, October 26, Alexander Galt, a Quebecker but an anglophone, moved

> That in the general legislature and its proceedings the English and the French language may be both especially employed, and also in the local legislature of Lower Canada and in the federal and local courts of Lower Canada.[10]

Galt's resolution hardly provided for universal bilingualism or the entrenched equality of French and English. It did not even apply to the public service. But in two institutions understood to be vital to the liberty of the citizen—parliament and the courts—the security of the French language would be guaranteed both in Canada East's and the federal parliaments and in the courts of Canada East.

Self-government in all local matters, security for educational and cultural institutions of Canada East, constitutional protection for the civil code, and a guarantee for the use of French as an official language— the conference had safeguarded most of the essential requirements of French Canada. One profound danger remained. If the cultural integrity, the essential institutions, even the language of French Canada all depended on the local legislature that Canada East was about to acquire as a province of the new confederation, then everything depended on the autonomy of that legislature in its relations with the new national government. Late in the evening on Tuesday, October 26, after a long day of wrapping up the list of provincial powers, Oliver Mowat introduced the remaining items on the list of federal powers the Canadian cabinet was proposing. These included two clauses that might have horrified advocates of strong, autonomous provinces, but particularly the francophone delegates and their constituency. Mowat moved that

> Any bill of the general legislature may be reserved in the usual manner for Her Majesty's assent, and any bill of the local governments may be in like manner be reserved for the consideration of the general government.

and

> Any bill passed by the general legislature shall be subject to disallowance by Her Majesty within two years, as in the case of bills passed by the said provinces hitherto; and in the like manner any bill passed by a local legislature shall be subject to disallowance by the general government within one year after the passing thereof.[11]

These two resolutions, eventually to be numbered 50 and 51 of the seventy-two Quebec Resolutions, seemed to repudiate all that Cartier's caucus required regarding the autonomy of the new province. The first part of each clause said that any bill passed by the new national government could be reserved for the examination of, and possible disallowance by, the British government—"her Majesty's assent" meaning the assent of her advisors, that is, the British cabinet—as if British North America were still simply a colonial dependence, with all its self-government existing at the whim of the mother country's politicians. Perhaps even more devastating for the new province of Quebec (and the other provinces as well) was the second part of each clause, which applied the same scrutiny to the new provincial governments. Their legislation could apparently be reserved for examination by "the general government," and then simply disallowed by it if the general government chose. If that were to be the case, then the provinces would not be autonomous at all, but clearly subordinate to the national legislature, which could supervise and override anything a provincial legislature chose to do, to the point of making the provincial government unworkable except at the will of the federal authorities. The reservation and disallowance resolutions seemed to make the elaborate list of powers conferred on the provinces merely a sham, if the exercise of them could be cancelled by the federal government whenever the provinces tried to use them. Confederation would indeed be a legislative union in disguise. Only a semblance of federalism would exist. Joseph Cauchon, generally sympathetic to the confederation plan, wrote in regard to disallowance, "We fear for the independence of the legislative actions of the provinces within the scope of authority given them by the plan. It is urgent that our ministers explain this vitally important point."[12]

According to Hewitt Bernard's notes, when Oliver Mowat presented these resolutions to the conference on Tuesday evening, New Brunswick's Edward Chandler, who had sought more for the provinces in the division of powers discussion only a day earlier, criticized them both, with the support of the provincial attorney general, John Mercer Johnson. Their colleague John Gray agreed with them, but Nova Scotian Jonathan McCully, who had earlier insisted on provincial responsible government, called the clauses "desirable." George-Étienne Cartier did not say a recorded word. Nor did Hector Langevin, or Étienne Taché or Jean-Charles Chapais, and both resolutions were quickly passed.

These resolutions certainly originated in the Canadian cabinet. They must have been worked out as the consensus agreement of the confederation coalition, and at Quebec, Cartier and his bloc did not break the unanimity the Canadians had maintained on major issues. Oliver Mowat would later describe the resolutions at Quebec on federal and provincial powers as "only as the best practicable in view of the different interests and sentiments of the members of the conference," but he did not speak against his own motion.[13] If the Canadians most committed to the autonomy of the future Ontario and the future Quebec had agreed that the disallowance and reservations resolutions were acceptable, they must have had reason to believe these powers were hardly as draconian as they seemed.

The first and fundamental reason why they could tolerate these resolutions lay in their collective experience of parliamentary life in British North America since the 1840s, and particularly since the political revolution of 1848. Responsible government—the principle that the governors general and lieutenant-governors must act on the advice of their elected councillors and not according to instructions from above—had established that the colonies would run their own affairs. But it went deeper than that. The 1848 achievements had established in the British North American provinces the fundamental principle of parliamentary democracy and constitutional monarchy: that an elected legislature, responsible to the people, was sacred, and that to interfere with it was tyranny. In Britain, Parliament recognized no superior authority. The Westminster parliament was supreme. Ever since it had deposed James II and crowned William III in the "Glorious Revolution" of 1688, monarchs reigned and Parliament ruled.

In British North America, it was slightly different. Britain had not delegated all powers to its colonies and their parliaments in 1848. Their self-government only extended to the domestic sphere, and Britain continued to run military policy, foreign affairs, and other imperial matters. But within the sphere of matters allocated to them, the colonial politicians of the 1840s vigorously asserted that they had as much right as Englishmen did to run their own affairs. The operations of parliaments were first and fundamental among those rights. The Canada West reformers William Warren Baldwin and his son Robert Baldwin had since the 1820s been arguing that once Britain created legislatures in its colonies, it surrendered the authority to abolish them, as the colonies had rights of representation that could not be taken from them without their consent. In Canada East, the lawyer and constitutional thinker Pierre Bédard had been making the same arguments at the beginning of the century: an elected legislature representing the people could not be interfered with in the exercise of its legitimate authority.[14]

As a result, the politicians of British North America had grown accustomed during the 1850s and 1860s to the autonomy of their provincial legislatures within the spheres allotted to them. All their legislation since 1848 had been subject to review and rejection by the British government, in theory, and that theoretical subservience was being restated in resolutions 50 and 51. In practice, however, such review and rejection had already become unacceptable, and by convention unconstitutional. It was reasonable, perhaps, for the delegates to conclude that the same chain of deference to the monarch applied in the clauses about federal disallowance of provincial legislation—with the same practical limitation imposed on them by the principle of responsible government. Reservation and disallowance preserved the hierarchy of a constitutional monarchy: from the provincial legislatures, through the new national government, through the British government, to the monarch herself. But one legislature could not oppress another, any more than the monarch could. Confederation was intended to cement the national autonomy of the new nation, not to impose a new subservience upon it. Cartier and his group had good reason to understand that the same would apply to reservation and disallowance with regard to the provinces.

The conference had already agreed that the provinces would be responsible governments. They had the same right not to be interfered with—within their sphere of responsibility—as any other responsible government. This seems to have been the understanding the Canadian cabinet had worked out regarding the reservation and disallowance

nal lawyers advising that the formal chain of
atures through to the monarch had to be
e practical politicians understanding the
retical meaning and its practical one. Even
received an assurance on this point, perhaps
gevin. Having initially called disallowance
explanation, he would ultimately conclude
ong as there is nothing here that conflicts
the local legislatures or invades or absorbs

the resolution on disallowance, Hewitt
A. Macdonald was as silent as George-
....................bly, as a skeptic about federal systems and a
believer in centralized power, he was attracted by the potential for the
central government to supervise the provinces. As a veteran drafter of
legislation and student of the British constitution, he had presumably
urged the Canadian cabinet to accept that a chain of authority was
necessary and proper. In private correspondence, he would sometimes
suggest the provinces would be no more important than municipal
governments, even that they would be abolished within his own life-
time. But he tended to say such things to like-minded supporters who
wished to hear them. In the conference, despite his earlier preference, he
consistently ruled out a legislative union as impossible: "That is just
what we do not want. Lower Canada and the lower provinces would
not have such a thing."[16] In future years, when he was prime minister of
Canada and warring with the provinces, Macdonald asserted the right
of the federal government to use the disallowance power but, as his own
minister of justice, he declared that disallowance actually had a very
limited scope. It was intended to prevent provincial acts that were
"altogether illegal or unconstitutional" or "clashing with the legislation
of the general parliament." At Quebec, he had said that the general
government would act like "a court of equity" to ensure fairness to all.[17]

WHEELBARROW OF BOOZE

Proceeds go to help Dennis Bondy and his surgery in Germany

Draw Will Take Place Wednesday June 22nd At The Fogolar Fundraiser

THANK YOU!!!

$10 OR 3 For $20

No. 0907

In setting out rules for disallowance, he seemed to be suggesting that the general government could exercise a court-like power to determine when provincial legislation went beyond its constitutional authority, and in power he would sometimes act that way. But the delegates had already addressed the question of courts. Indeed, courts of law, and the role of courts in arbitrating federal–provincial disputes, were very much on their minds.

TWENTY

Tuesday, October 25 to Wednesday, October 26: Rights and Courts

On Tuesday afternoon, October 25, having spent the morning on the educational rights of Protestant and Catholic minorities in Canada, the delegates around the table turned to consider questions of justice in the new nation and its provinces. The discussion did not feature stirring debates about the rights and freedoms of citizens or about a bill of rights that would put fundamental freedoms beyond threats from meddlesome or abusive governments in the new confederation. The constitutional discussions of 1864 were about creating a federal nation from the provinces of British North America, not about defining parliamentary government or setting out how that system defended freedom and provided justice. The politicians of 1864 understood that those matters had broadly been settled by the establishment of responsible government in the 1840s. Parliaments existed. Rights existed. No fundamental review seemed required. There was no resolution at Quebec about a rights charter.

A bill of rights already existed for British North America, in the form of the bill of rights that the English parliament had enacted in 1689 and which applied across the British Empire. Mostly, that bill of rights set out limits on what the Crown could do without parliamentary approval. It affirmed that without parliamentary sanction, the Crown could not change laws or establish courts, or maintain armies, or levy taxes. It could not interfere with parliamentary elections or limit the speech of parliamentarians. The bill of rights ensured that the Crown and its government could only govern with the support of the parliament in which the people were represented. These were parliamentary rights, not human or universal rights; indeed, some elements of the bill of rights, such as those preventing a Roman Catholic from inheriting the throne, were plainly discriminatory. The bill of rights was based on the conception of a representative parliament being the people's fundamental defence against tyranny and abuse by the Crown. Since Parliament represented the people, it was understood, a bill of rights that safeguarded the supremacy of Parliament provided all the protection for citizens' rights that was required. It followed, therefore, that Parliament was the ultimate lawmaker and guarantor of rights.

For the delegates in the conference chamber at Quebec, this was close to being the bedrock of their political beliefs. They did, however, have long, vexing experience with one question that the principle of parliamentary supremacy posed: which parliament? Since they were planning to be governed by three levels of parliament, they could not avoid the question of which parliament was supreme. Their new nation would still be part of the British Empire, governed by the imperial parliament in London. It would also have its new national parliament, autonomous within its sphere. Finally, within the federal system they were planning, provincial parliaments would hold specific powers and responsibilities. Canada would be the first state in the world where a federal system coexisted with sovereign regional parliaments.* No one

---

* In these years, the German federation was being assembled from the many principalities and German states, but the autocratic power of the Kaiser makes that federation hard to compare with the Canadian situation.

who served in a legislature of British North America could fail to be alive to the question of divided sovereignty and the competing rights of different parliaments. The vigour of the delegates' discussion about which government would control the residual powers, and the wrangle about shared or concurrent powers, testified to their awareness of that issue.

Canadians had lived with divided sovereignty for a long time, as colonials running their own affairs while also acknowledging the authority of the British parliament. Before 1848, British politicians and imperial thinkers often declared it was constitutionally impossible for a British colonial governor to take his orders from a colonial legislature while also being subject to the British government that had appointed him. That would be a fundamental denial of the sovereignty of Britain's parliament, they said.[1] But since the early 1800s, Canadian parliamentary reformers had insisted that Britain's colonial governors did indeed have to yield to colonial legislatures. Colonials had not forfeited the rights of Englishmen by emigrating, they argued. They were entitled to have their government answer to them through their legislatures. That argument had triumphed in the responsible government settlement of 1848, when it was accepted that each legislature could be sovereign *in its own sphere*. In 1848, Britain had merely declared its willingness, not its obligation, to accept the independent responsibility of local legislatures for local affairs. At that time, no constitutional document ratified the change in policy. Nevertheless, Canadian reformers insisted that the implementation of responsible government in British North America was a constitutional change—that once having accepted it, the British had surrendered the authority to meddle in the colonials' internal affairs.

In effect, British North American parliamentarians of 1848 had translated the principle of parliamentary sovereignty into the rule that every parliament was sovereign—at least, within its own sphere. Now that they were creating federal and provincial levels of parliaments within British North America, they could not escape the same conclusion. In dealing with Britain, they relied on tradition, on assertions of rights, even on veiled threats like Étienne Taché's well-remembered oratory about the last cannon shot,* to defend the autonomy of the colonial legislatures against British interference. Talking about a federal system for the new nation, however, delegates at Quebec talked increasingly about courts.

The conference was well provided with lawyers—twenty of the thirty-three delegates practised law. They took the law seriously, and they took professional pride in how the bar and the courts of British North America had developed and flourished. One of the delegates, indeed, had suddenly acquired a very direct interest in the judicial bench during the conference. On October 20, Vice-Chancellor James Esten, one of the superior court judges of Canada West, died in Toronto. As attorney general for Canada West, John A. Macdonald immediately offered the position to Oliver Mowat, who at that very time was busy presenting the resolutions on provincial powers, on minority schools— and on courts and judges. "I fear he will take it and leave me in the lurch," wrote George Brown on hearing of Mowat's opportunity—which may have been precisely Macdonald's motive for making the offer to one of Brown's most effective Reform supporters rather than to one of his Conservative allies.[2]

On Monday, October 24, a resolution introduced by Mowat (who had not yet accepted the judicial post) had established that one of the powers of the new provinces would be

> the administration of justice, and the constitution, maintenance and organization of the courts both of civil and criminal jurisdiction.

Each of the British North American provinces already provided its own courthouses and its court officers and prosecution services, and none of these powers was to be transferred to the new federal government. On Tuesday evening, however, Mowat presented another resolution affirming that

* See Chapter Six in this volume.

> All courts, judges and officers of the several provinces shall aid, assist, and obey the general government in the exercise of its rights and powers under this act, and for such purposes shall be held to be judges and officers of the general government.[3]

The next morning, it was further established that

> The judges of the courts of record in each province shall be appointed and paid by the general government, and their salaries shall be fixed by the general legislature[4]

and that

> The judges of the superior courts shall hold their offices during good behavior and shall be removable only on the addresses of both houses of the general legislature.[5]

The delegates were establishing a duality in the courts. All the courts would be built and administered by the provinces (and since their judges would be appointed from among the lawyers of the individual provinces, the judgeships of the smaller Maritime provinces were not about to be commandeered by well-connected lawyers from Canada.[†]) Yet all the judges who sat in these provincially administered courtrooms would be appointed and paid by the national government. The last resolution guaranteed the independence of the judiciary, something already established in most of the British North American provinces but never before given constitutional status.

Long after, federal appointment would be said to be a cynical plan by the lawyer-delegates to arrogate patronage powers and plum appointments for themselves and their friends when they became

---

† This was one of the resolutions that Hewitt Bernard neglected to note in his minutes. Probably moved and passed on Wednesday morning, October 26, it was included in the list of seventy-two resolutions at the close of the conference.

federal politicians. "No doubt the lawyers took a warm interest in the matter ... having before their eyes judgeships ... and other lucrative appointments," one anti-confederate politician would declare.[6] This was not entirely unfair. Certainly the lawyer-delegates were ambitious, either for themselves or for their partners and protegés, and they could see the rich possibility of future judgeships in the new judicial institutions they were planning. But confederation supporters would reply that local governments would be much more susceptible to local pressure to appoint "troublesome advocate(s) of the second, third, or fourth order of talent" rather than "the men of the highest order of qualification" that the more remote national government would be able to appoint. Joseph Cauchon also suggested federal appointment was intended to protect the interests of Protestant lawyers in Canada East.[7] Beyond questions of patronage, the delegates seem to have intended that judges in each province would have a national role. There would not be separate courts for federal and provincial matters. A judge would sit in a single province but would be responsible for interpreting both provincial and federal laws—part of a national judiciary and not a merely provincial one.

In any case, the rule of law, like financial and commercial matters, could be seen not as an attribute of local culture and pride (and therefore an appropriately provincial jurisdiction), but as one of the great impartial institutions underpinning a common national space within which shared prosperity could blossom. There was an exalted conception of the judiciary in the resolutions that gave the judges life appointments, security of tenure, and a guarantee of independence from political pressure. The delegates were aware that Canadians were to be the arbiters of their own national law. All the judges would "aid, assist, and obey the general government in the exercise of its rights and powers" and should therefore be national in their authority and their appointment.

One national role the judges were about to assume was constitutional interpretation. When discussing the division of powers, and again when considering what the federal power of disallowance would mean, delegates several times observed that, in the end, judges would interpret the constitution. Judges, that is, would determine when the national government or the provincial governments were exceeding the powers allocated to them. On Monday, discussing the division of powers, Robert Dickey of Nova Scotia said, "I propose a supreme court of appeal to decide any conflict between general and state rights." Indeed, on the previous Friday, when setting out federal government powers, the delegates had already voted to authorize the federal government to establish "a general court of appeal for the federated provinces."[8] Perhaps recalling that vote more clearly than Dickey, George Brown quickly agreed with him about reliance on the courts: "I would let the courts of each province decide what is local and what general government jurisdiction, with appeal to the appeal or superior court."[9] At another moment, Attorney General William Henry of Nova Scotia, in supporting John A. Macdonald's arguments for leaving the residual, undefined powers to the general government, declared, "[W]e shall be bound by an imperial act and our judges will have to say what is constitutional under it as regards general or local legislation." A day later, casting doubt on the need for the disallowance clause, Edward Chandler of New Brunswick observed plausibly, "Your courts will decide whether the local legislatures exceed their powers. Why require a second veto?"[10]

It would be 1875 before the federal government created the Supreme Court of Canada, empowered to hear appeals from the high courts of each province, but the delegates proved to be good prophets about the way that courts, rather than the federal government's disallowance power, would be the ultimate authority in settling federal–provincial disputes. Soon after confederation, as prime minister and minister of justice of Canada, John A. Macdonald declared that the disallowance power could and should be used only when the provinces clearly and flagrantly abused their authority and were obviously trespassing on powers only the federal government was authorized to use. In the House of Commons, Macdonald declared that though he had at first supported a legislative union in which the provinces had only a subordinate role, he had been overruled "by large majorities" and had come to accept that the federal government "had no right to interfere so long as the different provincial legislatures acted within the bounds of the authority which the constitution gave them."[11]

Macdonald continued to believe, however, that the federal government had authority to determine when a provincial government went beyond the bounds of its authority or interfered with "the general interests of the dominion."[12] It was on this point that the predictions of the delegates about relying on the courts to settle such disputes proved accurate. In the 1880s, John A. Macdonald, returned to power after five years in opposition, began using the disallowance power vigorously to shore up federal authority. Arguing that even on a matter where the province had the constitutional authority to act, the federal government could disallow a provincial law if it was plainly bad policy, he vetoed the Rivers and Streams Act, a bill passed by the Ontario government—which was then led by Oliver Mowat. Mowat by then had abandoned the judgeship given him by John A. Macdonald in 1864 to become premier of Ontario. Mowat did not for one moment accept that the federal government had the right to determine what was right and wrong in his province's legislation. He took the matter to court, and the courts agreed with him. A long series of trials and appeals ensued, in the courts of Ontario, in the new Supreme Court of Canada in Ottawa, and at the Judicial Committee of the Privy Council in Britain (which had yet not lost its role in settling Canadian cases).[13] Over and over, the courts declared that Ottawa could not disallow valid provincial legislation and, perhaps more important, that it was courts and not the federal government that would decide when a law exceeded the constitutional authority of the province. It took many years, but the principles of responsible government triumphed over the black letter resolution about the power of disallowance. A province's legislation could not be arbitrarily abolished. Courts and not politicians would be the ultimate arbiters of the boundaries of federal and provincial authority, as laid down in the Quebec Resolutions and confirmed in the British North America Act, 1867. As Cartier seems to have told his Bleu caucus, and as Joseph Cauchon predicted in his analysis of the Quebec Resolutions, Ottawa's House of Commons, with its permanent anglophone majority, lacked the authority, even if it had the will, to abrogate the fundamental constitutional powers of Quebec, or indeed of any province.

TWENTY-ONE

Tuesday, October 25: The Old Indian Chief

On the first Wednesday of the conference, just before she fell ill, Mercy Coles had joined a carriage tour setting out to see "the Falls of Lorette and the Indian Chief." Premier Gray of Prince Edward Island chaperoned the group, she reported. (He had called in sick to the conference, and Hewitt Bernard noted him "indisposed.") The others in the party were her mother, the wife of Canada West delegate William McDougall, and the one possible object of chaperoning, a young man named Crowther, Alexander Galt's private secretary who would visit Mercy diligently while she lay ill. It was raining at Lorette and they did not walk down to admire the beauty of the falls on the St. Charles River. Instead they continued on to Wendaké, one of the most remarkable Aboriginal communities in British North America.[1]

Until 1649, the Wendat nation, known to Samuel de Champlain as the Huron, had been the principal trading partners and military allies of the small new colony of New France. They did not live on the outskirts of Quebec then; their homeland lay on the shores of Georgian Bay, a long canoe voyage to the west. This nation of perhaps forty thousand farmers and traders directed much of the fur trade of the upper Great Lakes and took charge of delivering the furs down to Champlain's outpost at Quebec. The Wendat were one of the great powers of the Great Lakes region of North America, and they had allied themselves with New France in a long multi-sided struggle against the Haudenosaunee or Iroquois confederacy, based south and east of Lake Ontario, whose trade and military alliances were with the Dutch (and later English) of New York. By the late 1640s, however, the Wendat had been devastated by diseases that the French brought with them, and they were internally divided by conflicts over the Christian message brought to them by the Jesuit missionaries their French allies insisted they accept among them. Reduced in numbers and weakened by internal division, the Wendat nation was unable to sustain the war for trade and pre-eminence. It was overrun and dispersed by the victorious armies of the Iroquois in 1649. Many Wendat survivors were absorbed into the Iroquois confederacy to replace sons and daughters the confederacy had itself lost to disease and to the long war. Others retreated north or west, but some of the Christian Huron retreated with their French allies to the St. Lawrence valley. There they founded the village of Wendaké just north of Quebec City. When Mercy Coles and her friends visited in 1864, the community was already more than two hundred years old.[2]

Mercy Coles probably knew a little of this Huron history, but she was surprised by the home of "the old Indian Chief." Instead of being the teepee or wigwam she may have imagined "Indians" living in, it was a substantial home of a familiar kind: "the only sign of it being Indian was a tomahawk and the chief cap which they showed us." Mercy told her diary that the chief, whom she met seated with his wife, "an old woman 90 years of age," was "the last of the Huron tribe." That was an odd misconception, since hundreds of other members of the tribe lived all around him at Wendaké, but he was indeed old. Ondialerethe, or Simon Romain, had been chief since 1844. He showed them amulets said to have been presented by George IV (who had died in 1830) and bracelets given him by the Prince of Wales during the royal visit of 1860. Mercy purchased a wooden spoon to take home "as a curiosity." A week later, at the Tessiers' ball, her father told Feo Monck that Mercy was ill with diphtheria, "what with the ship and going to see an Indian encampment."[3]

There were no First Nations delegates in the conference room at Quebec. No chiefs from the Wendat or the Six Nations or the Cree or the Mi'kmaq had been invited even to observe what the white politicians were planning for them. The delegates talked ambitiously of expanding their confederation across to British Columbia and opening the lands of the northwestern plains for the sons and daughters of Ontario's crowded farming counties, but their plans took no account of the people who actually lived there. The Coles family's comments about Mercy's Wendaké visit reflect what most of the delegates understood about First Nations: they did not live up to their romantic image, they lived in "encampments," they were generally nameless, they carried disease, and they were rapidly dying out.

They were in fact not dying out, though waves of disease like those suffered by the Wendat in the 1640s continued to move through Aboriginal communities. In 1864, though the delegates probably never knew of it, smallpox had been ravaging the Pacific Northwest coast for two years, killing half of all the people living in what is now British Columbia, wiping out scores of long-established First Nations communities, and leaving only a few hundred survivors among long-powerful nations such as the Haida.[4] It was another scourge in a disease cycle seen across the continent for centuries. Yet, across the future Canada, stable, self-sufficient Aboriginal communities remained more the norm than the exception. The Inuit of the north remained almost unvisited and unknown, except in areas where whalers or explorers ventured. In the boreal forest, the Cree and other nations had maintained a fur-trade relationship with Europeans for centuries. Since the Hudson's Bay Company had seized a monopoly on the trade in the 1820s, terms of trade had worsened for the Cree trappers, but they continued to live a mostly traditional life, moving freely across their territories. On the plains, the Siksika or Blackfoot confederacy still hunted the great bison herds, disdaining the fur trade. Well provided with horses and firearms, they competed for supremacy with the rival Plains Cree and generally forbade Europeans access to their territories. Around the Red River settlement and along the rivers leading west toward the Rockies, the Métis—both the Scots Métis associated with the Hudson's Bay Company and the French Métis associated with the earlier French fur trade—had built their complex and still mostly autonomous society.[5] All these nations, and many more, were almost entirely ignored by the conference and those who attended it, except for Mercy's tourist excursion to Wendaké—and by two constitutional items. One was noted in the conference resolutions. The other was unspoken but underpinned the first.

On Tuesday evening, October 25, the delegates passed a resolution on federal powers that included the declaration

> It shall be competent for the general legislature to pass laws respecting:
> 1) The Indians.

In the final version of the Quebec Resolutions, this became subhead 29 of resolution 29, which placed among the federal responsibilities "Indians and lands reserved for the Indians."[6] Nothing more was written down about "the Indians," or lands reserved for them. No delegate initiated any discussion of this item. Still, no other group or community received this kind of specific attention in the seventy-two resolutions. There was no resolution empowering the new federal government to pass laws regarding German Canadians, or Nova Scotia fishing communities, or frontier settlers on the Saskatchewan River. George-Étienne Cartier said frequently that he wanted all the "races" of Canada—he meant the English, the French, the Scots, the Irish—to thrive independently in the new nation and never be forced to assimilate into a single identity. But there was no constitutional protection for anyone simply because they were Irish or French or Scots. All British North Americans were presumed to be subjects of the Crown, and to be equally subject to the laws of Canada and the provinces. So this brief sub-clause, "Indians and lands reserved for the Indians," did establish a unique constitutional status for the First Nations. They were not simply subjects like any other, but a constitutionally identified group concerning whom some special responsibility was delegated to the new federal government and not to the provinces. That responsibility had long preceded the constitutional discussions of 1864.

A century earlier, just after proclaiming the treaty that ended the Seven Years War and transferred New France from French to British rule, the British government issued the Royal Proclamation of 1763 in the name of George III. Much of the proclamation concerned routine details of administration in the king's new territories from Labrador to Florida. The last part of the Royal Proclamation, however, addressed relations with the First Nations of North America.

In 1763, Britain understood that the Aboriginal nations of North America could be powerful military allies or powerful enemies. In the recent war of conquest, most of the Aboriginal powers in northern North America, particularly those engaged in the fur trade through Montreal, had sided with France. With the war ended, Britain's Indian agents sought to reduce that hostility and reassure Aboriginal leaders about the security of their land and territory. The Royal Proclamation of 1763 confirmed as British policy that no subjects of the Crown could settle on First Nations land and presume they remained on British territory, under British law and protection. Only the Crown could negotiate for land with the First Nations, and only, as the Proclamation said, "in our name, at some public meeting or assembly of the said Indians to be held for that purpose by the governor or commander in chief of our colony." A year after the Proclamation, at Niagara Falls, a large gathering of First Nations, many of them former allies of New France, ratified a new peaceful relationship with the British based on respect for territory. To mark the significance of the agreement, the assembled First Nations produced "the two row wampum," a woven blanket of coloured shells depicting two peoples travelling parallel courses on the same river. Henceforth, it would be Crown policy that treaty negotiations had to precede any expansion of British territory in North America, and this policy became part of the constitutional inheritance of British North America. Long before 1864, many treaties had been negotiated between royal officials and the First Nations.[7]

In their very brief subheading about Indians and lands belonging to Indians, the delegates at Quebec were recognizing that century-old obligation to make and maintain treaties with the First Nations. It was embedded in the constitutional framework of their new nation. Given the inherent dignity—and nation-building importance—of future treaties, they agreed, the treaty-making power would pass down from the old imperial officers to the new federal government, not to the provinces. Indeed, a process for negotiating treaties was an essential companion to the resolutions that were committing the new nation to acquire the northwest plains and incorporate British Columbia into confederation. Before the railroad could proceed westward, before settlers could flow onto the plains, Canada would have to negotiate treaties with the First Nations for the right to use their lands. Since Crown lands had already been deemed provincial lands, the Quebec Resolutions were creating the odd situation that the federal government had the obligation to negotiate treaties with the First Nations, but that land so acquired would immediately become provincial, not federal, Crown land.

Treaties would not bring understanding or respect for the Aboriginal nations, however. To First Nations chiefs and headmen who accepted them, the treaties were sharing agreements. They saw their people beset by poverty and disease and the encroachments of settlers and entrepreneurs, and they calculated that by agreeing to share the bounty of the land with the newcomers, their people might be able to support and sustain themselves. Before and after confederation, nearly every treaty negotiation included promises such as "you may hunt and fish forever," or "the land will always be yours," even "as long as the rivers run and the sun shines." When the chiefs affixed their marks to the parchments, however, Canadians would interpret the treaty signings as ceremonies of surrender. The written texts that the treaty commissioners would file in Ottawa included the blunt, cold phrase "cede, release, surrender, and yield up ... all rights whatsoever." Within a decade of confederation, Canada would pass the Indian Act, in which Parliament gave the government and its agents almost unlimited power to control the lives of Aboriginal people battered by the collapse of the buffalo herds, the shrinking of the fur trade, and the continued inroads of sickness, starvation, inequality, and the advance of Canadian society and Canadian authority.

The eclipse of Aboriginal society and sovereignty, rather than treaty negotiations that would place obligations on Canada, was surely what the delegates were contemplating when they assigned to the federal government the authority to make laws regarding Aboriginal matters. It would take most of a century before First Nations began to persuade Canadian courts that the principles enshrined in the Proclamation of 1763 and the wampum of 1764 could bind Canada to a different interpretation of its responsibility for "Indians and lands reserved for Indians."[8]

TWENTY-TWO

Wednesday, October 26: The Money

Tariffs. Anyone governing a province of British North America in the 1860s cared about tariffs. Broadly speaking, the governments of those provinces collected no income tax, no corporate tax, no property tax. For their revenues, they depended on tariffs—that is, on the customs duties they charged at their borders and seaports when goods passed through. A tariff on imported goods set so high as to discourage imports and protect local producers from foreign competition was a "protective" tariff, but even governments that preached the virtues of free trade had little choice about maintaining what were called "revenue" tariffs, because such tariffs provided the revenue on which governments ran. In 1864, each British North American province's tariffs, whether for revenue or protection, were applied against other provinces as well as against outsiders. Goods shipped from Quebec to Halifax were subject to duty, as if they were being shipped to a foreign country.

One of the goals of confederation was to expand the British North American economy by breaking down the tariff barriers between the provinces. At the Russell Hotel dinner on October 15, the first statement made by Chairman Joseph of the Board of Trade, the host of the dinner, was that the merchants strongly desired "that the unequal and hostile tariffs of the several provinces should disappear. We wanted one tariff instead of five." In reply, delegates proudly listed all the resources and products their province would contribute to the general welfare of the new nation once they achieved commercial union. "We should bring a revenue to the common purse of something like $3,000,000," said Charles Tupper about Nova Scotia. Leonard Tilley boasted that the people of New Brunswick "were not coming in as paupers. They were coming to put something in ... that was worth having." With the tariffs removed and an intercolonial railroad from Montreal to Halifax guaranteed by confederation, trade between Canada and the Maritimes could begin to flow. "It was utterly impossible we could have either a political or a commercial union without it," said Tilley of the railroad, but he might have said the same about the tariff consolidation.[1]

Doing away with interprovincial tariffs would strengthen the economy of the united provinces, but provincial governments would still exist. Given the long list of powers and responsibilities the delegates were assigning to them, the provinces would need revenue. Somehow, the delegates had to square the circle of building up provinces while abolishing the tariffs that sustained them. In their listing of powers assigned to the federal and provincial governments, they had already assigned "duties of customs on imports and exports" and "excise duties" to the federal list. For the sake of confederation, provinces would not only lose the tariffs they levied on each other. They would also surrender to the federal government all their tariff revenues on foreign trade.

Sorting out money had always been Alexander Galt's forte. He made his start in British North America by putting the finances of British colonization companies on a sound footing.* He had successfully amassed the capital to invest in railroad and industrial projects in his hometown of Sherbrooke, Canada East. Serving as finance minister of the Province of Canada before confederation, Galt had boldly raised tariffs that put the government on a sound financial footing and, as it happened, protected local industries like his own.[2] As the financial expert of the Canadian cabinet, Galt presented the Canadians' plan for the finances of the new nation on Saturday, October 22. "Many questions and explanations were required by the other members, and all related to finance were replied to by Mr. Galt, who has all information on that point in his head and does not often require to refer to the printed statistics," wrote Andrew Macdonald, who kept the most detailed notes on the financial discussions. The Canadians' proposals were bold, and "there was a very general debate in which the leaders chiefly took part." It was Galt's plan that the confederation would acquire all the cash and securities of each province, and take title to "public works and property," including everything from canals and publicly owned railroads to light-houses and military armouries. In exchange, the federal government would assume all the debt and liabilities of each province, which were roughly equal across the provinces on a per capita basis, except in Prince Edward Island and Newfoundland, which were relatively debt-free and would be compensated for the difference.[3]

A critical item in the finance balance sheet was the taxation powers in the division of federal and provincial powers that the delegates had already approved. These authorized the federal government to raise money by "all or any other mode or systems of taxation," and also from all duties and tariffs levied at the borders of the new nation.[4] Galt was proposing to give the federal government the most significant source of revenues the provinces had, their customs tariffs, and also to give the

---

* The Galt family came to Canada to run the Canada Company in Canada West, which acquired tracts of land, recruited immigrants, and organized their settlement. Alexander Galt later managed the British American Land Company in Canada East.

treasury of the new national government unlimited options for any other kind of tax. The list of provincial powers, on the other hand, included the right to levy only direct taxation: income taxes, property taxes, and other levies on individuals and businesses. Direct taxes were largely unknown in the provinces in 1864. No provincial government was going to be eager to take on the administrative burden of collecting personal taxes from the population—or to be first to levy them on a population that was sure to resist the very concept. The Province of Canada had systems of municipal and county governments that assessed rates directly on local residents for schools and other local services. That funding would continue in the new regime. The Maritime provinces, however, had not created systems of local and municipal governments. Their schools, road maintenance, policing, and other local functions would have to be paid for by provincial governments that were about to lose their principal source of revenue, the tariffs.

Had the conference taken up the finances of confederation as its first agenda item, the meetings might have broken up immediately, or fallen into a struggle at least as long and heated as the Senate issue. Instead, the Canadians held back the financial issues until much had been agreed upon. As October came to an end, the delegates were increasingly anxious to wrap up a conference that was beginning to seem endless, and perhaps willing to stifle objections in order to keep the agenda moving. Still, these fundamental questions of public finance could not be avoided. "Mr. Tilley stated the objections he held against Mr. Galt's scheme," wrote Andrew Macdonald. "I admit the question ... is of great importance," Galt responded. Tilley and Brown and Galt discussed this matter "at length," and Galt's resolution on finances was tabled pending further discussion.[5]

Galt did have a solution for the financial crisis the loss of tariffs would produce for the provincial governments: federal subsidies. The new national government would collect all the tariff revenue, but it would redistribute much of it out to the provincial governments in order to keep them solvent. Galt's proposal was simple: 80 cents per head of population would be paid annually by the national government to each province. If the provinces needed or wanted more revenue, they would have to develop new sources. Since they would control their Crown lands, they could begin to replace tariffs with levies on the development of resources—timber, mining, and whatever other resources they held. As well, they would have that right to levy direct taxation on their citizens, when and if they were prepared to do so. In the meantime, Galt was proposing that the provinces be wards of the federal treasury.

In the first week of the conference, Andrew Macdonald had excused the incomplete state of his conference notes by explaining that he had been "engaged in compiling statistics of Prince Edward Island in dollars and cents" and "making up a number of statistical tables."[6] Statistics and tables compiled for the various provinces eventually became fodder for a committee of financial experts from each colony: Galt and Brown for Canada, Tupper and Archibald for Nova Scotia, Tilley for New Brunswick, Ambrose Shea for Newfoundland, and William Pope for Prince Edward Island. "The delegates especially learned in finance are also closeted by themselves," the Toronto *Globe*'s correspondent reported, "endeavouring, I suppose, to come to an understanding on difficult financial matters."[7] There was no quick solution, and two days later *The Globe* reported that "Galt and Brown were closeted until very late with Tupper, Tilley, Shea, and Pope." By Wednesday, October 26, this financial committee had made enough progress for Galt's resolution to be brought back to the conference table—amended, but not by much. The financial experts, all supporters of the confederation project, had accepted Galt's fundamental proposition: the provinces would live on subsidies from the new national government until they developed revenues of their own.

On Tuesday, October 25, however, the conference had agreed that "all lands, mines, minerals, and royalties," as well as rents from leases on Crown land, "shall belong to the local governments." The final text of the Quebec Resolutions gave the provinces authority to legislate not merely for direct taxation (as the original proposal had read), but also for "duties on the export of timber ... and of coals and other minerals."[8] This may have been the vital reassurance the provinces needed from the finance committee. Subsidies from Ottawa would remain the lifeblood of some provincial governments for years—inadequately, in the case of Nova Scotia particularly. In 1868, new terms would have to be negotiated to save that province from a financial crisis (and to appease the powerful anti-confederate bloc there, which protested having been "sold for 80 cents a head"). In the longer term, resource revenues would become a vital income source for the provinces, particularly those well endowed with timber and minerals. Once Canadian taxpayers became resigned to being subject to direct taxes on their property and income—by both federal and provincial taxmen—the provinces would become more independent of Ottawa's subsidies, and more in command of their own finances.

Wednesday's vote to approve the financial terms passed by five votes to one. Once more, Prince Edward Island had reverted to the position of lonely opposition it had adopted early in the conference. "It was impossible for the government to be carried on there with such limited resources," the Island delegates objected.[9] There was a deeper complaint as well. The Islanders believed they were being betrayed on the one financial incentive that had persuaded Islanders even to consider confederation: the land question.

The promise made at Charlottetown that the new confederation, out of its much larger financial resources, would provide a fund to assist the Island's tenant farmers in buying the land they had rented for generations had made some key Islanders into supporters of confederation. George Coles and Edward Whelan saw at once that a federal government, standing between Charlottetown and Westminster, could ensure that the proprietors were compelled to accept the buy-out offers made to them. They saw an end to the land war as the key condition that would enable them to sell confederation to Island voters—and perhaps return to office as the government of the new province of Prince Edward Island. But Galt put nothing about a land purchase into his financial proposals, and the Island delegates seem to have realized early in the Quebec City sessions that they would not be able to deliver the one thing their voters really needed from confederation. Edward Whelan continued to argue that confederation would be good for the Island and even solve the land problem eventually, but George Coles later said he told the conference that without a guarantee of funds to buy out the landlords, "they might as well strike Prince Edward Island out of the constitution altogether."[10]

On Wednesday, even as the final financial package was being passed, George Coles and Andrew Macdonald put forward a resolution that would commit the new federal government to a land purchase. "Prince Edward Island has no crown lands, mines, or minerals from which money can be realized," said Coles, so the concessions on resources meant little there. Andrew Macdonald observed that Islanders would have to contribute to the intercolonial railroad though it would bring them no benefit. "The only advantage he could see that would accrue to the people of his province under the proposed confederation would be to have the lands purchased."[11]

The resolution got no support. Hewitt Bernard did not even include it in his minutes or notes. Prince Edward Island was really and truly out of confederation.

TWENTY-THREE

Thursday, October 27: Roads East and West

Could a railroad contract be part of a nation's constitutional foundations? In the midst of their debates about the role of an upper house, the division of powers, and the implications of disallowance, the delegates at Quebec had no doubt that it should be:

> The general government shall secure without delay the completion of the Intercolonial Railway from Rivière du Loup through New Brunswick to Truro in Nova Scotia.[1]

This resolution was probably moved and passed on Thursday, October 27, but in the rush of the last day's discussions, Hewitt Bernard neglected to make note of it, or to say whether it produced any comment from the delegates. The previous day, Andrew Macdonald had said in his critique of the financial resolutions that, being "an insular province," the Island was indifferent "whether the Intercolonial Railroad is built at all or not," so the Island delegates probably dissented once more on this resolution.

They were surely alone. In the plan of confederation, the railroad east to Nova Scotia was as vital as federalism or rep by pop.

In the 1860s, railroads were the most important lever for economic development. Railroad executives and railroad lawyers had made a point of being present in Quebec City throughout the conference, attending the balls and dinners, and offering transportation to take the delegates wherever they chose to go after the Quebec sessions. This was hardly an expression of altruism. All railroads depended on government support. Any railroad investor could see how much the federation, so much larger, better financed, and more ambitious than any of the provinces alone, could do to support railroad development.

The Intercolonial Railway, from Montreal to the Maritimes, was the key railroad of the confederation project, for the grim secret of confederation in 1864 was how little trade was actually carried on between the provinces that would form the new nation. For all of them, trade was mostly outward, to Britain or the United States rather than with each other. The ambition to change this was strong, and railroads were the means to do so. It was not just Montreal that intended to export its wares down the new railroad to Atlantic Canada. Anti-confederate Maritimers would warn of being flooded with Canadian exports (with good reason as it proved), but they had export ambitions of their own. Halifax could see itself becoming a northern Boston, a centre of shipping, finance, and manufacturing for the new nation. Small industries in steel, sugar refining, and coal mining were already springing up around Nova Scotia, and New Brunswick saw a bright future in the much-expanded market confederation promised. A railroad line that finally enabled year-round communications between the Maritime provinces and Canada was the vital prerequisite to all that. British North Americans had been talking about an intercolonial rail line for years, and their discussions had always broken down over how to share the very substantial costs. It was certain that Canada, so much larger and more developed than the Maritimes, would have to bear much of the cost of the railroad—as much as five-sixths, went a common estimate. But Canadian governments naturally balked at assuming such a financial burden when the Maritimes could still place tariff barriers against their products whenever the political currents so dictated.

The intercolonial railroad project also became drawn into the local politics of Canada West and Canada East. George Brown had long protested that Canada West, the richest and largest part of Canada, provided most of the revenues of the Province of Canada, but could not control how its own money was spent, since it had only half the votes in the legislature. As a result, Canadian government interest in an intercolonial line to the Maritimes had often been denounced by the Canada West reformers as another plot to spend Canada West's money on a project to benefit Montreal and the Maritimes. Brown had long insisted on linking the railroad to constitutional reform. Until there was representation by population, with or without a federal system, Brown argued, Canada West would never support railroad plans it did not control but would have to pay for. That was a powerful argument in Canada West's elections, and had helped kill negotiations whenever Maritime and Canadian politicians discussed railroad development. Canadian intransigence on the intercolonial railroad had been embittering Canada–Maritime discussions for years.

Suddenly, with federalism and rep by pop on offer, George Brown withdrew his veto on funding an Atlantic railroad. Canada West's share of control over the project was assured, and the federal union promised precisely the kind of free-trading economy that Brown always preferred over tariffs and trade barriers. Some of Brown's old allies, notably Antoine-Aimé Dorion and Christopher Dunkin of the Canada East Rouges and Reformers, would continue to criticize what seemed to be another giveaway to the railroad barons by their friends and agents in the government. Dorion would argue that confederation was little more than "a decent pretext" to "resuscitate the question of the intercolonial railroad" and wondered how politicians who had refused to contribute seven-twelfths of the cost of the road a few years earlier were now offering ten-twelfths. Confederation, he sneered, was mostly "another long haul at the public purse for the Grand Trunk."[2]

John A. Macdonald could not resist underlining how Brown, his old enemy and now his cabinet colleague, had changed sides on the railroad question. "Brown's confession of faith in favour of the railroad at Toronto has astounded his supporters, and dismayed a good many of them who have hitherto been educated by him to oppose it," he would write rather meanly in November 1864. But Brown—who might have retorted that Macdonald's acceptance of federal union was no less shocking to the supporters he had educated against that—rightly understood that the whole question had been transformed by the confederation plan. Once confederation and tariff abolition fell into place, the intercolonial railroad was a sure thing, and the means to pay for it were now at hand, even without endless begging for British guarantees.[3]

In the years when Brown had been attacking the intercolonial railroad project leading eastward, he had also been boosting plans for expansion into the west. It was another point where Cartier and Brown were in agreement and Macdonald more cautious. Cartier, like Brown, liked the ambition in western expansion and saw it as good for the business of Montreal, while Macdonald told a railroad executive in 1865 that "the country is of no present value to Canada. We have unoccupied land enough to absorb immigration for many years." Only the threat of American expansion justified westward moves by Canada, he then thought. At the beginning of the conference, however, the delegates had approved Brown's resolution on "provision being made for the admission into the union on equitable terms of the North-West Territory, British Columbia and Vancouver Island." Now, near the end of the conference, as if to bookend the commitment to the eastern railroad, the delegates returned to their westward aspiration:

Communication with the North-Western Territory, and the improvements required for the development of the trade of the Great West are regarded by this conference as subjects of the highest importance to the federated provinces, and shall be prosecuted at the earliest possible period that the state of the finances will permit.[4]

This was a much more hedged commitment than the firm guarantee to fund the Intercolonial Railway. There was no promise of a western rail line, though the United States had recently laid plans for its own railroad to the Pacific.[*] The resolution carefully specified that confederation's western commitment was only to be fulfilled when it seemed financially possible. Still, in less than a decade, their cautious promise would produce a confederation that did indeed stretch to the Pacific. By then, the government of Canada was fully committed to the Pacific railroad that was hardly imaginable in the meeting room in Quebec City.

---

[*] Approved by President Lincoln in the midst of the Civil War, the American transcontinental railroad was completed in 1869.

TWENTY-FOUR

Thursday, October 27: The Rush for the Trains

On the afternoon of Wednesday, October 26, Feo Monck went from the governor general's residence at Spencer Wood into the city. The weather had never really improved during the conference. Tuesday had been "wet as usual, very dark and damp," and there were hard frosts and icicles most nights. But even when overcast, Quebec City could be beautiful, and Feo was charmed by the sunset: "There was an extraordinary light from the setting sun on Point Lévis and the Isle of Orléans. It made them look perfectly pink. I never saw anything more beautiful and curious, as the sky was quite grey at the time."[1]

Everyone was tired: tired of the weather, tired of the hours in conference, tired of each other's company. There were no more balls and parties. Small groups of delegates were doubtless still negotiating over dinner at the Stadacona Club or walking the esplanade at the cliff's edge. But none of the diarists bothered to scribble out the details. Mercy Coles, now mostly recovered, focused on her health, her correspondence with home, and the forthcoming move to Montreal. Feo Monck had largely given up on the conference and its delegates, who were consumed by the work still to be done, and turned her interest to "Captain Pemberton, who has gone to Montreal to try and prevent his friend from marrying some girl."[2] On October 22, Edward Whelan had told his newspaper readers he still had many interesting notes to send them about the city, but he wrote only one more letter, and in it he admitted he had little of interest to tell. The division of powers issue and the financial matters had "led to the most wearisome discussions ... until one or two hours after midnight." He later excused his silence by declaring that after the bachelors' ball of October 21, "nothing further of any importance remains to be noted during the time the delegates remained in Quebec." Still the work went on. "The delegates regularly sit for ten hours a day, and not an hour is wasted in futile debates," reported *La Minerve*. "They are there alone, without access to the public and needing neither to charm audiences nor to seek the attention of the press or the voters. It is not like parliamentary debate, where time often has to be wasted. Still, they move ahead only slowly."[3] In the last days, Hewitt Bernard became even more hard pressed to keep up with the record of proceedings, and he failed to note the discussion and passage of several resolutions.

By Thursday, October 27, the end was in sight, the work nearly done. During the final week, several nagging details had been attended to piecemeal. On Tuesday, October 25, the delegates had confirmed that in the few areas where both the provinces and the new national government shared jurisdiction, federal legislation would be superior to provincial—that is, in case of a direct conflict in agriculture, immigration, or public works, provincial legislation could not countermand federal legislation. Another matter addressed that day, however, would soon spark controversy:

> The local legislature of each province may afterwards from time to time, alter the electoral districts of the provinces for the purposes of representation in the House of Commons and distribute the number of representatives to which the province is entitled in any manner such legislature shall think fit.[4]

Proposing that the provincial legislatures should define constituency boundaries for the national government seemed on the face of it like a contradiction of the principle that the federal and provincial governments would be separate, each managing its own affairs. The conference had already decided that, for the time being, voting requirements and electoral processes in each province would be applied in federal elections as well, perhaps simply to ensure that the first federal election could be held smoothly. That was only a temporary measure, until a federal parliament existed and was able and inclined to take charge of its own electoral rules. As proposed in this resolution, however, the constituency boundary rule was permanent. "Hereafter, from time to time" the provinces would be able to control and change federal constituency boundaries at will.

Within days of the completion of the conference's work, Macdonald was telling everyone he could that, on this point, Bernard's record of the Quebec Resolutions, as signed by the delegates and distributed to the provincial governments and to Britain, was not what the conference had agreed on. "In looking over our resolutions," he wrote to Premier Tupper of Nova Scotia early in November, "I see a mistake has been made. We have given power from time to time to the local legislatures to alter the constituencies sending members to the general parliament. Now this is an obvious blunder and must be corrected." It would be dangerous, he insisted, to allow provincial governments to adjust federal constituencies whenever they chose. What if a province simply eliminated the federal constituency of a member who had offended it?[5]

Some weeks later, William MacDougall wrote in his official capacity as provincial secretary of the Province of Canada that the text of the resolution as presented to the Canadian legislature had been revised, "because it was found that the resolution, as expressed in the original report, did not convey the true meaning of the conference." He reported that "communication was had with leading members of the government of the several Maritime provinces," and all had agreed to confirm federal control of federal constituencies.[6] Unfortunately, the legislatures of the different provinces found themselves debating different versions of the seventy-two resolutions, as this change had not been incorporated into the official record of the resolutions in every province, or even reviewed by every delegate. It was not a fatal error, but it raised doubts about the integrity of the process—and about the politicians who rewrote resolutions out of their own conviction that their passage had been a "blunder." Eventually the adjustment allowing the federal government, not the provinces, to fix federal constituency boundaries would be confirmed when Canadian delegates went to Britain to supervise the transformation of the resolutions into a legislative bill.

Also on Tuesday, methodically nailing down the small essential details a federal constitution required, the delegates had agreed that the power of pardon would be vested in the lieutenant-governor of each province. In the 1860s, there was, practically speaking, no right of appeal for anyone convicted of a criminal offence. Criminal trials were jury trials, and it was believed no judge should countermand what a jury had decided. As a result, the only escape from a criminal conviction was a petition to the Crown for a pardon or clemency. The conference had agreed that criminal law was a federal power, but the courts were to be administered provincially. Giving the power of clemency to the province confirmed once more that the provincial courts would govern federal as well as provincial law. To give the royal power of clemency to provincial lieutenant-governors—that is, to the cabinets that advised them—was a powerful affirmation of the stature of the provinces.

This would later become one of the relatively few resolutions approved at Quebec City that would yield to the insistence of British constitutional authorities and colonial officials. When British officials—centralists almost to a man and largely oblivious to the Canadian political realities that underpinned the federal union—examined the seventy-two resolutions, they recommend greater centralization in almost everything, but the provincialization of the pardon power seemed particularly to shock them. Pardoning wrongdoers was a matter of royal prerogative.

Though the royal power had long been exercised locally by British North American politicians, the British disliked seeing it delegated down the hierarchy to a level of government they barely acknowledged. If it were not to be vested in the Queen's British advisors, they urged, it should at least be given to the governor general of Canada, who would be advised by the Canadian cabinet but would at least be named by the British government.

The British North Americans rarely gave in to the relentless Colonial Office demands for greater centralization, and the British government usually deferred to them. On the pardoning power, however, the British persuaded the delegates who had gone to London to confirm the final terms for the British North America Act.* The colonials yielded to the imperial arguments, and accepted that the power of pardon would be held by the governor general of Canada and not by the local lieutenant-governors. It would be members of the federal cabinet who would frequently face agonizing decisions about whether to commute a judge's death sentence or to let it proceed. In 1885, when Louis Riel was about to hang, it was John A. Macdonald's government that refused to commute the sentence, despite great pressure from the province of Quebec upon the francophone ministers. Had the pardon power been in the hands of the territorial government of the Northwest, his fate would have been even more certain.

On Wednesday, October 26, in the midst of the financial debates, the delegates found time to make two decisions about federal and provincial capital cities that would have momentous consequences for the cities concerned. The provincial capitals of the Atlantic provinces would remain unchanged, but confederation required new capital cities for Canada West, Canada East, and for the new nation itself. The delegates affirmed that Ottawa, where new parliament buildings were already under construction, would become the seat of the federal capital. Toronto would be the capital of the new province that had been Canada West,

* The London Conference, when the delegates met again, is discussed in the next chapter.

and Quebec City would become the capital of the new province to succeed Canada East. The press had already made mention of these choices, so they must have been predetermined within the Canadian cabinet. The delegates passed them without any recorded discussion, and the destinies of all three cities, and of several other contenders, were permanently transformed.

Ottawa had been chosen to be the future capital of the Province of Canada in 1857, after bitter battles that pitted supporters of Toronto, Kingston, Montreal, and Quebec City against each other and often against the government. All these cities had hosted the government of the Province of Canada in turn. Each believed itself to be the natural capital of the province. Beset by these rivalries, the hard-pressed government of the day made a brief, temporary abdication of responsible government. It asked Queen Victoria—meaning in reality the British government—to make the choice that bedevilled the colonial legislature. Cartier and Macdonald, then in government, hoped that sheltering behind Queen Victoria would silence the opposition. They could safely trust that British officials, relying on their advice, would present the Canadian government's preference, Ottawa, as if it were the Queen's personal choice. This pious fraud was counterproductive in the short term. MPs from all the losing cities were furious when the "royal" preference for Ottawa was announced, and a motion regretting the Queen's choice brought down the Canadian government, though the choice of Ottawa survived. When the delegates at Quebec City had to consider a capital for the new nation they were planning, however, the choice was close to inevitable, given the need to balance the interests of Canada East and Canada West, and given the work already in progress in Ottawa. Few of the delegates meeting at the plain and cramped parliament in Quebec City had seen the construction site on the remote shores of the Ottawa River, but they had heard of the work being done, the expenditures being made, and the spectacular buildings already arising where the Rideau Canal dropped down a flight of locks to the Ottawa River.[7]

Choosing Toronto as the capital of the new province of Ontario, the delegates disappointed Kingston. Kingston and its vicinity had long been a Conservative stronghold, but Macdonald, disgusted by the fights over the capital that had hamstrung governments for years, did not fight hard for his hometown, either in 1857 or in 1864. Toronto, the province's principal city, in the heart of Reform country, became its centre of government as well. For the new province of Quebec, however, the delegates bypassed Montreal, already well on its way to becoming the economic and cultural centre of Quebec. They chose Quebec City as the centre of government for the new province. Quebec City would be spared from becoming a purely folkloric and touristic city, living on past glories. It preserved its role as a capital city, the capital of francophone North America and the new province of Quebec.

As they boldly determined the destinies of cities, the delegates flinched from choosing a name for the new country. They voted to ask the Queen "to determine the name and rank of the federated provinces." This request was probably once again slightly fraudulent. The Queen and her advisors would turn to her British North American advisors, and Canada was almost certain to be the name. In 1864, "Canada" still referred only to the Province of Canada, and the delegates from the Atlantic provinces did not consider themselves "Canadians." Canadians were the people they were negotiating with.[*] It would take time for the name of Canada, applied to the whole country, to take hold, and a pretence of deferring to the Queen's choice might quell objections. There was no plausible alternative to "Canada," though newspaper correspondents amused themselves for the next few years proposing names. Elgin, Cabotia, Borelia, Alberta, Tuponia, Laurentia, Western Britain, and Transatlantica were just a few options proposed by readers of the Toronto *Globe* in response to its reports from the Quebec Conference. In

---

[*] From the time of Jacques Cartier and long before, "Canada" had referred to the lands along the river he named St. Lawrence. "Canadian" meant, roughly, townspeople, and the corn-growing farmers then inhabiting the St. Lawrence valley did indeed live in substantial towns, including Stadacona near the site of Quebec City.

the long run, the power of Canada East and West and the undoubted preference of its representatives for "Canada" tipped the scales, with the support of British officials who were more familiar with that name than any other.[8]

The "rank," or title, of the new nation was a more vexed question, and both the Canadian cabinet and the conference delegates flinched from determining it. What was the new nation to be? There was no easy label for a colony that was no longer a colony, or for a group of provinces that were no longer merely a province. "Kingdom of Canada" was proposed during the London Conference, but the British government disapproved. It said the Americans might object to having a monarchy so close to them on the North American continent, but there was no evidence that the Americans followed the discussion at all or cared much about it. Almost certainly it was the British colonial officials themselves who objected to calling Canada a kingdom. Those still determined to preserve an imperial authority that had mostly been ceded doubtless found "kingdom" an unwarranted presumption on the part of the colonials. Those who foresaw a rapid transition to independence probably assumed that Canada would soon cease to be a monarchy. Eventually "dominion," probably the suggestion of Leonard Tilley, emerged as a plausible alternative. Ambitious British North Americans could appreciate the symbolism in the Old Testament phrase "dominion from sea even unto sea and from the river unto the ends of the earth." Imperialists appreciated the preservation of a hint of empire in the opportunity to continue including Canada in the traditional British phrase "our dominions beyond the seas."*

By Thursday, time had grown exceedingly short. The conference delegates had agreed to move to Montreal for the next day, Friday, October 28, when they would attend a military parade in their honour, followed by yet another lavish dinner and ball. Most of the delegates'

---

* In the long run, the imperial connotations prevailed, with "dominions beyond the sea" being incorporated into the monarch's title to include everything from autonomous states like Canada to the most directly ruled colonial outposts, so that "dominion" came to be associated with dependent rather than independent status.

families and some of the delegates caught the 4 P.M. train to Montreal
on Thursday. For those who stayed on, the last few hours of the conference were thinly attended and very badly recorded. "As Your Excellency
is aware," provincial secretary McDougall would write to one of the
lieutenant-governors some months later, trying to explain the errors in
the official record, "the proceedings of the conference toward the close of
its deliberations were very much hurried." Andrew Macdonald, the only
Prince Edward Islander still in Quebec City, recorded that "a number of
resolutions which had been under consideration at previous sessions
were adopted this morning and the whole read over."[9]

Among the resolutions approved by the remaining delegates were two
that directed how approval of their constitution-in-embryo would proceed.
Resolution 70 declared that

> the sanction of the Imperial and Local parliaments shall be sought for
> the union of the Provinces, on the principles adopted by the conference.

And Resolution 72 provided that

> the proceedings of the conference shall be authenticated by the signa-
> tures of the delegates, and submitted by each delegation to its own
> government, and the chairman is authorized to submit a copy to the
> governor general for transmission to the secretary of state for the
> colonies.[10]

Did the delegates consider how their constitution might one day be
amended? Apparently not. The delegates provided no amending
processes, and it seems they never discussed one. The formalities of
amendment were clear enough: the Quebec Resolutions were to become
official through an act of the Imperial parliament, so any future change
would also require British parliamentary action. Having just designed
their own constitution for the Imperial parliament to pass, the British
North Americans would not tolerate changes unless they originated in

Canada, but they set out no rules to guide the new federal parliament and the provincial legislatures in such a process. They also neglected to provide a mechanism by which the new territories they intended Canada to acquire could eventually accede to provincial status and a place in the constitution. During 1864, the British North Americans had more or less spontaneously developed a process for writing a constitution—something never before achieved in Britain or its empire. In the conference's last moments, perhaps they trusted to similar creativity from the Canadians of the future.

In these final resolutions, the delegates at Quebec were underscoring, as their final statement, that they were indeed delegates, holding no independent authority to make either constitutions or nations. As delegates of the provincial legislatures of the provinces of British North America, it was their responsibility to provide their deliberations and recommendations to the legislatures. Only the legislatures, the elected representatives of the people of each province of British North America, could lend official sanction to confederation and the constitution the delegates had drafted for it. And only the British parliament could formally make the resolutions into law. Let the legislatures adopt the principles of the Quebec Resolutions and the imperial parliament ratify them, these resolutions declared, and confederation would be made "on the principles adopted by the conference."

And then the rush was on: to vacate the parliament building, clear out of the Hotel St-Louis, and cross the river to Lévis station, where the night train for Montreal awaited. George Brown, the indefatigable correspondent who had not written to his wife for ten days—such were the pressures of business in the last half of the conference—caught the frantic mood in a scribbled note studded with exclamation marks.

> All right!!! Conference through at six o'clock this evening. Constitution adopted—a most creditable document—a complete reform of all the old abuses and injustices we have complained of!! Is it not wonderful?

~~French Canadianism~~ the old French domination entirely extinguished!*
I have only a moment to write you as I am just starting for Montreal....
They are crying to me to hurry and my baggage is gone down. There
they are again![11]

Brown managed to continue on for another three pages before running
for the carriage.

* In the manuscript letter, "French Canadianism" is crossed out and "the old French
domination" substituted.

TWENTY-FIVE

From the Quebec Resolutions to the British North America Act

Mercy Coles, her strength reviving as she and her mother boarded the Thursday train for Montreal, anticipated a renewal of festivities ahead. Still recuperating and warned not to talk, she was kept entertained throughout the trip by politicians and civil servants. Next morning at the St. Lawrence Hotel in Montreal, "an immense place," where John A. Macdonald had intervened personally to ensure her family enjoyed a premium room, she breakfasted with Mr. Tilley, and Mr. Crowther, Alexander Galt's personal secretary, came by to remind her of the dance she had promised him in Quebec City. On Friday evening, Mercy was finally able to attend Montreal's confederation ball and keep that promise. But it rained heavily in Montreal as it had in Quebec, and so the military review and fireworks planned in honour of the delegates was cancelled.[1]

The leading delegates on the overnight train reached Montreal early Friday morning. At the St. Lawrence Hotel, they renewed their conference sessions, wrapping up unfinished details, reviewing the resolutions, and affixing signatures. With that, the constitutional outline for a new nation was effectively done, and the business sessions of the Quebec Conference were over.

But the social side of the confederation project they had launched at Charlottetown and continued in Quebec City was not yet done. After a grand reception in Montreal and much speechmaking, the delegates and their party travelled on to Ottawa to visit the still-unfinished parliament buildings, now intended to serve the new nation and not just the Province of Canada. Then they continued on across Canada West to Toronto, Hamilton, and even Niagara Falls. At dinners and public meetings at every stop, they began to reveal to the public the outline of what they had done at Quebec. On November 2, in Toronto, George Brown had the privilege of summarizing the Quebec City agreement before a large crowd of enthusiastic supporters in his hometown. Great, roaring cheers greeted his proud declaration that the conference had accepted and endorsed "that so long desired, so long earnestly contended for, reform—representation by population." Equally popular with the Toronto crowd was his announcement that, with confederation, Toronto would become the capital of a new province. But he did not flinch from acknowledging—"I announce it frankly"—that, after opposing it for years as being of little benefit to Canada West, he had accepted the intercolonial railroad as a condition of union. "Without the Intercolonial Railway there could be no union of these provinces," he said, quickly adding that the great northwest, potentially the future home of many Ontarians, would also be welcomed into the union. He explained that the delegates had agreed on a federal union, "a general legislature to which should be committed matters common to all the provinces, and local governments and legislatures for the several sections, to which should be committed matters peculiar to their several localities." By committing "local matters to local control," he argued, "we will secure the peace and permanence of the new confederation much more effectually than could possibly have been hoped for from a legislative union." Then, loyal to the compromises he had accepted, he defended a strong central government in language that may have surprised some of his old followers. "There will be no danger of the two bodies coming into collision," he added optimistically. Brown even made the case for the federal upper house with its life-appointed members, declaring that making the upper house appointive would ensure that the government answered exclusively to the truly representative lower house.

Brown knew that, within days, newspapers across British North America—including his own—would publish detailed summaries of the seventy-two resolutions, and he warned that opposition to confederation was sure to erupt from those who had not participated in drafting them. "Let not gentlemen think we are past all danger. We have still to meet the legislatures of the different provinces; we have still to encounter the prejudices of the people of the different provinces, and it requires the greatest harmony of action to obtain a favourable result."[2]

The delegates planned a quick ratification for the confederation plan. All the provincial legislatures would meet early in 1865. If they each approved confederation on the Quebec terms, the British government would formally be requested to draft—with British North American guidance—a statute that would bring the new nation into being. It was soon clear that the British government was ready and willing. Immediately after the Quebec meetings, Governor General Monck had sent the Quebec resolutions to Edward Cardwell, the British secretary for the colonies. In his comments, Monck hedged a little on the delegates' firm commitment to a federal regime for the new nation, fearing that his masters remained cool to federalism. Early in December 1864, however, Cardwell's reply was full of praise for the Quebec Resolutions. The British government accepted the British North American plan as "in the deliberate judgment of those best qualified to decide on the subject, the best framework of a measure to be passed by the imperial parliament."[3]

At home in British North America, the response was hardly so welcoming. The resolutions had to be ratified by each of five provincial legislatures, and the political struggle quickly became intense in almost all of them. In Canada West, with Brown's Grits and Macdonald's Tories supporting the plan, support for ratification was certain. There were prominent politicians, including former premier John Sandfield Macdonald, who opposed the plan, and some who insisted it must be put to the electorate and not solely to the legislature—something the delegates, staunch parliamentary democrats, refused to consider.

In Canada East, opposition was more widespread and more visceral. Antoine-Aimé Dorion of the Rouges published a manifesto against confederation barely two weeks after the close of the conference. Kept out of the coalition in June 1864—and unwilling to be part of it, in any case—Dorion was uncompromisingly opposed. It was not only the Parti Rouge that stood opposed. The publication of the Quebec Resolutions initially caused alarm in many among the Roman Catholic clergy and even among Bleu supporters, who discovered how Cartier and the Bleus had abandoned positions they had declared for years were essential to French Canada's survival. The union in which Canada East held an equal share was being abandoned. French Canada would be a permanent minority in an English-majority nation. For many, the issue was not simply whether the planned federation would be too centralized or decentralized. It was the survival of French civilization in North America.

The response of Atlantic Canada quickly promised disaster for confederation and its supporters. In New Brunswick, Premier Leonard Tilley, even with a majority government and the support of key opposition leaders, could not persuade the independent-minded legislature to join him in supporting confederation. With the legislative term nearly expired, he called an election on the confederation question instead—and was overwhelmingly defeated by a wave of anti-confederate feeling across the province. In Nova Scotia, Premier Charles Tupper also led a majority government and he had the support of opposition leader Adams Archibald for the confederation project, but they too led backbenchers determined to make their own judgment. Losing more Conservative backbenchers than he could replace from Reform supporters, Tupper could not assemble a majority of legislators behind the Quebec plan. He settled on delay, and did not put the confederation plan to the legislature that year. In Prince Edward Island, Premier Gray, his confidant William Henry Pope, and Edward Whelan from the opposition continued to support federal union. But with most of the Island delegates, including George Coles, refusing to endorse confederation, with the promise of the intercolonial railroad meaning little, and with no solution to the land problem on offer, Island rejection of union was near total. Despite the work of Frederic Carter and Ambrose Shea, Newfoundland proved not at all interested in union with the distant mainland provinces, and the Quebec Resolutions were not put to the legislature.

The extent of opposition to confederation suggested that although thirty-three delegates had been cramped and crowded in the room provided them in the parliament building at Quebec, they had in fact been too few, not too many, for the task assigned them. The Quebec Conference might have benefited from a bigger room, even more delegates, and even more parties and factions. In all the provinces, opposition to confederation would be dominated by politicians and factions left out of the discussion of the federal plan. In Canada East, Dorion and the Parti Rouge stood out, but there were also leading anglophone politicians such as Christopher Dunkin and Lucius Huntington, who preferred the united Province of Canada over minority status in a new French-majority province. New Brunswick's delegation, though bipartisan, had failed to include the growing Irish-Catholic population, the Acadians, and the mercantile community of Saint John. Doubt and opposition flared up among all of them. Charles Tupper of Nova Scotia, who had come to Quebec with a delegation of lawyers, soon found that the tariff changes and the threat of Canadian competition had turned the business community of Halifax and the shipowners of Halifax, Lunenberg, and Yarmouth against him.

Opposition leader Adams Archibald remained a staunch confederation supporter but found himself dumped as leader of the Reformers, while his replacement, William Annand, organized the anti-confederation forces of Nova Scotia. Early in 1865, the anti-confederation "Botheration Letters," of Joseph Howe, the retired giant of Nova Scotian reform politics, appeared in Annand's newspaper, the *Morning Chronicle*—after Annand had fired his editor, the delegate and confederation advocate Jonathan McCully.

The debate the Canadian legislature held on the Quebec Resolutions early in 1865 demonstrated the gulf that had opened between those who participated in the closed-door debates on confederation and those who had not. Rouge leader Antoine-Aimé Dorion had indeed long been interested in a federal solution to the problems of the Province of Canada. He had worked to build alliances with George Brown's Reformers long before Cartier had. But his doubts about the motives of confederation's architects were profound. In the parliamentary debate, he accused Macdonald and Cartier of accepting Brown's federalism projects merely to retain office. "These gentlemen only found out that confederation was a panacea for all evil, a remedy for all ills, when their seats as ministers were in danger," he charged.[4] Macdonald and Cartier responded that he was the one reneging on his principles, and Dorion, acknowledging his previous interest, shot back, "I do not say that I shall be opposed to their confederation for all time to come.... I am opposed to this confederation now."[5] Dorion engaged in a long, very specific dissection of the recommendations of the Quebec Resolutions—and every point was one that had been debated intensely in the long sessions of the conference.

He began by denouncing the upper house, designed, he feared, "to restrict the control and influence of the people" by "substituting a chamber nominated by the crown." Dorion had not participated in the Quebec discussions where the reformers successfully argued for an appointive upper house, not to make it strong, but to render it weak and ceremonial, unable to challenge the authority of the more truly representative lower house. Dorion aimed his upper-house critique directly at his former allies among the Reformers of Canada West, arguing that none of them would dare take such a proposal to their supporters in an election. But it was Reformers, and particularly George Brown, who argued most effectively that appointment would strengthen the voice of the people and handcuff the upper house. Brown's fellow Reformer Alexander Mackenzie, for his part, regretted that "all the members from Lower Canada" had not "united with us and studied out a new system" instead of going into "unqualified opposition."[6]

Dorion protested that confederation would become an endless guarantee of Canadian largesse for the railroad contractors, particularly the Grand Trunk, to build railroads that would mostly benefit the Maritimers. Once again, he was taking up arguments the Canada West reformers had used before the confederation conferences, but without taking into account what the convention delegates had come to recognize: that there could be no federation without transportation links between the provinces, and that the end of internal tariffs on trade between the provinces almost surely guaranteed that the Canadians who put up the money would be well rewarded by the growth of trade between the Canadas and the Atlantic provinces.

On the vital question of federalism and the powers of the provinces, Dorion insisted that he had always supported "a real confederation, giving the largest powers to the local governments and merely a delegated authority to the general government."[7] He hammered effectively at the powers the Quebec Resolutions had given the central government. Disallowance, "which gives the general government control over all acts of the local legislature," would make it impossible for the provinces to endure, he charged, and particularly impossible for Quebec to defend the language, the legal code, and the distinct institutions of the French-Canadian people. Early in the coalition, Reformers from Canada West and Bleus such as Hector Langevin had shared these fears. In the conferences, however, they had come to accept that the compromises and balances made at Quebec would simultaneously provide for a strong central government able to build a coherent national economic space, and strong provincial governments that could defend local interests. Langevin, in his own contribution to the debate on the Quebec Resolutions, insisted that the French Canadians were "a separate people" who must control their own affairs—and made that into an argument in favour of the plan he had debated and discussed at Quebec. Dorion, not having been there, could not believe.[8]

In the Maritime provinces, opponents of the Quebec Resolutions included both advocates of legislative union, who found the central government proposed in the Quebec plan impossibly weak, and federalists, who found it impossibly centralizing. In this, they were not so different from their colleagues who had been delegates. Both provincial rights advocates—such as Edward Chandler—and strong centralists—such as Charles Tupper—had made themselves heard around the table at Quebec. The difference was that those who had participated in the long days of debate at Quebec had come to trust that the Quebec compromise was feasible, and indeed essential, a victory neither for Macdonaldian centralists nor Brownian provincial rights advocates. Those who had been outside the room, whichever side they favoured, remained full of doubt.

The commitment to submit the delegates' plan to the legislatures of British North America initially seemed a disaster for the Quebec Resolutions. Throughout the Atlantic provinces, leaders and delegates found the proposal rejected by their own legislative colleagues. Even Cartier in Canada East had not initially been certain that his usually reliable Bleu caucus would follow his lead should public opinion turn against the confederation plan. In the longer term, however, the consensus that the multi-party Quebec delegates had found proved more resilient than the doubts and protests of the anti-confederates.

Between 1864 and late 1866, the debate in the British North American provinces went on, with only the Province of Canada committed to confederation, but outside factors began to conspire against the anti-confederates. The British government, now strongly in favour of uniting the British North American provinces—and letting them take responsibility for their own affairs—had to defer to what the local legislatures would decide about confederation, but British support and British influence, both political (in the work of lieutenant-governors) and economic (in the urgings of British business leaders with colonial investments to protect) undermined the loyalty arguments some anti-confederates deployed against the new federal nation proposed at Quebec City.[9]

Events surrounding the looming Northern victory in the American Civil War also undermined those who argued confederation was unnecessary. Six weeks after the Quebec Conference, the American Confederate raiders who had attacked St. Albans, Vermont, and then fled to Canada, came to trial in Montreal. The American Union government, angry over the raids but mollified by the Canadians' proceedings against them, sought to have the Confederate raiders handed over to American justice. There was no lack of Confederate sympathy in Montreal, however, and the soldiers had excellent legal counsel, including the noted lawyer John Abbott—a future prime minister of Canada.

Abbott and his colleagues presented the Montreal magistrate, Charles-Joseph Coursol, with a flaw in the extradition treaty between Canada and the United States. To the horror of the American representatives in the courtroom in December 1864, Coursol endorsed this argument. He concluded he had no jurisdiction, and not only freed the prisoners but gave them back the money they had plundered from the banks of St. Albans. The raiders quickly vanished. In the aftermath, Magistrate Coursol, "that wretched prig of a police magistrate," in the words of John A. Macdonald, was blamed for the fiasco and actually suspended from office. He was, however, soon reinstated and eventually exonerated. Coursol was well connected: he was the son-in-law of Premier Taché and a protegé of George-Étienne Cartier, who had charge of the case as attorney general for Canada East. Cartier had travelled to Washington immediately after the Quebec Conference to pacify the American government about the St. Albans matter, but he declined to charge the raiders with violating Canadian neutrality. Since British North America was officially neutral in the American Civil War and acknowledged the Confederacy as a belligerent power, it may have been good law to refuse the extradition of the prisoners as common criminals.[10] Indeed, Cartier may have calculated that for Canada to enforce American criminal law against soldiers engaged in an act of war might actually have strengthened annexationist attitudes on both sides of the border, and that having the whole matter dropped on a technicality was a good way to make the problem disappear.[11] If so, it was a serious miscalculation.

American fury against the escape of the St. Albans raiders was enormous, and anti-Canadian sentiment surged again in the American north. The ten-year-old Canadian–American reciprocity treaty, by which many goods crossed the border duty-free, was up for renewal. After the freeing of the St. Albans prisoners, its prospects for approval by the American congress collapsed—though they had never been high, as the treaty benefited Canada more than the United States, particularly during the Civil War, when the Union army's hunger for Canadian grain and pork was enormous. Talk in British North America about the dangers of American military action against Canada surged again.

There was, however, a silver lining for the confederation cause. Fear of the United States tended to engender support for pro- rather than anti-confederation arguments. Dorion and other critics easily demonstrated that British North America would be just as vulnerable to American attack whether it comprised one government or a dozen. Still, the spectre of a large, very well-armed, and hostile power directly to the south suggested to many that the provinces had to pull together or be swept into the American orbit. That sentiment was encouraged, after the American war finally ended in 1865, by the Fenian raids. The American veterans of Irish descent who began attacking British North America in an attempt to support Irish independence were extensively infiltrated by both American and Canadian police agents, and they mounted only one substantial attack on Canada. But they made it easy for supporters of confederation to question the patriotism of those who opposed confederation while British North America was under attack.

As the confederation struggle continued in the legislatures, in the newspapers, and in elections and by-elections, the matter of trust became central. In the Canadian legislature, some of the Rouges concentrated not on the details of the Quebec Resolutions but on the accusation that, whatever the details might be, the real aim was to silence, dispossess, and assimilate the French Canadians and put an end to French and Catholic civilization in North America. "The policy of England has ever been aggressive, and its object has always been to annihilate us as a people," declared Joseph Perrault. "And this scheme of confederation is but the continued application of that policy on this continent. Its real object is nothing but the annihilation of French influence in Canada."[12] Others among the Rouges accused George-Étienne Cartier of having betrayed his country, French Canada.

Perrault, and other Rouges who followed his arguments, spoke to deep fears, and were able to show abundant justification for such fears from their long descriptions of the history of French–English conflicts in North America. But the most effective and articulate responses came from the francophone delegates who had participated in the conferences. The days and weeks they had spent with the other delegates from the provinces of British North America had indeed bred in them the kind of understanding that Edward Whelan expressed when, in the midst of the Quebec sessions, he suddenly saw why it was impossible to anglicize the French Canadians and that they would have to be accepted as they were.

There were similar charges in Atlantic Canada—declarations that the Canadians could not be trusted, and that a nefarious plot underpinned the bland language of the confederation resolutions. It was a plan from the "oily brains" of Canadians, a plot against Maritime prosperity, charged Albert Smith, a Reformer who had broken with Tilley and become a leader of the anti-confederate forces in New Brunswick. "Canadians are disloyal," declared an opposition member in Nova Scotia; Nova Scotians were the ones truly loyal to the Queen and to Britain. A fellow anti-confederate Nova Scotian, however, argued that better terms would be available from the Americans just down the seacoast. The most exotic charge of all, perhaps, came from Newfoundland, where it was declared that, with confederation, the sons of Newfoundland would all be conscripted into Canada's armies "and would leave their bones in the deserts of the west." But the doubts, accusations, and suspicions of the anti-confederates were confronted across the provinces by Quebec Conference delegates who had gotten over such fears and prejudices. They accepted the confederation compromises and argued that the other provinces might be partners as much as rivals and competitors.

In New Brunswick, the anti-confederates who had swept Leonard Tilley from office early in 1865 all shared a distrust of the Quebec Resolutions, but some of them saw that the solution was a true legislative union, while others insisted on stronger provincial rights. The government led by Albert Smith fell apart as it confronted the very issue that the delegates at Quebec had wrestled with: the balancing of local and national authority. When another election was held in the spring of 1866, the confederates won an even more decisive victory than their rivals had the year before. In Nova Scotia, there was no election, but there too the supporters of confederation in the Conservative and the Reform parties began to occupy the moderate middle ground. By 1866, a substantial majority of the Nova Scotian legislators agreed to support a union. Both Nova Scotia and New Brunswick passed resolutions leaving open the possibility of "better terms" than those offered by the Quebec Resolutions. But both agreed to empower delegates to travel to Britain and negotiate the best terms they could, and the Canadian parliament had already made it clear that it could accept only minor changes to the principles of the Quebec Resolutions.

In the fall of 1866, therefore, with Prince Edward Island and Newfoundland still rejecting confederation, delegations from Canada, New Brunswick, and Nova Scotia travelled to Britain. At the London Conference, they reviewed changes to the Quebec plan and oversaw the work of the British parliamentary draftsmen who took the language of the seventy-two Quebec Resolutions and turned them into a parliamentary bill, the British North America Act of 1867.

TWENTY-SIX

Brown, Cartier, Macdonald: Who Should Lead the Confederation?

"The great reason why I have been able to beat Brown," wrote Prime Minister John A. Macdonald a few years after confederation, "is that I have been able to look a little ahead, while he could on no occasion forego the temptation of a temporary triumph."[1] This is one of the vivid Macdonald aphorisms of which the reverse seems to be at least as true. Of the two men, Macdonald was the supremely flexible politician, skilled at reading trends of popularity and politics and adjusting his course in order to keep himself close to power and able to influence events. Macdonald built his successful forty-five-year political career on a long succession of temporary triumphs. Brown, by comparison, was a stubborn man and a less adroit politician. He had a handful of policies that he stuck to through thick and thin, popular or unpopular. As a result, he was frequently out of power for long stretches, defending unpopular ideas and derided, not least by Macdonald, as a "political impossibility" for his refusal to adapt.

Brown had committed himself to representation by population in the early 1850s, when the policy condemned him not only to the margins of power but to accusations of being a bigot and a francophobe, "brought out here from Scotland" in the words of one of his many enemies in Canada East "to cast the flaming torch of discord between the two populations and to inflame them one against the other."[2] Similarly, by committing himself wholeheartedly to federalism in 1859, Brown had condemned himself to five more years in the political wilderness, seeking to revive a policy that had been an impractical dream for decades, if not generations. In August 1864, after chairing one of the Canadian cabinet sessions on confederation policy, he wrote to his wife about the satisfaction of seeing his long-held ideas about federalism and rep by pop finally achieving the success to which he had looked forward throughout his years of failure:

> For perhaps the first time in my political life I indulged in a regular chuckle of gratified pride (no higher sentiment) at the thought of my presiding over such a discussion by such men, there not being one man at the table who had not openly derided the idea of such a scene ever occurring in our lifetime. I could not help recalling many furious scenes in which several of those around me had bitterly denounced me for even proposing the consideration of the very subject they were then engaged in settling under my presidency![3]

Many politicians speak of their desire to retire from the struggle, but Brown may have been more sincere than most when he wrote to Anne Brown again in November 1864. He described "great times" in Toronto, when he had the honour of leading the speakers in "the first time that the confederation scheme was really laid open to the public." He predicted that "there is a good chance of carrying it." He then concluded, "At any rate, come what may, I can now get out of the affair and out of public life with honour."[4] A few months later, with the Quebec Resolutions being approved by the Canadian legislature, he repeated his insistence that these great events—"for great they are, and history will tell the tale of them"—would not tempt him to remain in office. "On the contrary, every day makes me more anxious to get quit of politics forever."[5]

As he saw the successful achievement of confederation approaching, Brown became ready to abandon the perks of office and quit the government coalition he had reluctantly entered. He contended that the coalition had been formed solely to present the confederation project. With that measure accomplished, he wanted to return as soon as possible to the normal state of party rivalry between his Reform friends and their Conservative rivals. During and after the Quebec Conference, he noted potential allies among the Reformers of the Maritime provinces: Leonard Tilley of New Brunswick, Adams Archibald of Nova Scotia, and perhaps George Coles and Andrew Macdonald of Prince Edward Island. Should confederation succeed and become accepted in French Canada, he saw, the Reformers of Canada West might even renew their old alliance with Antoine-Aimé Dorion and the Rouges. To this end, Brown resigned from the coalition government in December 1865. He did not even attend the conference in London where the Quebec Resolutions were translated into a parliamentary act.[6] To his regret, however, not all his party supporters left office with him. Both William McDougall, a fellow Reformer but not close to Brown, and William Howland, who had succeeded Oliver Mowat in the cabinet when Mowat became a judge, preferred to retain their cabinet seats, even though an increasingly Conservative government happily used them to retain the mantle of the great confederation coalition.

George Brown lacked the political suppleness, probably, that a successful Canadian leader required. In the Quebec Conference, he seems to have annoyed or alienated potential supporters on several occasions. He did not succeed in the alliance building that would have been necessary to have forged a Reform-centred alliance, and seemed almost unwilling to try. His friend and ally Alexander Mackenzie was eager to rebuild ties to the Rouges as the beginning of a strong national Reform Party, but Brown wanted out. He agreed to run in the first election for the new national parliament, but would serve no longer—and in fact was defeated, so that he never served in the Ottawa parliament buildings. Even in the first few months of confederation there were rumours that Macdonald's government would collapse and Brown would be sent for, but Brown was no longer awaiting the call. Despite all the honours and appointments Canada could offer, he said he would rather be editor of *The Globe*: "Party leadership and the conducting of a great journal don't harmonize."[7]

On February 27, 1865, during the Canadian parliament's debate on the Quebec Resolutions, Christopher Dunkin, an erudite lawyer from the Eastern Townships and a confederation skeptic, was pointing out to the Canadian legislature just how difficult it would be to assemble a united cabinet for the new confederation, considering all the different regional, economic, and cultural interests that would have to be represented. The skills of "the cleverest politician" would be required simply to form a government, he said. If that talented man could hold a cabinet together a year or two, he ought to go to Britain and teach the political alphabet to Prime Minister Palmerston, who would be an amateur by comparison. Who could possibly build and maintain a cabinet representing "so many sections" in the new confederation?

George-Étienne Cartier instantly took up the challenge, claiming, "There will be no difficulty."

"The Hon. gentleman never sees a difficulty in anything he is going to do," Dunkin shot back.

"And I have been generally correct in that. I have been pretty successful," responded Cartier.

"The Hon. Attorney General East probably thinks he will be able to do it," Dunkin taunted a little later in his outline of all the obstacles that would arise.

"I have no doubt I can," replied Cartier. "I do feel equal to the work of forming an executive council that will be satisfactory to Upper and Lower Canada as well as to the lower provinces."[8]

In February 1865, Cartier was thinking of himself, speaking of himself, as the future prime minister of Canada, the man who would be choosing cabinet ministers. He had reason to. He had long experience in politics and had been hugely successful. He led the largest bloc of politicians in the Province of Canada, and he was working amiably with George Brown, who led the second-largest bloc but was planning and promising to withdraw from political leadership. Cartier had been among the first to see the potential in the union of all the British North American provinces on a federal basis: protection for French Canada's vital interests, as well as the makings of national greatness and economic expansion. To achieve federation, Cartier had abandoned the political arrangements French Canada had relied on since the 1840s. Despite that, he was confidently expecting to see the Quebec Resolutions approved, not only by his loyal Bleu caucus but by some of the opposition Rouges as well, with the support of most of the Catholic clergy, many of the leading newspapers, and probably a solid majority of Canada East voters as well. He fully intended to remain in national politics, and was bold enough already to be talking of the large, ambitious, and risky national projects about which John A. Macdonald was temperamentally cautious: expansion into the west, trade links that would span the continent, a vast new economic empire for Montreal. Cartier was confident he had the strategic vision for a confederated Canada.

In the end, Cartier lost out on his ambition to lead the new nation. On July 1, 1867, John A. Macdonald became prime minister of Canada, with the task of forming the cabinet over which Cartier and Dunkin had sparred. Cartier became minister of militia and defence. In truth, he was nearly co-premier, with a free hand on many matters. He would take the lead on the acquisition of the Northwest Territories from the Hudson's Bay Company and the admittance of British Columbia into confederation in 1871, and he first proposed Canada's commitment to build a railroad to the Pacific Ocean. By that time, he was already weak with the kidney disease that killed him in 1873, when he was not yet fifty-nine. He never had the opportunity to be first among equals.

He tried, surely. There was that bold reply to Dunkin during the confederation debate. At that time, Cartier was working closely and well with George Brown, his old enemy. Premier Étienne Taché had already suffered the first of the health breakdowns that would kill him in June 1865, and there may have been quiet discussions about forming a Cartier–Brown ministry to link the two strongest parties in the government.[9] In the end, however, another figurehead prime minister, Narcisse Belleau, succeeded Taché—Brown, Cartier, and Macdonald having in effect vetoed each other's leadership again. Belleau held the prime ministership until he became first lieutenant-governor of the new province of Quebec on July 1, 1867.

Cartier seems to have continued to contend for the leadership, even during the London Conference of late 1866 and early 1867. Cartier's deputy, Hector Langevin, described himself working grimly to prevent any alliance of English-Canadian delegates and British officials that might try to dilute the Quebec Resolutions or erode the guarantees Langevin believed had been secured for French Canada. Langevin—in his own words, "growling" and "biting" to protect the draft bill—began to resent how rarely Cartier was sitting alongside him in the conference room fighting the battle for French Canada. Cartier, he and Alexander Galt told each other, was devoting himself "so much to society that we do not get much work out of him." Premier Belleau heard that Cartier was spending every evening among "the dukes, lords, MPs, countesses, duchesses, and marquesses."[10]

Cartier cannot have been merely socializing, not at this critical juncture when the language of the Canadian constitution was being finalized in constant revisions by the British parliamentary draftsman and the Canadian delegates. The dukes, lords, and ladies would not take an interest in the detailed language of the bill. They would hardly even influence its chances of being passed in the British Commons and

Lords, since the strong support of the British government and most parliamentarians made that a virtual certainty. These men and women from the high society around Westminster, however, might be able to influence who came to be preferred and promoted by the British establishment, and even the Queen, as the leader of the new confederation. But if such was Cartier's aim when he abandoned his fellow Bleu delegates to haunt the salons of London, he was surely too late. There was another contender for the leadership of the new confederation, and Cartier was up against a master.

John A. Macdonald may have failed to appreciate the blossoming of support for confederation in the spring of 1864, but when the movement took hold in the Canadian legislature and cabinet and particularly after it prospered at Charlottetown and Quebec, he seized every temporary triumph available to put himself close to the direction of the movement. He accepted federalism, while continuing to urge the necessity for strong central government. He quickly secured agreement that including the Maritime provinces (and not merely "federalizing" the Province of Canada) would be the Canadian coalition's first object. He worked intensely at the conference planning, talked skillfully and persuasively in the conferences, and lobbied tirelessly and effectively in the backrooms as well as at every social occasion.

He fought hard for his advantages. He got his friend and secretary to keep the minutes of the conference. He moved Oliver Mowat, "in all respects the very man Mr. Brown most needed as an adviser," out of the conferences and into a judgeship.[11] When he saw the developing alliance between Cartier and Brown in 1865, he helped encourage the quarrels that led to Brown's resignation from the government—to Cartier's regret—and still managed to keep Brown's more pliable fellow Reformers in the coalition. He worked to set himself slightly apart from his allies as well. At the London Conference, with Prime Minister Belleau back in Canada, he assumed the chair of the delegates' sessions, though Cartier growled that only the accident of Macdonald having been an MP and a cabinet minister slightly earlier than Cartier enabled him to claim the leadership. Finally, with confederation confirmed, he accepted the offer of the prime ministership from Governor General Monck, who told him there would be no more joint premierships as in the Province of Canada. On the eve of July 1, 1867, when Lord Monck bestowed a knighthood on him, while giving lesser honours to all the other makers of confederation, Cartier and Alexander Galt were furious and declined the decorations offered them.* Macdonald blandly declared he had to accept, and though Galt joined Macdonald's first cabinet as minister of finance, he resigned within months, bitter over his belief that Macdonald had betrayed him in a banking crisis. After confederation, only Cartier among Macdonald's potential rivals for leadership retained power and independent authority within the cabinet, but he soon became ill. After his death, Macdonald would be unchallenged for twenty years.

Hector Langevin, for all his suspicions of Macdonald's centralizing ambitions, described John A. Macdonald at London as "the man" of the conference, elegant, persuasive, and popular. A British deputy minister who observed Macdonald was greatly impressed with his powers of management and adroitness, and thought him the "ruling genius" among the delegates. He was certainly the British choice as leader of the new Canadian confederation. They admired his abundant political and administrative skills. They shared his commitment to strong central government for the new nation. They appreciated his carefully deferential manner toward British authorities, and were confident he was a supporter of empire who would restrain impulsive movements toward Canadian independence. He had become the overwhelming favourite of the British, and he would continue to play the imperial card skillfully as long as he held office.

It was not up to the British to impose a prime minister, of course.

---

* Brown, offered nothing, wrote, "I don't care one straw for a ribbon or a title as a Canadian, which I always expect and wish to be," and indeed he declined later offers of honours and titles.

Lord Monck invited Macdonald to assemble a cabinet and become the first prime minister of the new nation, but his choice was determined by what he calculated the politicians would accept. Macdonald had done the work to build the broadest possible network of supporters. Cartier retained the support of the Bleus, but Macdonald had secured the loyalty of McDougall and Howland (who had refused to resign with Brown), and built strong alliances with Charles Tupper, Leonard Tilley, and other leaders of the Maritimers who would soon be represented in the new House of Commons and cabinet.

Simply by being a French Canadian, George-Étienne Cartier was almost fatally handicapped in any competition with Macdonald for support among the British. No matter how vigorously he insisted that as a French Canadian he was the equal of every other British subject, and no matter how he worked his persuasive charms on British politicians and hostesses, he would always have his French "race" (people of the mid-nineteenth century spoke of race as we might of ethnicity) held up against him. Not only by the British. Two decades later, when the Liberal Party of Canada chose Wilfrid Laurier as its leader, Laurier himself accepted the job very reluctantly. Even in 1887, Laurier was convinced that English Canada would never accept a French Canadian as prime minister, and when he left office in 1911 predictions were made that there would never be another.

The British surely favoured Macdonald, but they would have deferred to the British North Americans if they had insisted on another candidate. By 1867, Macdonald's support was spread very widely. The man who had insisted in 1864 that only a legislative union could serve Canada's needs had become by 1867 the inevitable man for the new confederation. "Until confederation, I never knew what it meant to govern," Macdonald once said, and from 1867 until the end of his life in 1891, he did wield a profound impact on how the British North America Act was interpreted and understood. It may not have been Macdonald's constitution in 1867, but increasingly it became so during his decades in office. As prime minister, Macdonald was able to declare the meaning of confederation without the contrary voices that had made themselves heard in the cabinet of the Great Coalition and deliberations of the Quebec Conference.

In February and March 1868, already surpassed and sidelined by Macdonald but not entirely resigned to that situation, Cartier renewed his correspondence with George Brown, sharing views of how confederation had been achieved. Brown opened the discussion: "Lower Canada was the difficulty in the way, and you were the only man in Lower Canada who, when the crisis arrived, had the pluck and the influence to take the bull by the horns. You ran the risk of political death by the bold course you took. Mr. Macdonald ran no risk whatsoever." Cartier responded with similar compliments. He endorsed Brown's declaration that his own fifteen-year struggle for constitutional reform "won the battle," and even suggested that Brown ought to be back in the House of Commons, "where some difficulty might spring up before long and your presence in the House might be so useful." Cartier, though a senior member of the Macdonald cabinet, seems still to have had in mind a Cartier–Brown or Brown–Cartier alternative.[12]

Brown declined all interest, and the suggestion remained within their private correspondence. Brown and Cartier, however, might have agreed that while Macdonald got to rule on the cases, it was to a significant degree they who had made the rules. In the spring and summer of 1864, the Cartier–Brown alliance was based on a federal vision of British North America. Despite Macdonald's strong preference, they had embedded a federal principle in the constitution that he was obliged to accept and that has shaped Canada ever since.

After the Conference: What Became of Them All?

George Brown

George Brown lost an election in 1867 and never sat in the Canadian House of Commons. He was later appointed to the Senate of Canada, but he preferred being publisher of *The Globe*, husband to Anne, and father to Maggie. He died in 1880, after being shot by a disgruntled employee. Anne Brown, Maggie, and their other children all eventually returned to Scotland, where Anne died in 1906.

George-Étienne Cartier

George-Étienne Cartier served in John A. Macdonald's cabinet from 1867 until his death in 1873. He was honoured with a baronetcy in 1869.

George Coles

Mercy Anne Coles's father opposed confederation in 1865 and the anti-confederate movement carried him back to the premier's office.

He developed a mental illness soon afterwards, had to retire from politics, and died in an asylum in 1875.

Mercy Anne Coles

Mercy Anne Coles never found a husband at the confederation conferences. When they ended, she travelled though the United States with her parents. She never married, and spent the rest of her life in Charlottetown, where she died in 1921.

John A. Macdonald

John A. Macdonald was prime minister of Canada from 1867 to 1873 and from 1878 until his death on June 6, 1891, at the age of seventy-six.

Charles Monck

Viscount Monck, the last governor general of British North America, was also the first governor general of Canada. He retired from that office in 1868 and returned to his large but debt-burdened estates in Ireland.

Frances ("Feo") Monck

Feo Monck enjoyed her year in North America, but returned happily to Ireland in the spring of 1865 and never returned to Canada.

Oliver Mowat

In 1872, Oliver Mowat left the judgeship he received in 1864 and became premier of Ontario. He never lost a provincial election and remained premier until 1896, when he joined Wilfrid Laurier's cabinet in Ottawa. At his death in 1903, he was lieutenant-governor of the province.

Leonard Tilley

Leonard Tilley, a Reformer in New Brunswick politics, remained in the confederation coalition and became a cabinet minister in John A. Macdonald's Conservative governments. As finance minister, he introduced the national policy of tariff protection and struggled to finance the Canadian Pacific Railway.

Charles Tupper

Charles Tupper moved from provincial to federal politics in 1867. A close ally of Macdonald's, he eventually succeeded him as prime minister. The last survivor of the delegates to the Quebec Conference, he died in Britain in 1915.

Edward Whelan

Edward Whelan continued to support confederation, and lost his seat in the Prince Edward Island legislature in 1867. He died suddenly the same year, just forty-four years of age.

APPENDIX:
The Quebec Resolutions[1]

1. The best interests and present and future prosperity of British North America will be promoted by a Federal Union under the Crown of Great Britain, provided such Union can be effected on principles just to the several Provinces.

2. In the Federation of the British North American Provinces, the system of Government best adapted under existing circumstances to protect the diversified interest of the several Provinces, and secure efficiency, harmony and permanency in the working of the Union, would be a general Government, charged with matters of common interest to the whole country; and Local Governments for each of the Canadas, and for the Provinces of Nova Scotia, New Brunswick and Prince Edward Island, charged with the control of local matters in their respective sections. Provision being made for the admission into the Union, on equitable terms, of Newfoundland, the North-West Territory, British Columbia and Vancouver.

3. In framing a Constitution for the General Government, the Conference, with a view to the perpetuation of our connection with the Mother Country, and to the promotion of the best interests of the people of these Provinces, desire to follow the model of the British Constitution, so far as our circumstances will permit.

4. The Executive Authority or Government shall be vested in the Sovereign of the United Kingdom of Great Britain and Ireland, and be administered according to the well-understood principles of the British Constitution, by the Sovereign personally, or by the Representative of the Sovereign duly authorized.

5. The Sovereign or Representative of the Sovereign shall be Commander-in-Chief of the Land and Naval Militia Forces.

6. There shall be a General Legislature or Parliament for the Federated Provinces, composed of a Legislative Council and a House of Commons.

7. For the purpose of forming the Legislative Council, the Federated Provinces shall be considered as consisting of three divisions: 1st Upper Canada, 2nd Lower Canada, 3rd Nova Scotia, New Brunswick and Prince Edward Island; each division with an equal representation in the Legislative Council.

8. Upper Canada shall be represented in the Legislative Council by 24 members, Lower Canada by 24 members, and the 3 Maritime Provinces by 24 members, of which Nova Scotia shall have 10, New Brunswick 10, and Prince Edward Island 4 members.

9. The colony of Newfoundland shall be entitled to enter the proposed Union, with a representation in the Legislative Council of 4 members.

10. The North-West Territory, British Columbia and Vancouver shall be admitted into the Union on such terms and conditions as the Parliament of the Federated Provinces shall deem equitable, and as shall receive the assent of Her Majesty; and in the case of the Province of British Columbia or Vancouver, as shall be agreed to by the Legislature of such Province.

11. The members of the Legislative Council shall be appointed by the Crown under the Great Seal of the General Government, and shall hold office during life: if any Legislative Councillor shall, for two consecutive sessions of Parliament, fail to give his attendance in the said Council, his seat shall thereby become vacant.

12. The members of the Legislative Council shall be British subjects by birth or naturalization, of the full age of thirty years, shall possess a continuous real property qualification of four thousand dollars over and above all incumbrances, and shall be and continue worth that sum over and above their debts and liabilities, but in the case of Newfoundland and Prince Edward Island, the property may be either real or personal.

13. If any question shall arise as to the qualification of a Legislative Councillor, the same shall be determined by the Council.

14. The first selection of the Members of the Legislative Council shall be made, except as regards Prince Edward Island, from the Legislative Councils of the various Provinces, so far as a sufficient number be found qualified and willing to serve; such Members shall be appointed by the Crown at the recommendation of the General Executive Government, upon the nomination of the respective Local Governments, and in such nomination due regard shall be had to the claims of the Members of the Legislative Council of the Opposition in each Province, so that all political parties may as nearly as possible be fairly represented.

15. The Speaker of the Legislative Council (unless otherwise provided by Parliament) shall be appointed by the Crown from among the Members of the Legislative Council, and shall hold office during pleasure, and shall only be entitled to a casting vote on an equality of votes.

16. Each of the twenty-four Legislative Councillors representing Lower Canada in the Legislative Council of the General Legislature, shall be appointed to represent one of the twenty-four Electoral Divisions mentioned in Schedule A of Chapter first of the Consolidated Statutes of Canada, and such Councillor shall reside or possess his qualification in the Division he is appointed to represent.

17. The basis of Representation in the House of Commons shall be Population, as determined by the Official Census every ten years; and the number of Members at first shall be 194, distributed as follows:

Upper Canada	82
Lower Canada	65
Nova Scotia	19
New Brunswick	15
Newfoundland	8
Prince Edward Island	5

18. Until the Official Census of 1871 has been made up, there shall be no change in the number of Representatives from the several sections.

19. Immediately after the completion of the Census of 1871, and immediately after every Decennial Census thereafter, the Representation from each section in the House of Commons shall be re-adjusted on the basis of Population.

20. For the purpose of such re-adjustments, Lower Canada shall always be assigned sixty-five members, and each of the other sections shall at each re-adjustment receive, for the ten years then next succeeding, the number of Members to which it will be entitled on the same ratio of representation to population as Lower Canada will enjoy according to the Census last taken by having sixty-five Members.

21. No reduction shall be made in the number of Members returned by any section, unless its population shall have decreased, relatively to the population of the whole Union, to the extent of five per centum.

22. In computing at each decennial period the number of Members to which each section is entitled, no fractional parts shall be considered, unless when exceeding one-half the number entitling to a Member, in which case a Member shall be given for each such fractional part.

23. The Legislature of each Province shall divide such Province into the proper number of constituencies, and define the boundaries of each of them.

24. The Local Legislature of each Province may, from time to time, alter the Electoral Districts for the purposes of Representation in such Local Legislature, and distribute the Representatives to which the Province is entitled in such Local Legislature, in any manner such Legislature may see fit.

25. The number of Members may at any time be increased by the general Parliament,—regard being had to the proportionate rights then existing.

26. Until provisions are made by the General Parliament, all the laws which, at the date of the Proclamation constituting the Union, are in force in the Provinces respectively, relating the qualification and disqualification of any person to be elected, or to sit or vote as a Member of the Assembly in the said Provinces respec-tively; and relating to the qualification or disqualification of voters and to the oaths to be taken by voters, and to Returning Officers and their powers and duties,—and relating to the proceedings at Elections,—and to the period during which such elections may be continued,—and relating to the Trial of Controverted Elections, and the proceedings incident thereto, and relating to the vacating of seats of Members, and to the issuing and execution of new Writs, in case of any seat being vacated otherwise than by a dissolution—shall respectively apply to Elections of Members to serve in the House of Commons, for places situate in those Provinces respectively.

27. Every House of Commons shall continue for five years from the day of the return of the writs choosing the same, and no longer; subject, nevertheless, to be sooner prorogued or dissolved by the Governor.

28. There shall be a Session of the General Parliament once, at least, in every year, so that a period of twelve calendar months shall not intervene between the last sitting of the General parliament in one Session, and the first sitting thereof in the next Session.

29. The General Parliament shall have power to make Laws for the peace, welfare and good government of the Federated Provinces (saving the Sovereignty of England), and especially laws respecting the following subjects:

1. The Public Debt and Property.

2. The Regulation of Trade and Commerce.

3. The imposition or regulation of Duties of Customs on Imports and Exports,—except on Exports of Timber, Logs, Masts, Spars, Deals and Sawn Lumber from New Brunswick, and of Coal and other minerals from Nova Scotia.

4. The imposition or regulation of Excise Duties.

5. The raising of money by all or any other modes or systems of Taxation.

6. The borrowing of money on the Public Credit.

7. Postal Service.

8. Lines of Steam or other Ships, Railways, Canals and other works, connecting any two or more of the Provinces together or extending beyond the limits of any Province.

9. Lines of Steamships between the Federated Provinces and other Countries.

10. Telegraphic Communication and the Incorporation of Telegraph Companies.

11. All such works as shall, although lying wholly within any Province be specially declared by the Acts authorizing them to be for the general advantage.

12. The Census.

13. Militia—Military and Naval Service and Defence.

14. Beacons, Buoys and Light Houses.

15. Navigation and shipping.

16. Quarantine.

17. Sea Coast and Inland Fisheries.

18. Ferries between any Province and a Foreign country, or between any two Provinces.

19. Currency and Coinage.

20. Banking—Incorporation of Banks, and the Issue of paper money.

21. Savings Banks.

22. Weights and Measures.

23. Bills of Exchange and Promissory Notes.

24. Interest.

25. Legal Tender.

26. Bankruptcy and Insolvency.

27. Patents of Invention and Discovery.

28. Copy Rights.

29. Indians and Lands reserved for the Indians.

30. Naturalization and Aliens.

31. Marriage and Divorce.

32. The Criminal Law, excepting the Constitution of Courts of Criminal Jurisdiction, but including the procedure in Criminal matters.

33. Rendering uniform all or any of the laws relative to property and civil rights in Upper Canada, Nova Scotia, New Brunswick, Newfoundland and Prince Edward Island, and rendering uniform the procedure of all or any of the Courts in these Provinces; but any Statute for this purpose shall have no force or authority in any Province until sanctioned by the Legislature thereof.

34. The Establishment of a General Court of Appeal for the Federated Provinces.

35. Immigration.

36. Agriculture.

37. And generally respecting all matters of a general character, not specially and exclusively reserved for the Local Governments and Legislatures.

30. The General Government and Parliament shall have all powers necessary or proper for performing the obligations of the Federated Provinces, as part of the British Empire, to Foreign Countries arising under Treaties between Great Britain and such Countries.

31. The General Parliament may also, from time to time, establish additional Courts, and the General Government may appoint Judges and Officers thereof, when the same shall appear necessary or for the public advantage, in order to the due execution of the laws of Parliament.

32. All Courts, Judges and Officers of the several Provinces shall aid, assist and obey the General Government in the exercises of its rights and powers, and for such purposes shall be held to be Courts, Judges and Officers of the General Government.

33. The General Government shall appoint and pay the Judges of the Superior Courts in each Province, and of the County Courts in Upper Canada, and Parliament shall fix their salaries.

34. Until the Consolidation of the Laws of Upper Canada, New Brunswick, Nova Scotia, Newfoundland and Prince Edward Island, the Judges of these Provinces appointed by the General Government shall be selected from their respective Bars.

35. The Judges of the Courts of Lower Canada shall be selected from the Bar of Lower Canada.

36. The Judges of the Court of Admiralty now receiving salaries shall be paid by the General Government.

37. The Judges of the Superior Courts shall hold their offices during good behaviour, and shall be removable only on the Address of both Houses of Parliament.

38. For each of the Provinces there shall be an Executive Officer, styled the Lieutenant Governor, who shall be appointed by the Governor General in Council, under the Great Seal of the Federated Provinces, during pleasure: such pleasure not to be exercised before the expiration of the first five years except for cause: such cause to be communicated in writing to the Lieutenant Governor immediately after the exercise of the pleasure as aforesaid, and also by Message to both Houses of Parliament, within the first week of the first Session afterwards.

39. The Lieutenant Governor of each Province shall be paid by the General Government.

40. In undertaking to pay the salaries of the Lieutenant Governors, the Conference does not desire to prejudice the claim of Prince Edward Island upon the Imperial Government for the amount now paid for the salary of the Lieutenant Governor thereof.

41. The Local Government and Legislature of each Province shall be constructed in such manner as the existing Legislature of each Province shall provide.

42. The Local Legislature shall have power to alter or amend their consitution from time to time.

43. The Local Legislature shall have power to make laws respecting the following subjects:

    1. Direct taxation, and in New Brunswick the imposition of duties on the Export of Timber, Logs, Masts, Spars, Deals and Sawn Lumber; and in Nova Scotia, of Coal and other minerals.

    2. Borrowing money on the credit of the Province.

    3. The establishment and tenure of local offices, and the appointment and payment of local officers.

    4. Agriculture.

    5. Immigration.

    6. Education; saving the rights and privileges which the Protestant or Catholic minority in both Canadas may possess as to their Denominational Schools, at the time when the Union goes into operation.

    7. The sale and management of Public Lands excepting Lands belonging to the General Government.

    8. Sea Coast and Inland Fisheries.

    9. The establishment, maintenance and management of Penitentiaries, and of Public and Reformatory Prisons.

    10. The establishment, maintenance and management of Hospitals, Asylums, Charities, and Eleemosynary Institutions.

    11. Municipal Institutions.

    12. Shop, Saloon, Tavern, Auctioner and other Licences.

    13. Local Works.

    14. The Incorporation of Private or Local Companies, except such as relate to matters assigned to the General Parliament.

    15. Property and civil rights, excepting those portions thereof assigned to the General Parliament.

    16. Inflicting punishment by fine, penalties, imprisonment or otherwise, for the breach of laws passed in relation to any subject within their jurisdiction.

    17. The Administration of Justice, including the Constitution, maintenance and organization of the Courts,—both of Civil and Criminal Jurisdiction, and including also the Procedure in Civil matters.

    18. And generally all matters of a private or local nature, not assigned to the General Parliament.

44. The power or respiting, reprieving, and pardoning Prisoners convicted of crimes, and of commuting and remitting of sentences in whole or in part, which belongs of right to the Crown, shall be administered by the Lieutenant Governor of each Province in Council, subject to any instructions he may, from time to time, receive from the General Government, and subject to any provisions that may be made in this behalf by the General Parliament.

45. In regard to all subjects over which jurisdiction belongs to both the General and Local Legislatures, the laws of the General Parliament shall control and supersede those made by the Local Legislature, and the latter shall be void so far as they are repugnant to, or inconsistent with, the former.

46. Both the English and French languages may be employed in the General Parliament and in its proceedings, and in the Local Legislature of Lower Canada, and also in the Federal Courts and in the Courts of Lower Canada.

47. No lands or property belonging to the General or Local Governments shall be liable to taxation.

48. All Bills for appropriating any part of the Public Revenue, or for imposing any new Tax or Impost, shall originate in the House of Commons or House of Assembly, as the case may be.

49. The House of Commons or House of Assembly shall not originate or pass any Vote, Resolution, Address or Bill for the appropriation of any part of the Public Revenue, or of any Tax or Impost to any purpose, not first recommended by Message of the Governor General or the Lieutenant Governor, as the case may be, during the Session in which such Vote, Resolution, Address or Bill is passed.

50. Any Bill of the General Parliament may be reserved in the usual manner for Her Majesty's Assent, and any Bill of the Local Legislature may, in like manner, be reserved for the consideration of the Governor General.

51. Any Bill passed by the General Parliament shall be subject to disallowance by Her Majesty within two years, as in the case of Bills passed by the Legislatures of the said Provinces hitherto; and, in like manner, any Bill passed by a Local Legislature shall be subject to disallowance by the Governor General within one year after the passing thereof.

52. The Seat of Government of the Federated Provinces shall be Ottawa, subject to the Royal Prerogative.

53. Subject to any future action of the respective Local Governments, the Seat of the Local Government in Upper Canada shall be Toronto; of Lower Canada, Quebec; and the Seats of the Local Governments in the other Provinces shall be as at present.

54. All Stocks, Cash, Bankers' Balances and Securities for money belonging to each Province at the time of the Union, except as hereinafter mentioned, shall belong to the General Government.

55. The following Public Works and Property of each Province shall belong to the General Government, to wit:—

    1. Canals.
    2. Public Harbours.

3. Light Houses and Piers.

4. Steamboats, Dredges and Public Vessels.

5. River and Lake Improvements.

6. Railways and Railway Stocks, Mortgages and other debts due by Railway Companies.

7. Military Roads.

8. Custom Houses, Post Offices and other Public Buildings, except such as may be set aside by the General Government for the use of the Local Legislatures and Governments.

9. Property transferred by the Imperial Government and known as Ordnance Property.

10. Armories, Drill Sheds, Military Clothing and Munitions or War; and

11. Lands set apart for public purposes.

56. All lands, mines, minerals and royalties vested in Her Majesty in the Provinces of Upper Canada, Lower Canada, Nova Scotia, New Brunswick and Prince Edward Island, for the use of such Provinces, shall belong to the Local Government of the territory in which the same are so situate; subject to any trusts that may exist in respect to any of such lands or to any interest of other persons in respect of the same.

57. All sums due from purchasers or lessees of such lands, mines or minerals at the time of the Union, shall also belong to the Local Governments.

58. All assets connected with such portions of the public debt of any Province as are assumed by the Local Governments shall also belong to those Governments respectively.

59. The several Provinces shall retain all other Public Property therein, subject to the right of the General Government to assume any Lands or Public Property required for Fortifications or the Defence of the Country.

60. The General Government shall assume all the Debts and Liabilities of each Province.

61. The Debt of Canada, not specially assumed by Upper and Lower Canada respectively, shall not exceed, at the time of the Union, $62,500,000; Nova Scotia shall enter the Union with a debt not exceeding $8,000,000; and New Brunswick with a debt not exceeding $7,000,000.

62. In case Nova Scotia or New Brunswick do not incur liabilities beyond those for which their Governments are now bound, and which shall make their debts at the date of Union less than $8,000,000 and $7,000,000 respectively, they shall be entitled to interest at five per cent on the amount not so incurred, in like manner as in hereinafter provided for Newfoundland and Prince Edward Island; the foregoing resolution being in no respect intended to limit the powers given to the respective Governments of those Provinces, by Legislative authority, but only to limit the maximum amount of charge to be assumed by the General Government; provided always, that the powers so conferred by the respective Legislatures shall be exercised within five years from this date, or the same shall lapse.

63. Newfoundland and Prince Edward Island, not having incurred Debts equal to those of the other Provinces, shall be entitled to receive, by half-yearly payments, in

advance, from the General Government, the Interest at five per cent on the difference between the actual amount of their respective Debts at the time of the Union, and the average amount of indebtedness per head of the Population of Canada, Nova Scotia and New Brunswick.

64. In consideration of the transfer to the General Parliament of the powers of Taxation, an annual grant in aid of each Province shall be made, equal to 80 cents per head of the Population, as established by the Census of 1861; the population of Newfoundland being estimated at 130,000. Such aid shall be in full settlement of all future demands upon the General Government for local purposes, and shall be paid half-yearly in advance to each Province.

65. The position of New Brunswick being such as to entail large immediate charges upon her local revenues, it is agreed that for the period of ten years, from the time when the Union takes effect, an additional allowance of $63,000 per annum shall be made to that Province. But that so long as the liability of that Province remains under $7,000,000, a deduction equal to the interest on such deficiency shall be made from the $63,000.

66. In consideration of the surrender to the General Government by Newfoundland of all its rights in Mines and Minerals, and of all the ungranted and unoccupied Lands of the Crown, it is agreed that the sum of $150,000 shall each year be paid to that Province, by semi-annual payments; provided that the Colony shall retain the right of opening, constructing and controlling Roads and Bridges through any of the said Lands, subject to any Laws which the General Parliament may pass in respect of the same.

67. All engagements that may before the Union, be entered into with the Imperial Government for the defence of the Country, shall be assumed by the General Government.

68. The General Government shall secure, without delay, the completion of the Intercolonial Railway from Rivière-du-Loup, through New Brunswick, to Truro in Nova Scotia.

69. The communications with the North-Western Territory, and the improvements required for the development of the Trade of the Great West with the Seaboard, are regarded by this Conference as subjects of the highest importance to the Federated Provinces, and shall be prosecuted at the earliest possible period that the state of the Finances will permit.

70. The sanction of the Imperial and Local Parliaments shall be sought for the Union of the Provinces, on the principles adopted by the Conference.

71. That Her Majesty the Queen be solicited to determine the rank and name of the Federated Provinces.

72. The proceedings of the Conference shall be authenticated by the signatures of the Delegates, and submitted by each Delegation to its own Government, and the Chairman is authorized to submit a copy to the Governor General for transmission to the Secretary of State for the Colonies.

NOTES

ONE: October 10, 1864: La Vieille Capitale

1. Anthony Trollope, *North America*, Vol. 1 (London, 1862), Ch 4: Lower Canada. Consulted at www.gutenberg.org/files/1865/1865-h/1865-h.htm.
2. Phillip Buckner, "Charles Tupper," in *Dictionary of Canadian Biography* online (hereafter *DCB*).
3. Library and Archives Canada, MG24-B40, R2634-0-9-E. George Brown fonds, letters of George Brown, 1864 (hereafter "Brown Letters"), Brown to Anne Brown, 13 September 1864.
4. Frances Elizabeth Owen (Feo) Monck, *My Canadian Leaves: An Account of a Visit to Canada in 1864–1865* (Toronto, Canadian Library Service, [1873] 1963), hereafter "Monck, *Leaves*," p. 11, 29 May 1864.
5. Edward Whelan, *The Union of the British Provinces* (Summerside PEI, Pioneer Publishing, [1865] 1949) (hereafter "Whelan, *Union*"), pp. 57–8.
6. Whelan, *Union*, pp. 57–8.
7. Joseph Bouchette, quoted in John Hare, Marc Lafrance, and David-Thierry Riddel, *Histoire de la Ville de Quebec 1608–1871* (Montreal, Boreal, 1987), p. 7.
8. Library Canada and Archives, MG24-B66, R2663-0-6-E, Mercy Anne Coles, "Reminiscences of Canada in 1864" (hereafter "Coles Diary") 5 October 1865.
9. Thomas C. Keefer, *The Philosophy of Railroads*, (Toronto, W.H. Armour and Co., 1850) p. 3.
10. George Ross, *Getting into Parliament and After* (Toronto, William Briggs, 1913), pp. 46–7.
11. Brown Letters, Brown to Anne Brown, 25 February 1864.
12. Henry James, *Collected Travel Writings: Great Britain and America* (Boston, Library of America, 1993), Quebec (visited 1871), pp. 767–76.
13. Brown Letters, 23 February, 2 March, 13 May 1864.
14. Brown Letters, 5 September 1864.
15. Coles Diary, 11 October 1864.
16. Peter Waite, ed., "Edward Whelan Reports from the Quebec Conference," *Canadian Historical Review*, 42 (1961), pp. 23–45 (hereafter "Whelan, *Reports*"), 11 October 1864.
17. The description of the city draws on *Histoire de la Ville de Quebec*, pp. 257–84; Paul Linteau, René Durocher, and Jean-Claude Robert, *Quebec: A History*

1867–1929 (Toronto, Lorimer, 1983), pp. 126–36; and Luc Noppen, *Québec de roc et de pierres: La Capitale en architecture* (Québec, Editions MultiMondes/ Commission de la Capitale Nationale de Quebec, 1998).

18. Trollope, *North America*, Vol. 1, Ch. 4; Artemus Ward, *His Book His Travels* (London, Gordon Routledge and Sons, 1865), p. 144.

19. Isabella Bird, *The Englishwoman in America* (Toronto, University of Toronto Press, [1856] 1966), Ch. 12, viewed at www.gutenberg.org/cache/epub/7526/pg7526.html.

20. Bird, *Englishwoman in America*, Ch. 12.

21. Whelan, *Reports*, p. 40.

22. Monck, *Leaves*, p. 76.

TWO: Before the Conference 1: John A. Macdonald's Worst Summer

1. Brown Letters, Brown to Anne Brown, 29 August 1864. What follows draws from Brown's long and detailed description.

2. Brown Letters, Brown to Anne Brown, 15 August 1864. Whelan, *Union*, p. 42 (speech at Halifax, 12 September 1864).

3. There are many Macdonald biographies. A brief, accessible one is J.K. Johnson and P.B. Waite, "John A. Macdonald," in *DCB*.

4. Noted by Ged Martin, *John A. Macdonald: Canada's First Prime Minister* (Toronto, Dundurn, 2013) pp. 81–2.

5. Ged Martin, *John A. Macdonald*, pp. 81–2.

6. J.M.S. Careless, *Brown of The Globe*, Vol. 2: *Statesman of Confederation* (Toronto, Dundurn, 1989, 1963), pp. 120–1, quoting *The Globe* of 15 March 1864.

7. Careless, *Brown of The Globe*, Vol. 2, p. 128.

8. Brown Letters, Brown to Anne Brown, 18 June 1864.

THREE: Before the Conference 2: George Brown's Best Summer

1. The best guide to Brown remains Careless, *Brown of The Globe*.

2. Brown Letters, Brown to Anne Brown, 5 August 1864.

3. Brown Letters, Brown to Anne Brown, 15 August 1864.

4. Brown Letters, Brown to Anne Brown, 26 April 1864.

5. Michael Cross, *A Biography of Robert Baldwin: The Morning Star of Memory* (Toronto, Oxford University Press Canada, 2012) is a recent summary.

6. Careless, *Brown of The Globe*, Vol. 1: *Voice of Upper Canada*, pp. 314–22.

7. Brown Letters, Brown to Anne Brown, 26 August 1864.

FOUR: Before the Conference 3: The Veto Power of George-Étienne Cartier

1. Alastair Sweeny, *George-Étienne Cartier* (Toronto, McClelland & Stewart, 1976), p. 212, quoting Stafford Northcote of the Hudson's Bay Company.
2. On Cartier's career, Sweeny, *George-Étienne Cartier* and Brian Young, *George-Étienne Cartier, Montreal Bourgeois* (Montreal, McGill-Queen's University Press, 1981).
3. J.-C. Bonenfant, "Sir George-Étienne Cartier," in *DCB*.
4. John Boyd, *Sir George-Étienne Cartier* (London, Macmillan, 1917) p. 159, quoting Cartier's words to a Montreal public meeting, 10 August 1846.
5. At the Royal Colonial Institute in London in March 1869, Cartier said that he had said the same thing to Queen Victoria "ten or twelve years ago." Boyd, *Cartier*, p. 299. Sweeny, *George-Étienne Cartier*, p. 131, dates that to 1858.
6. Galt's 1858 plan, *Documents on Confederation*, pp. 15–19.
7. W.L. Morton, *Monck Letters and Journals 1863–68: Canada from Government House at Confederation* (Toronto, McClelland & Stewart, 1970, Carleton Library Vol. 52), p. 43.
8. The novel *Lady Cartier* by Micheline Lachance (Montreal, Quebec-Amerique, 2004) sympathetically imagines Hortense Cartier's life.

FIVE: September in Charlottetown: John A. Bounces Back

1. Monck, *Leaves*, p. 81, 20 October 1864.
2. Library and Archives Canada, RG1 E1, State Minute Books, Canada Executive Council 1841–67, Minutes of Executive Council, State Book AA Volume 89, May 1864–January 1865 (hereafter "Executive Council Minutes"), 20 September to 8 October 1864.
3. Janet Ajzenstat, ed., *Documents on the Confederation of British North America* (Montreal, McGill-Queen's University Press, 2009, based on the 1969 edition, G.P. Browne, ed.), hereafter "*Documents on Confederation*," pp. 93–126. Coles's diary frequently notes Macdonald's hospitality to Mercy and the Coles family.
4. Ged Martin, "John A. Macdonald and the Bottle," *Journal of Canadian Studies* 40 (2006), 162–85.
5. Whelan, *Union*, p. 111.
6. Executive Council Minutes, 17 October 1864.
7. Quotation from Phillip Buckner, "Charles Tupper," in *DCB*.

SIX: Monday, October 10: Étienne Taché in the Chair

1. Brown letters, Brown to Anne Brown, 10 October 1864.
2. Halifax *Morning Chronicle*, 24 September 1864, "Quebec (from our correspondent)," p. 2.

3.   Halifax *Morning Chronicle*, 24 September 1864, "Quebec (from our correspondent)," p. 2.

4.   Halifax *Morning Chronicle*, 5 November 1864, quoting reports from the Montreal *Gazette*, p. 2.

5.   Halifax *Morning Chronicle*, 5 November 5 1864, quoting reports from the Montreal *Gazette*, p. 2; Whelan, *Reports*, p. 27, 10 October 1864.

6.   Jacques Monet, *The Last Cannon Shot* (Toronto, University of Toronto Press, 1969), pp. 3–4, 228–9.

7.   Brown Letters, Brown to Anne Brown, 26 August, 1864.

8.   *Documents on Confederation*, p. 58.

9.   Canada, House of Commons, *Debates*, 1885, p. 1132–1444, 16–29 April 1885, reports the debate; Colin Grittner, "Macdonald and Women's Enfranchisement," pp. 27–57 in Patrice Dutil and Roger Hall, eds, *Macdonald at 200: New Reflections and Legacies* (Toronto, Dundurn, 2014) argues for Macdonald's sincere commitment.

10. Province of Canada, Legislative Assembly, *Parliamentary Debates on the Subject of the Confederation of the British North American Provinces* (Quebec, Hunter Rose, 1865, reprinted Ottawa, Queen's Printer, 1951), hereafter "*Canadian Debates*," p. 426 for Alexander Mackenzie's view.

11. Whelan, *Union*, p. 109.

12. *Documents on Confederation*, p. 131 (Tupper) and p. 60 (resolution).

13. Executive Council Minutes, 22 October 1864.

14. Brown Letters, Brown to Anne Brown, 17 October 1864.

15. Coles Diary, 10 October 1864.

16. Coles Diary, 10 October 1864. Whelan, *Reports*, p. 28. *Constitution, Rules and Regulations of the Stadacona Club* (Quebec, *Morning Chronicle* 1868), article 2 at p. 3.

SEVEN: Monday, October 10: Viscount Monck's Dinner Party

1.   Jacques Monet, "Charles Stanley Monck," in *DCB*; Gregory Barton, *Palmerston and the Empire of Trade* (New York, Pearson, 2012) describes Palmerston's views on empire.

2.   Barbara Messamore, *Canada's Governors General 1847–78: Biography and Constitutional Evolution* (Toronto, University of Toronto Press, 2006).

3.   Monck, *Leaves* and Coles Diary, 10 October 1864.

4.   Robin W. Winks, *The Civil War Years: Canada and the United States*, 4th ed. (Montreal, McGill-Queen's University Press, [1960] 1998), pp. 69–103 on the *Trent* Affair; Doris Goodwin Kearns, *Team of Rivals* (New York, Simon & Schuster, 2005), on Seward generally, and at pp. 396–401 on his actions in the *Trent* incident.

5.   Winks, *Civil War Years*, pp. 119 and 284.

EIGHT: Tuesday, October 11: How to Run a Constitutional Conference

1. *Documents on Confederation*, p. 94.
2. Joseph Pope, *Memoirs of John A. Macdonald* (Toronto, Musson, 1894), p. 298, notes Drinkwater's shorthand skills; Coles Diary, 10 October 1864.
3. *Documents on Confederation*, pp. 93–4.
4. *Documents on Confederation*, pp. 94–8 (Macdonald's speech) and pp. 133–4 (Andrew Macdonald notes).
5. *Documents on Confederation*, pp. 98–9.
6. Morton, *Monck Letters and Journals*, p. 161.
7. *La Minerve* (Montreal), 11 October 1864, "La convention constitutionelle"; Whelan, *Reports*, p. 32.
8. Coles Diary, 13 October 1864.
9. Whelan, *Reports*, p. 32.

NINE: Wednesday, October 12: What Federalism Means

1. *Documents on Confederation*, p. 61.
2. Whelan, *Reports*, p. 31.
3. Douglas Owram, *The Promise of Eden: The Canadian Expansionist Movement and the Idea of the West, 1856–1900* (Toronto, University of Toronto Press, 1992).
4. *Documents on Confederation*, Andrew Macdonald notes, p. 134.
5. Coles Diary, 13 October 1864.
6. Whelan, *Reports*, p. 34.

TEN: Thursday, October 13: Nations and Empires

1. *Documents on Confederation*, pp. 62–3.
2. *Documents on Confederation*, p. 135; Whelan, *Reports*, p. 33.
3. *Documents on Confederation*, Minutes, p. 63.
4. *Documents on Confederation*, Minutes, p. 63.
5. *Documents on Confederation*, Minutes, p. 63.
6. *Documents on Confederation*, pp. 135–6; Whelan, *Reports*, pp. 33–4.
7. Lawrence H. Officer and Lawrence B. Smith, "Canadian-American Reciprocity Treaty of 1855 to 1866," *Journal of Economic History* 28(4) (Dec. 1968), pp. 598–623.
8. Brown to Macdonald, 22 December 1864, in Joseph Pope, *Memoirs of Sir John A. Macdonald* (Toronto, Musson Books, 1894), p. 290.
9. *Documents on Confederation*, p. 95.
10. Jean-Pierre Kesterman, "Alexander Tilloch Galt," in *DCB*.
11. John Ralston Saul, *Louis-Hippolyte LaFontaine and Robert Baldwin* (Toronto, Penguin, 2010), pp. 58–9.

12. *Documents on Confederation*, p. 64.

13. *Documents on Confederation*, p. 65.

14. Coles Diary, 14 October 1864.

15. *Le Courrier du Canada*, 12 October 1864.

16. Bird, *Englishwoman in America*, Ch. 12.

ELEVEN: Friday, October 14: An Upper House

1. "Le Temps," *Le Courrier du Canada* (Quebec), 14 October 1864, p. 2.

2. Whelan, *Reports*, pp. 34–5.

3. Whelan, *Reports*, p. 35. *Documents on Confederation*, pp. 65 and 136.

4. Coles Diary, 17 October 1864.

5. Whelan, *Reports*, p. 36.

6. Whelan, *Reports*, pp. 36–7. Coles Diary, 15 October 1864.

7. Monck, *Leaves*, p. 79.

8. Whelan, *Reports*, p. 36.

9. Brown Letters, Brown to Anne Brown, 15 October 1864.

TWELVE: Saturday, October 15 to Sunday, October 16: The Work to Be Done

1. Brown Letters, Brown to Anne Brown, 15 October 1864.

2. *Documents on Confederation*, p. 66.

3. *Documents on Confederation*, pp. 136–7.

4. Whelan, *Union*, pp. 62–79, reprints the speeches.

5. Whelan, *Reports*, p. 37.

6. Whelan, *Reports*, pp. 34–5.

THIRTEEN: Monday, October 17: Representing the Regions

1. *Documents on Confederation*, pp. 66–7.

2. *Documents on Confederation*, p. 138.

3. Brown Letters, Brown to Anne Brown, 17 October 1864.

4. *Documents on Confederation*, p. 68.

5. Brown Letters, Brown to Anne Brown, 17 October 1864.

FOURTEEN: Tuesday, October 18: The Senate Defined

1. Coles Diary, 18 October 1864.

2. *Documents on Confederation*, pp. 97–8.

3. *Documents on Confederation*, p. 68.

4. *Canadian Debates*, pp. 421–6 (Mackenzie and Brown), p. 35 (Macdonald).
5. *Canadian Debates*, pp. 25–45.
6. *Documents on Confederation*, p. 68.
7. *Documents on Confederation*, pp. 68–72.

FIFTEEN: Wednesday, October 19: Were the Confederation Makers Democrats?

1. The assertion can be found in the work of many distinguished scholars of Canadian politics, including, among others, A.R.M. Lower, Bruce Hodgins, Reginald Whittaker, George Woodcock, Peter Russell, and Phillip Buckner.
2. *Documents on Confederation*, p. 72.
3. *Documents on Confederation*, Minutes, pp. 72–3, discussion, pp. 106–10.
4. *Documents on Confederation*, discussion of 19 October 1864, pp. 106–10.
5. Whelan, *Union*, p. 12, speech of John H. Gray of New Brunswick. *Documents on Confederation*, pp. 151–2 has Andrew Macdonald's report of the discussion on 26 October 1864.
6. Francis P. Bolger, *Prince Edward Island and Confederation* (Charlottetown, St. Dunstan's University Press, 1964), p. 61, quoting *The Protestant* of Charlottetown.
7. *Documents on Confederation*, p. 137.
8. Whelan, *Reports*, pp. 39–40.
9. Monck, *Leaves*, pp. 80–1.
10. Whelan, *Reports*, p. 43.
11. Coles Diary, 20 October 1864.

SIXTEEN: Thursday, October 20: The Mechanics of Democracy

1. Winks, *The Civil War Years* has a detailed account; *The Globe* (Toronto) carried early stories on 22 and 24 October 1864.
2. Executive Council Minutes, 21 October 1864. Monck, *Leaves*, 24 October 1864.
3. Quoted in "The Vermont Raid: Further Details of the Outrage," *The Globe* (Toronto), 26 October 1864, p. 1.
4. Winks, *The Civil War Years*, particularly pp. 300–3.
5. *Documents on Confederation*, p. 81.
6. Whelan, *Union*, p. 69.
7. *Canadian Debates*, p. 55; Cartier expressed a similar view at the Quebec Conference: *Documents on Confederation*, pp. 128–9.
8. *Documents on Confederation*, Macdonald, pp. 94–5.
9. *Documents on Confederation*, pp. 110–12.
10. *Documents on Confederation*, p. 74.
11. *Documents on Confederation*, pp. 112–13.
12. *Documents on Confederation*, p. 113.

13. From 14 April, 1871 to 11 April, 1872. Parliament of Canada website: www.parl. gc.ca/ParlInfo/compilations/parliament/InterSessions.aspx?Parliament= c71b65a3-05fa-4e52-8d61-7cba67362e87

14. *Documents on Confederation*, pp. 85–6.

15. *Documents on Confederation*, pp. 85–6.

16. *Report of the Earl of Durham on British North America, 1839* (London, Methuen, 1902), p. 211; Janet Ajzenstat, *The Canadian Founding: John Locke and Parliament* (Montreal, McGill-Queen's University Press, 2007), pp. 59–60, emphasizes that in Canada responsible government is not a convention but constitutionally entrenched.

17. Donald Swainson, "James Cockburn," in *DCB*.

18. J. Keith Johnson, "John A. Macdonald," in J.M.S. Careless, ed., *The Pre-Confederation Premiers* (Toronto, University of Toronto Press, 1985), pp. 197–245.

19. James Young, *Public Men and Public Life in Canada* (Toronto, 1912), p. 225.

20. *Documents on Confederation*, p. 75.

21. *Documents on Confederation*, p. 114.

22. Careless, *Brown of* The Globe, Vol. 2, pp. 232–3.

23. *Documents on Confederation*, p. 114.

24. *Documents on Confederation*, p. 114.

25. Whelan, *Union*, pp. 80–2.

26. *Documents on Confederation*, p. 76.

SEVENTEEN: Friday, October 21 to Monday, October 24: Ottawa and the Provinces

1. *Documents on Confederation*, pp. 76–9.

2. Kesteman, "Galt," in *DCB*.

3. *Documents on Confederation*, pp. 15–19, has the Galt–Cartier federal plan of 1858.

4. *Documents on Confederation*, pp. 15–19.

5. *Documents on Confederation*, pp. 119–20.

6. "The Bachelors' Ball," *The Globe* (Toronto), 22 October 1864, p. 2.

7. Monck, *Leaves*, p. 82; Coles Diary, 22 October 1864.

8. Whelan, *Reports*, pp. 40–1.

9. *Documents on Confederation*, pp. 81–4.

10. Janet Ajzenstat, Paul Romney, Ian Gentles, and William Gairdner, eds., *Canada's Founding Debates* (Toronto, Stoddart, 1999), hereafter *"Founding Debates,"* pp. 272–3.

11. *Documents on Confederation*, pp. 122–5.

12. *Documents on Confederation*, pp. 122–6.

13. *Documents on Confederation*, p. 123.

14. *Documents on Confederation*, pp. 122–5.

15. *Documents on Confederation*, p. 125.
16. *Documents on Confederation*, pp. 82, 123–4.

EIGHTEEN: Sunday, October 23: The Work Still to Be Done

1. *The Chronicle* (Halifax), 29 October 1864 (on Shea and Carter); *The Globe* (Toronto), 25 October 1864 (on McDougall). Brown's views on McDougall are in the Brown Letters for August 1864.

NINETEEN: Tuesday, October 25 to Wednesday, October 26: What Quebec Needed

1. *Documents on Confederation,* p. 123 (Tupper) and p. 124 (Macdonald).
2. Joseph Cauchon, *L'Union des provinces de l'Amérique Britannique du Nord* (Quebec, A. Coté, 1865), p. 45. (My translation.)
3. "A False Alarm," *The Globe,* 30 August 1864, p. 2.
4. *Documents on Confederation*, p. 82.
5. Cauchon, *Union des provinces*, p. 120.
6. Brian Young, *The Politics of Codification: The Lower Canadian Civil Code of 1866* (Montreal, McGill-Queen's University Press, 1994).
7. Cauchon, *Union des provinces*, p. 92.
8. *Documents on Confederation*, p. 88.
9. Cauchon, *Union des provinces*, p. 129ff; Monet, *Last Cannon Shot*, describes the language struggle of the 1840s.
10. *Documents on Confederation*, p. 88.
11. *Documents on Confederation*, p. 86
12. Cauchon, *Union des Provinces*, p. 133.
13. Charles Biggar, *Oliver Mowat: A Biographical Sketch* (Toronto, Warwick Bros. and Rutter, 1905), p. 132.
14. Ajzenstat, *The Canadian Founding*, particularly Ch. 6.
15. Cauchon, *Union des Provinces*, pp. 104 and 133.
16. *Documents on Confederation*, p. 124.
17. Robert Vipond, *Liberty and Community: Canadian Federalism and the Failure of the Constitution* (Albany, SUNY Press, 1991), pp. 113–18.

TWENTY: Tuesday, October 25 to Wednesday, October 26: Rights and Courts

1. Francis Bond Head, who helped provoke the 1837 rebellion in Upper Canada, asserted this view strongly. Head, *A Narrative* (Toronto, McClelland & Stewart, 1969), pp. 42 and 50.
2. Brown Letters, Brown to Anne Brown, 27 October 1864.
3. *Documents on Confederation*, p. 85.

4.   *Documents on Confederation*, p. 87.

5.   *Documents on Confederation*, p. 87.

6.   *Founding Debates*, p. 143, John Casey in the Newfoundland legislature.

7.   *Canadian Debates*, pp. 387–8 (Hector Langevin in the Province of Canada legislature); Cauchon, *Union des provinces*, p. 104.

8.   *Documents on Confederation*, p. 123 (Dickey) and earlier discussion, p. 120.

9.   *Documents on Confederation*, p. 123.

10.   *Documents on Confederation*, p. 126.

11.   Macdonald in 1873, quoted in Vipond, *Liberty and Community*, p. 122.

12.   Vipond, *Liberty and Community*, pp. 29–30.

13.   John T. Saywell, *The Lawmakers: Judicial Power and the Shaping of Canadian Federalism* (Toronto, University of Toronto Press, 2002).

TWENTY-ONE: Tuesday, October 25: The Old Indian Chief

1.   Coles Diary, 13 October 1864.

2.   B.G. Trigger, ed., *Handbook of North American Indians*, Vol. 15: *Northeast* (1978), article "Huron-Wendat"; Georges Sioui, *Huron-Wendat. The Heritage of the Circle* (Vancouver: British Columbia University Press, 1999).

3.   Coles Diary, 13 October 1864; Monck, *Leaves*, p. 81, 20 October 1864.

4.   Cole Harris, *The Resettlement of British Columbia: Essays on Colonialism and Geographical Change* (Vancouver, UBC Press, 1997) surveys Aboriginal depopulation in B.C.

5.   Gerald Friesen, *The Canadian Prairies: A History* (Toronto, University of Toronto Press, 1984), pp. 91–128 on Métis society.

6.   *Documents on Confederation*, p. 85.

7.   Olive Patricia Dickason and David T. McNab, *Canada's First Nations: A History of Founding Peoples from Earliest Times* (Don Mills, Ontario: Oxford University Press, 4th edition, 2009).

8.   J.R. Miller, *Compact, Contract, Covenants: Aboriginal Treaty-Making in Canada* (Toronto, University of Toronto Press, 2009) and John S. Long, *Treaty No. 9: Making the Agreement to Share the Land in Far Northern Ontario in 1905* (Toronto, University of Toronto Press, 2010) stand out in a growing literature on this subject.

TWENTY-TWO: Wednesday, October 26: The Money

1.   Whelan, *Union*, pp. 62–79.

2.   Kesteman, "Alexander Galt," in *DCB*.

3.   *Documents on Confederation*, pp. 79–81 (Bernard minutes), pp. 120–2 (Bernard notes), and pp. 143–6 (Andrew Macdonald notes).

4.   *Documents on Confederation*, p. 78.

5.   *Documents on Confederation*, pp. 145–6.

6. *Documents on Confederation*, p. 137.
7. "Latest from Quebec," *The Globe* (Toronto), 24 October 1864, p. 1.
8. *Documents on Confederation*, p. 160.
9. *Documents on Confederation*, p. 150.
10. Ian Ross Robertson, *The Tenant League of Prince Edward Island* (Toronto, University of Toronto Press, 1996); Christopher Moore, *1867: How the Fathers Made a Deal* (Toronto, McClelland & Stewart, 1997), pp. 84–7; Whelan, *Reports*, pp. 42–3 for his view and Coles's.
11. *Documents on Confederation*, pp. 151–2.

TWENTY-THREE: Thursday, October 27: Roads East and West

1. *Documents on Confederation*, pp.153–65; Resolution 68, on the Intercolonial Railway, undated.
2. *Canadian Debates*, p. 251.
3. Joseph Pope, *Correspondence of John A. Macdonald* (Toronto, Oxford University Press Canada, 1921), pp. 13–15, Macdonald to Charles Tupper, 14 November 1964.
4. *Documents on Confederation*, p. 168 (another resolution not covered in Bernard's minutes).

TWENTY-FOUR: Thursday, October 27: The Rush for the Trains

1. Monck, *Leaves*, p. 83.
2. Monck, *Leaves*, p. 83.
3. Whelan, *Reports*, p. 43; Whelan, *Union*, p. 83; *La Minerve*, 22 October 1864.
4. *Documents on Confederation*, p. 84.
5. Pope, *Correspondence of Macdonald*, pp. 13–15, Macdonald to Tupper, 14 November 1864.
6. *Documents on Confederation*, pp. 176–8.
7. David B. Knight, ed., *Choosing Canada's Capital: Conflict Resolution in a Parliamentary System* (Montreal, McGill-Queen's University Press, 1991).
8. *Documents on Confederation*, p. 165; Names: *The Globe* (Toronto), 22 October and 1–9 November, 1864.
9. *Documents on Confederation*, p. 176 (McDougall) and p. 152 (Macdonald).
10. *Documents on Confederation*, p. 165.
11. Brown Letters, Brown to Anne Brown, 27 October 1864.

TWENTY-FIVE: From the Quebec Resolutions to the British North America Act

1. Coles Diary, 28 and 29 October 1864.
2. Whelan, *Union*, Brown's speech, pp. 183–203.

3. *Documents on Confederation*, Edward Cardwell to Monck, 3 December 1864, pp. 168–71.

4. *Canadian Debates*, p. 252.

5. *Canadian Debates*, p. 248.

6. *Canadian Debates*, p. 245 (Dorion) and p. 239 (Mackenzie).

7. *Canadian Debates*, p. 250.

8. *Canadian Debates*, p. 386.

9. Ged Martin, *Britain and the Origins of Canadian Confederation 1837–67* (Vancouver, UBC Press, 1995) is the best study.

10. The legal issues are set out in Dale Gibson, "Free Trade in Criminals: Canadian–American Extradition before 1890," in William Kaplan, Donald McRae, eds., *Law, Policy, and International Justice: Essays in Honour of Maxwell Cohen* (Montreal, McGill-Queen's University Press, 1993), pp. 144–86.

11. Cartier biographer Alastair Sweeny makes the case at http://www.canadachannel.ca/cartier/index.php/Siamese_Twins_-_Growing_Dangers, accessed September 15. 2014.

12. *Canadian Debates*, p. 589.

TWENTY-SIX: Brown, Cartier, Macdonald: Who Should Lead the Confederation?

1. Pope, *Correspondence of Macdonald*, p. 161, Macdonald to M.C. Cameron, 3 January 1872.

2. *Canadian Debates*, speech of Joseph Perrault, p. 589.

3. Brown Letters, Brown to Anne Brown, 26 August 1864.

4. Brown Letters, Brown to Anne Brown, 7 November 1864.

5. Brown Letters, Brown to Anne Brown, 14 and 15 March 1865.

6. Careless, *Brown of* The Globe, Vol. 2, Chapter 6.

7. Careless, *Brown of* The Globe, Vol. 2, p. 266 and p. 242.

8. *Canadian Debates*, pp. 498–9.

9. Richard Cartwright, *Reminiscences* (Toronto, William Briggs, 1912), p. 41; J.M.S. Careless's judgment on this point, *Brown of* The Globe, Vol. 2, pp. 262–8.

10. Andrée Desilets, Hector Langevin, *Un père de la confédération Canadienne* (Quebec, Presses de l'Université Laval, 1969), p. 164.

11. Cartwright, *Reminiscences*, p. 42.

12. Careless, *Brown of* The Globe, Vol. 2, pp. 262–7, quotes their letters and analyzes their positions.

Appendix

1. Library and Archives Canada, http://www.collectionscanada.gc.ca/confederation/023001-7104-e.html

ACKNOWLEDGMENTS

This book began with a brief conversation with Diane Turbide of Penguin Canada and then a discussion over coffee with Margaret MacMillan and Robert Bothwell about the History of Canada series, in which they planned to cover a series of surprising or important moments from Canadian history. I knew at once that the moment I wanted was this one: a day-by-day, debate-by-debate, dinner-and-dance-by-dinner-and-dance exploration of the meeting in Quebec City, a century and a half ago, from which came the constitution under which Canadians still live. I am grateful to Diane, Margaret, and Robert for their interest, support, patience, and good counsel throughout. I also thank my agent, Dean Cooke, the editorial and production team at Penguin Canada, Professor Janet Ajzenstat for her confederation scholarship and for various conversations, and Anne McDonald for her perceptive reading of Mercy Coles's diary.

INDEX